E. B. Beravale initially achieved success in real estate and later went on to become an owner of thoroughbred race horses. Throughout her years in business, she was also very active as a volunteer for numerous organisations, serving on and chairing various committees. She has been a well-known London hostess for more than 20 years. She enjoys countryside pursuits such as riding and gardening. The author is very fond of reading and research, and has written on self-improvement, personal development and traditional etiquette. E.B. Beravale is currently a director of Beravale Enterprises and makes her home between Windsor in the UK and Tuscany, Italy, residing with her husband and their daughter.

This book is lovingly dedicated to the many, many wonderfully supportive people who have touched my life in positive ways, from friends and relations to strangers in distant countries. A special thanks to those whom I have not yet met, but who have decided that this book is worth reading - may we meet in the spirit of creating a more positive and pleasant world. This book is especially dedicated to my beloved husband and daughter, for joy is what they continually bring, and life is meant to be filled with happiness.

For those who wish to have, be, do and share anything they choose, I decided to create a comprehensive programme called *Living Royally—Happiness and Success through Personal Management* to help people take life to the next level. Inner improvement, outer appearance, surroundings, health, well-being, and financial freedom are some of the areas which have enabled us to enjoy everything from travelling the six continents in luxury, to establishing an incredible personal life. If finding your bliss means a special vocation, a wonderful home life, material assets, healthful lifestyle, pleasing location, social status, or all of these blessings—this book can help you make it happen!

E.B. Beravale

Living Royally

Happiness and Success Through Personal Management

AUSTIN MACAULEY PUBLISHERS®

LONDON * CAMBRIDGE * NEW YORK * SHARJAH

Copyright © E.B. Beravale 2024

The right of E.B. Beravale to be identified as author of this work has been asserted by the author in accordance with sections 77 and 78 of the Copyright, Designs and Patents Act 1988.

All rights reserved. No part of this publication may be reproduced, stored in a retrieval system, or transmitted in any form or by any means, electronic, mechanical, photocopying, recording, or otherwise, without the prior permission of the publishers.

Any person who commits any unauthorised act in relation to this publication may be liable to criminal prosecution and civil claims for damages.

The story, the experiences, and the words are the author's alone.

A CIP catalogue record for this title is available from the British Library.

ISBN 9781035816064 (Paperback)
ISBN 9781035816071 (Hardback)
ISBN 9781035816088 (ePub e-book)

www.austinmacauley.com

First Published 2024
Austin Macauley Publishers Ltd®
1 Canada Square
Canary Wharf
London
E14 5AA

In memory of three great mentors: Dr Wayne Dyer, Mr Bob Proctor, and Mr Jim Rohn.

Table of Contents

Introduction	11
Part I: Personal Development Creating Your Best Self	15
Chapter 1: Your Name	18
Chapter 2: Inner Improvement	23
Chapter 3: Outer Appearance	78
Part II: Lifestyles	119
Chapter 4: Personal Surroundings	122
Chapter 5: Tangible Surroundings	172
Part III: Underlying Basics for Greater Joy	191
Chapter 6: Health and Well-Being	194
Chapter 7: Financial Freedom	213
Appendices	250
Index	288

Introduction

Welcome! Of all the stars in our vast universe, we find ourselves as co-creators of integrity and excellence, sharing this incredible planet. At times many of us have wondered why exactly we are here, but as life goes by, the curiosity often fades, and we have a tendency to simply accept things the way they are. A lifestyle might grow on us, or situations may simply be taken for granted.

Let us go back for a moment to a time in our youth, when we were closer to the source... when we were dreamers. Can you remember the things that first inspired you? The times when your body first shivered from sheer emotional joy? The futuristic ideals which you imagined? Now, return to the present. Do you still become inspired easily, or shiver from pure emotion? More importantly, how many of your ideals have already become a reality? If you can think of a fair list, congratulations!

You're on the right track and naturally you should continue to prosper. If your self-analysis was less positive, do not despair—change and progress will manifest whenever you truly decide to bring it about. Always remember, in a free society, **you create your world.** We may at times experience pain from matters beyond our control such as the loss of a loved one; but with respect to our own lifestyle, sadness and joy are the direct result of what one has sent out to the universe. I once heard a quote:

You will realise the Vision (not the idle wish) of your heart be it base or beautiful, or a mixture of both, for you will always gravitate toward that which you, secretly, most love. Into your hands will be placed the exact results of your own thoughts.

If any fatalist is frightened by the above concept, or prefers to believe in excuses for failure such as 'tough-luck' and 'ill-fortune'... let them enjoy their opinion unto themselves. As for those who have courage, heightened by spiritual faith and determination of action—let them move onward and upward, to the royal life which they deserve; indeed, which we are ALL worthy of.

Gandhi said, "Be the change that you wish to see in the world." This book will suggest many different ways to improve one's lifestyle and achieve success. Some people may wonder at the ambiguity of the word success—let it mean whatever is right for you. If success means a happy disposition, a special vocation, a wonderful family, material assets, a healthy lifestyle, social status, financial independence or all of the above—so be it. All of those topics will be covered.

Take whatever is right for you at this point in time and leave the rest behind. One person may want to improve in an area which would appear relatively unimportant to the next individual. My purpose is to help people to find the information which they desire to bring their life to the next level.

Probably the most significant and sensitive area will be for people to analyse how they have utilised their time thus far. What is one's current position, what thoughts and actions have brought them to this point, and how do they wish to proceed from here? The first thing that absolutely must be done is to dispel any existing blame and accept total responsibility for our own behaviours. ***We are where we are—because on a conscious or sub-conscious level, that is what we have chosen.***

This work on personal management is designed to provide suggestions for those who are looking for ways to improve their lifestyle. Although some concepts will likely be familiar to those who have already begun the journey, this book has combined various ideas to produce a more complete guide and system of reference. I believe that there are many excellent sources of material available which can help to improve and transform one's life. For those who are just beginning this road of discovery, I hope to make the path more visible.

I must confess to having written the original draft of this book some years ago, but I wanted to put my programme to the test before proceeding to publish it for others. Now completely satisfied with the results that I have experienced in my own lifestyle and witnessed in the lives of others, I want to share the information with all who would desire to use it. In my own spirit of living royally, I have experienced everything from travelling the six continents in luxury, to the ownership of many high-quality assets and establishing an incredibly joyous family and social life.

Although many of us are in the habit of reading through books rapidly, it is important to note that the best results are usually achieved when we take more time. Whenever one comes across a particular idea, which may be of importance to them as an individual, it is better to write notes, complete the exercises, and truly make life happen. This is the age of information and it's wonderful to have knowledge, but equally important, is taking the required action. Like a heavy meal, this book needs to be digested slowly. Read a section and underline or highlight items, so you may later re-read it or take action if it is something which pertains to you. Every time we read something we can understand more, because we are always operating at a higher state of awareness. Later, move on to the next topic which interests you.

As already mentioned, ***use whatever is best for you in the present.*** If you are at the chapter on appearance, and you realise that your clothing wardrobe needs work, lay the book aside for a day and deal with your closets. If you have trouble keeping appointments, or with the prioritisation of your activities, stop at the time-management section, and work on this as long as necessary. Only you know what areas of your life you want to concentrate on and you are free to go back and forth.

Some parts of this book will be helpful to those who are just starting out at an early age, while other sections may inspire someone who is more senior. It is not necessary to read 'hints on how to give up smoking' in the Appendix if one has never used cigarettes, although they may want to suggest the book to a friend who is currently trying to break the habit and establish a healthier lifestyle. There are different pieces in the 'pie' of life and it is good for us to have a comprehensive knowledge and find good balance in various areas. A chapter which is insignificant to you today, may seem very important one year from now.

If several proposals from this book benefit your lifestyle, then it will have been worth reading. I read an enormous amount of selected material from which I generally gain at least one inspiring thought or piece of new information. Authors write to express what they have learned and hopefully to help others find a quicker and easier road to results by sharing experiences from our own challenges and eventual success. This is no longer my book, but yours to gain inspiration from and perhaps help someone else.

I was recently asked if I knew my purpose in life and the answer flowed from me straight away "To leave this world a more beautiful, civilised, peaceful and happier place than it has ever been before." Together let us make it so!

Part I
Personal Development Creating Your Best Self

There is one strong theme throughout this book, which is: always make a point to treat yourself, the way you feel that you deserve to be treated. In other words, if you wish to be rich—imagine and begin to live that way, even if you are not wealthy yet. Turn 'pauper' consciousness into 'prosper' consciousness. ***WE ATTRACT INWARDLY WHAT WE PROJECT OUTWARDLY.*** Don't be afraid to give yourself the privileges which the world has to offer. The universe is filled with an unlimited supply… enough wealth and natural beauty for everyone. There is no need or reason for poverty and lack to exist on this planet.

Whenever I pray for myself and others, I ask that God let us grow holier, healthier, happier and wealthier. If everyone possessed those blessings: the esteem which comes with integrity; being fit and in good health; filled with joy, and financial freedom, they would understand why the earth could be called Eden. Affirmative prayers also require ***ACTION***; consequently, I hope that the following chapters will motivate and encourage readers to make ***personal choices*** which will bring them closer to a life of harmony and fulfilment.

I will present many hints on how to experience a good life and be a part of 'royal living' but before we proceed to subjects like socialising, entertainment, enjoying our occupation, and greater independence, it may be best to start with some basics. Creating your best self is an excellent preparation for entering into the elite world of the success oriented.

This is achieved by inner improvement such as developing a classic behaviour and positive mental attitude. Outer appearance is also of great significance, for this is how you will be perceived during those vital first impressions… of which there should be many more in your exciting social future!

To encourage people to take complete responsibility for who they are, we begin with a brief word on Onomatology.

Chapter 1
Your Name

Onomatology—Who Are You?

We all know how significant first impressions are. There are three personal components which become obvious on most introductory meetings. First, our *appearance*—the clothes we wear, our face, our hair, scent, eye contact and motions. Second, our *voice*—one's tone, manner, and level of intellect become readily apparent through the speech we choose to practise. The third distinct characteristic of an introduction will be one's *name* and title.

When determining how you want to live—first consider who YOU are. What is your name, what does it represent, and most important of all—is it to your liking?

Many names are carefully chosen and reflective of their family's history—even my pedigree dog and thoroughbred racehorses were given names related to their bloodlines. Multitudes of people are pleased with the names that others have chosen for them, but I've also met many individuals who were not content.

In order to have a healthy self-esteem, one must feel good about the names which they use. To be convinced of this subject's significance, visit the library and observe how many 'name' books exist. In the past, much of the available information dealt primarily with the linguistic origins and etymology of names. Today, we are aware of a more unique form of onomatology… we study the ***connotations which our names carry, and how they affect our life***. I do not refer to numerology or speculation, but to actual psychological reaction. Test your knowledge of this onomatology theme right now. Picture two females:

A—Is a very dignified woman of graceful carriage. She is polished, soft-spoken, and regal. Her hair is elegantly swept back off her face. She is wearing a formal gown, and entering a Viennese ballroom.

B—Is a fresh-faced youth with hair windswept by the breeze. She is wearing comfortable casual clothing and chumming outdoors with her tomboy-friends. She has a vigour for life, is very pleasant and down-to-earth.

Both of the females described were equally wonderful characters; however, they possessed considerably different natures. Which one is named Bonny-Jo, and which one is Lady Victoria? If you guessed that Victoria is A and Bonny-Jo is B… then you clearly understand the connotations which names can carry.

The book "Baby Boomer's Name Game" summed it up this way: "What's in a name? Among other things—the difference between success or failure in the business world. Or between social acceptability and an emotional, educational, even sexual handicap. Names are far more than mere identity tags. They are charged with hidden meanings and unspoken overtones, that will profoundly help or hinder your child in relationships and in life."

The book goes on to say about the name game: "Before you could start playing—your parents played—using you as a pawn. The name put upon the new-born is a clear indication of where his parents want him/her to go."

Oh, how true that is… but what if we grow up to be very different from what our guardians envisioned? Consider how much we change naturally as we mature. Five-year-old 'Eddie' may insist on being called 'Ned' when he becomes 15. By the age of 30—he may prefer the more distinguished sound of 'Edward.'

Sometimes people with a long-syllabled name, Elizabeth for example, might choose to use a permanent shorter substitute such as: Beth, Betty, Elise, Eliza, Elsie, Libby, Lillibet, Lisa, or some other variation. Fortunately, people will usually ask *you* who you are, rather than making a rude or common assumption. One should never shorten another person's name unless they have specifically asked—more on this later.

Not all given names offer such a variety of options; therefore, it is advantageous to provide descendants with at least three legal Christian names. If a child has only one given name like **John** Doe, and is not content with this, he has no option but to use it, or suffer the expense and paperwork of applying for a legal replacement. If he is initially christened: **Jonathan Edward Cameron** Doe, he has far more legal choices, and likely will never desire to file a name change by deed poll. He can be—Jonathan E. Doe, J. Edward Doe, John E.C. Doe, or he may drop the Jonathan altogether and be—E. Cameron Doe, or Edward C. Doe. He can choose one of his three full names, or pick a short form, like—Ned, Ed, Cam, Ron, or John. He has numerous possibilities without the tension of legalities.

Chosen names can easily be re-arranged to suit our taste, but one's surname is quite another matter. A person's last name may represent their bloodline and heritage, but what if they simply feel that it is not appropriate: foreign to their current citizenship; ordinarily common; or just plain unattractive? Mr Doe should feel free to change it, either partially or completely. Although this is seldom done aside from marriage, there is no reason why people cannot create their own surname—the beginning of a great new heritage perhaps? One of the secrets to living like royalty is learning to exercise free-choice toward any positive improvements.

In entrepreneurial business seminars, I have noticed that many instructors stress the importance of remembering and using peoples' names. I agree that addressing someone by their correct name will show respect and help to establish an amicable relationship more rapidly. It is said that 'familiarity breeds contempt' so perhaps we should consider this when deciding whether to use someone's 'given' or 'surname.' It is inadvisable to become too familiar too quickly. New contacts and business acquaintances should be addressed as 'Mr Doe.' If a close friendship is established, Mr Doe will ask you to please call him "John."

When business people are introduced to someone for the first time, they often repeat the name out loud. "How do you do, Mr Doe," as this will help one to remember it. Remember that during initial introductions, it is correct and courteous to always use titles with surnames.

While living in Italy, I came to appreciate the deep personal respect which people show towards one another—whether in a shop or out walking and greeting a stranger with "buon giorno," everyone is addressed as Signor, Signora, or Signorina—good morning Sir, Madame, or Miss.

If a person has difficulty pronouncing names which originate from foreign countries, they should not be embarrassed to ask for guidance. Learn to enunciate correctly and respect all nationalities. Also, never take the liberty of altering someone's name without their suggestion. If a fellow's name is Robert, but he prefers to be called 'Bob' he should be the one to make that recommendation to you. If a woman introduces herself as Pamela, we have no authority to call her 'Pam,' unless **she** insists upon it. Everyone has the right to determine their own name—we must not dictate to anyone. Presumptuousness will only repel potential business contacts or friendships.

While on the subject of shortening first names, it should be noted that this practise is more common amongst children or in very casual situations. Aristocratic types generally consider short 'pet-names' befitting to their 'pets.' A Lady Elizabeth, Prince Alexander and Sir Michael might appropriately reserve 'Bessy' for the cow, 'Alix' for the cat, and 'Spike' for the dog.

The different aspects of onomatology make for fascinating study. It is important to show respect for every individual's name, and *although we are free to re-arrange our own, we should never distort anyone else's.* Those who design their own personal happiness, know that *A NAME IS PART OF WHO WE ARE*, and like most things, it is a private matter for each individual to establish. Royal Sovereigns, Popes, and clergy, have long utilised their power in selecting names for themselves—you have the same right if you feel the desire.

As additional information, I will list some title prefix samples for reference:

Envelopes
C.J.B. Smith, Esq. or:
Mr Charles Smith—man
Mrs Charles Smith—married woman
Mrs Betty Smith—divorced woman
Mrs C.J.B. Smith—widowed woman
Mr and Mrs Tom Jones or for example:
Prof and Mme T. Jones—married couple
Miss Jane Doe—unmarried woman
Prof or Dr Simon Doe
Prof or Dr Jane Doe

Letters
Dear Mr Smith
Dear Mrs Smith
Dear Professor and Mrs Jones
Dear Miss Doe
Dear Dr Doe
Dear Prof Doe
Dear Sir or Madam

<u>In person</u> (during introductions for example)
Mr Smith
Mr and Mrs Smith
Professor Jones
Madame Jones
The Doctor and Mrs Doe
Sir Charles
Lord Smith
Lady Smith—title by marriage
Lady Jane—inherited title single
Betty Lady Smith—title divorced

Chapter 2
Inner Improvement

Mind

WHAT IS MIND?

Before we proceed, and get involved in the fascinating powers of conscious and unconscious thought, it may be best to first discuss the question which baffles many. ***Does the mind belong to the brain/body, or to the spirit/soul?*** A fascinating question indeed.

Science offers proof that the physical brain is connected with thought; and spiritual study provides evidence that mind is uncontainable and definitely related to infinite intelligence. It is likely that the spirit is a source from infinite, super intelligence, while the brain as a human part, serves as a transmitter and receiver of frequency, energy and vibration which travel instantaneously. Albert Einstein said, "Anyone who becomes seriously involved in the pursuit of science becomes convinced that there is a spirit manifest in the laws of the universe, a spirit vastly superior to that of man." He also said, "Everything is energy and that's all there is to it. Match the frequency of the reality you want, and you cannot help but get that reality. It can be no other way. This is not philosophy, this is physics."

Every time you think a thought, you broadcast a frequency and every event which happens in your life, is an indicator of what you are vibrating. If you would like to study further information on the difference between conscious 'physical' and subconscious 'uncontainable' thought, I have provided a supplement as Appendix 2 at the back of this book.

How Does the Mind Work?

A simple analogy may be to compare our brain to a radio. It is a communication device enclosed in a relatively small compartment. The music, like thought, is not contained within the radio itself; but rather, the waves are received by selected transmitters. Similarly, our mind can tune in to different stations, as one so desires. The only way to prevent the radio from transmitting is to physically damage it. Likewise, the brain's retrieval system can become damaged by outside force such as disease, surgery, shock, or accident.

Let's assume that your radio is in good repair, i.e., your physical brain is functioning properly. You can send or receive thoughts at free will. Not all radios have the same receiving distance or power—likewise with the human brain's frequency. Some people possess super radar capabilities, and may even be referred to as being psychic. It might seem amazing that a psychic can discuss one's present life with such accuracy, but this is not surprising, for their super radar can pick up your current thoughts quite easily. Future predictions are always more difficult because the subject himself may be uncertain of his own desires.

In my youth, I once did an experiment at a psychic fair. I first visited one booth and enquired about my future—at the same time I concentrated deeply that I wanted three children. As you may have already guessed, the woman predicted that I would have three children. I then went to another psychic, and concentrated on a desire to have five children. When I asked about my future, the fellow said that I would have five children! Co-incidence? Perhaps… but most fortune tellers realise that whatever we constantly **THINK** about, we will eventually find a way to **BRING** about, thus making some predictions come true.

This is only a theory as with many human assumptions. Some people believe that psychics possess ordinary minds, and do not have stronger radar receiving capabilities. They suspect that psychics receive their information from outside entities which go around gathering information for them and channelling through them. Who knows? This is beside the point—we do know that ideas are everywhere, uncontainable, and like a radio, our brain can pick up various signals. So, let us concentrate on this subject, and how we can use this information to the betterment of our lives.

RE-PROGRAMMING

If you have ever read positive mental attitude (PMA) self-help books, or attended that sort of lecture, one of the first things you probably learned was 'never watch the news on television.' The reason of course, is to avoid negative brainwashing since most news is designed to shock you rather than inspire you. Once images have been recorded in your mind's data bank, you can dismiss the notion of erasing them, although time can help them to fade away. The brain is a permanent computer file. Unless the retrieval system becomes damaged or destroyed by outside force, memories will always be accessible. Although thoughts seem to disappear from our conscious mind, they may be summoned to re-appear at an instant.

The more frequently a thought has been introduced to one's mind, the easier it will be for the retrieval of that concept. With repetition, the sub-conscious will find no difficulty in grasping thoughts and handing them over to one's conscious mind. Consider this carefully—images, if dwelt upon, may continually reappear.

Every time a person sits down to watch negative news or film coverage, they are making those very ideas more accessible to their mind. This is a powerful human capability which should not be taken lightly. *YOU ARE WHERE YOU ARE TODAY, BECAUSE AT SOME POINT IN TIME, YOU HAVE THOUGHT ABOUT IT.* It is necessary to stress the danger in watching TV news—it is often long, repetitive, and consists of too many vivid negative pictures which are easily recorded by the brain.

Every truly cruel, or extremely violent act which I have ever seen, I have viewed on film or TV. The most violent scenes which are stored in some people's brain data banks were first observed through television or film. Repeated viewing can actually cause the inability for some persons to determine the difference between fiction and reality. When some particular thought, action, or scene is planted too frequently, the sub-conscious mind may accept it as correct or normal. *THE SUB-CONSCIOUS MIND IS NOT A DECISION MAKER… IT SIMPLY EATS THE MENTAL FOOD WHICH IT IS SERVED.* Be careful what you feed it repeatedly!

If one is a news addict, break away gradually by listening to something like BBC radio or Classic FM—it will cover major occurrences, by being brief and to the point. Avoid too much local TV or radio news—i.e.: you don't need to hear about the young adolescent down the street who robbed the grocery. That is not global business; it is not our business; it is police business.

The judicial system will handle such concerns, it has nothing to do with you, unless you were the thief or the victim, in which case you will already know the 'news.' It is a waste of one's thinking capabilities to fill their minds with useless information when they could be concentrating on more intelligent matters.

If one has had a lot of negative mental programming in their past, they needn't worry. One can easily replace negative thoughts with positive images and hand them over to their conscious mind on a permanent and constant basis. As soon as one discontinues the retrieval of negative images, and no longer uses them, their mind will no longer bother to summon them. Those thoughts will become like distant radio waves which are no longer in the vicinity of your station.

Let me illustrate with an example: Many years ago, I began to use calculators for all types of mathematical solutions, metric conversion, and mortgage equations. As a consequence, I lost the ability to instantly retrieve solutions to simple 'times-table' questions. This can be both bad news and good news.

The challenging part is to work continuously with healthy, positive thoughts, in order to keep these beneficial 'waves' coming to your receiver on a permanent basis. The good news is—you can ***stop receiving negative waves and make them non-existent in your life***. If one stops watching negative programming, those destructive images will eventually fade out of their mind. Of course, ***visual*** is not the only mental influence, consider what one reads for example. A simple action like throwing out the tabloids and beginning to read something related to affluence like 'Town and Country,' may create immediate changes in one's mental perception.

Another influencing factor is personal self-talk, and one will require a strong mind to have total control over this. Once a person has mastered positive change and control, they need never again despair about negative thoughts which they have had in the past. The past is irrelevant and non-existent in the present. The future, of course, will be determined by whatever one is ***currently*** feeding their mind.

How do we gain this discipline over our minds? Like most things… by **REPETITION**. Riding a horse, ballroom dancing, playing the piano… the more lessons one takes… the more adept they become, because practise develops skill. Become unconsciously competent by doing something over and over again. We must use our mind positively ***EVERY*** day to become an efficient thinker. Avoid negative input; concentrate on a positive lifestyle, and use affirmations.

My husband and I begin every morning with something positive whilst enjoying our tea or cappuccino. Sometimes we read to one another from an educational book, and at other times we prefer to listen to a good motivational speaker … or we simply relax whilst watching one of the videos with beautiful, affluent pictures and affirmations—YouTube now offers some very fine selections.

MIND POWER

The mind will usually put one in the position of their desires. We know that our situation eventually gravitates towards what we think about. If you should notice that you have not fulfilled desires which you repeatedly premeditated, it is likely for the reason that more intense thoughts were pulling events in a different direction. For example, if one employee wants their company to remain a franchise and continually thinks and plans to that effect, but 20 other minds are determined that the company become a private business, then in all likelihood the majority will win. Or it may simply be one desire over another.

For example: A man is infatuated with a woman and constantly thinks and schemes to win her attentions, but she has a powerful and true love for another man—the latter, burning desire and true love vibration will be the most likely to influence the future course of events.

Our life is connected, perhaps even a direct result, of our thoughts. Neville Goddard said, "The moment man matches the beliefs of any state, he fuses with it, and this union results in the activation and projection of its plots, plans, dramas, and situations." One should not let the outside world control their thoughts, but rather keep their mind on the goal they truly want: your state must be stronger than your environment.

Faith plays a major role in the process—your belief will create the fact. One should feel as though they have already acquired or achieved the goal and never think about the 'lack of it.' Do not be preoccupied about 'how' something will come to you—the universal laws are vast and many opportunities will not be visible on the radar screen of what you currently 'see.' Just let yourself feel good in the knowing that everything already exists, and imagine that feeling until it arrives.

In the book "Ask and It Is Given" by Ester and Jerry Hicks, one reads, "The only reason anything has manifested into a physical, tangible, definable, truth is because someone has given enough attention to it to make that so. But just because someone else has managed to create their truth, it does not mean it has any relationship to you or to what you will create."

Do you believe that if every person on the planet concentrated only on love and peace, that hatred and war would continue to exist? Of course, it would not! As the collective group of ideas change, so too will the reality change.

People with poor, negative, foolish or even superstitious thoughts generally suffer the consequences of such mentality. Those with wholesome and beautiful thoughts tend to experience good and beautiful lives; or sometimes they are cured from disease solely because of their faith in healing. When one understands this principle, they might easily assume more control over their feelings and circumstances.

People who believe that they are unlucky or cursed, are… by their own ignorance. Have you ever noticed that it's only the people who choose to be superstitious, which have all the bad luck? It is a weakness of the mind to fall prey to evil or nonsensical thoughts—why anyone would choose superstition is beyond reason. ***The best way to predict your future is to create it.*** Practise positive self-talk, imagery, affirmations—ask and you will receive… thinking makes it so.

There is much consequence to being open minded, and I believe that in general this trait is better than narrow vision. However, one must not become 'empty' minded. This is when the mind is like a hollow cavity which absorbs anything and everything without scrutiny. Of course, like any cavity, if we allow too much rubbish to enter, it will eventually become rotten and useless. The best defence is to remain unconvinced until the new idea has shown merit.

All new ideas should become public knowledge, available to be tried and proven. Beware of the know-it-all expert who is an authority on the subject which must be kept secret. They have a simple explanation for everything, but no recognition or evidence. This is often the scenario of people who promote 'occult'—the word itself meaning 'concealed and hidden.' ***The truth is never hidden.***

Everyone is different and everyone creates their own reality. If an individual is very superstitious, they may find that they always have bad luck on Friday the 13th. If one believes in Guardian Angels, that person may experience enormous protection and safety. They will find themselves in the right place at the right time, and will not be standing in the middle of the road when a vehicle runs a red light.

Why do some people see ghosts, auras, aliens, etc. whilst others do not? They see them because they believe they can, and so the subconscious, always answering as it does, will produce the vision for that person—*people cannot see anything manifest which is outside of their belief system.* Remember, not only does our subconscious mind create our reality, but everyone's reality is therefore different.

Know also, that *your luck is determined by your expectations.* The stream of plenty always flows towards the open, expectant mind, so always tell yourself and others that you are lucky, to inculcate this into your vibration. I have been doing this for years and have won all sorts of things. Once I was at a charity raffle and bought five tickets. From the whole room and various prizes offered, my name was drawn four times and people began to look at me with wonder.

The wonderfully brilliant, late Bob Proctor said, "You are God's highest form of creation. You are a living breathing creative magnet. You have the ability to control what you attract into your life." He and I not only shared this belief, but we also shared a favourite book, the original version of "Think and Grow Rich" by Napoleon Hill. It was probably my first real introduction to…

The Law of Attraction

In recent years, the Law of Attraction became much more widely known after people read the book or viewed the film called "The Secret." However, the Law of Attraction was working in my life long before I even knew what it was. Steve Jobs said you can only connect the dots by looking back. When I did this, I realised that the events which had manifested in my life, were all things or situations (good or not) that I had previously spent much time thinking about with passion and feeling. Napoleon Hill's secret to success was defining **your** dream and having a burning desire for it to manifest.

If you could imagine something and believe without any **doubt**, then you could *have, be* or *do* anything—as he wrote, "Whatever the mind can conceive and believe, the mind can achieve." The Bible states in Mark 11:24 "Therefore, I say unto you, all things, whatsoever you ask when ye pray, *believe that you shall receive*, and they shall come unto you."

Aside from belief, the power to change your circumstances lies in your ***imagination***. What will the greatest year of your life look like—see it happening ***next*** year, envision your future and remember that what you think about, you become. Neville Goddard spoke about the Law of Assumption in his book "The Power of Awareness" where he explained: "The future becomes the present when you imagine that you already are what you will be when your assumption is fulfilled." In other words, we must ***mentally live in our positive future*** before it occurs.

Everything we think about with emotion is a vibration (earlier discussed under brain thought transmissions) and when you put out a vibrational frequency, the universe moves to match it, with similar people and situations. Whatever you move toward, moves toward you: success, intellect, understanding, etc. This is known as The Law of Attraction and it will work whether you are consciously applying it or not, for its principle is that whatever you secretly desire, desires you.

Have you ever noticed in yourself or someone else, that when having recently fallen in love and brimming with joy, we become extremely attractive to others whom we meet? This is because ***happiness and manifestation belong together*** and we often hear that the first step in making a dream come true, is feeling the good and happy thoughts of already having it in your possession. Think about love and feel loving—you will attract love; think about problems and you will attract more of them.

The frequency you transmit will be picked up by other people on a similar vibrational level. You might eventually associate with like-minded people— Napoleon Hill's idea of forming a "Mastermind" group was very good. More than 20 years ago, I would meet with associates every Wednesday morning at 7.30 a.m. in an elegant hotel café to brainstorm together. I was an estate agent at the time and the other members were mortgage brokers, financial planners, lawyers, bankers and builders—all of us involved in the housing market. You may wish to create your own Mastermind group because the results from business discussions, referrals and support can be very beneficial. You will attract the circumstances and surroundings to fit your personality, and your environment will gradually change to match the kind of person you become.

The Law of Attraction is continually in motion, and for this reason one must also learn never to operate out of fear or lack—that is the act of thinking about what you ***don't*** want. Acknowledge your thoughts, then simply turn away from the things you don't want and do not give them any feeling; instead, learn to concentrate on all of the things that you *do* love. Think or say out loud frequently "I love my family", "I love my house", "I love my neighbourhood", "I love my vocation", "I love laughter", "I love happy people", "I love nature", "I love my new car" …put forward good thoughts and focus on what you enjoy or want and life will respond to you.

Whenever you do feel in a bad or sad place, refuse to stay discouraged—write down all of the things you are grateful for because you will no longer be able to feel bad when concentrating on the good. Do something kind for somebody else; like the law of cause and effect, only good will come back to you, especially the wonderful feelings we get when we have helped another person or done a good deed. Sing along to some wonderful music or listen to affirmative meditations on YouTube – I highly recommend those posted by Jessica Heslop. Another way to feel better is by changing your physiology—see Chapter 3.

Know your desire—what exactly do you *really* want; immerse into the field of *already having* it through the process of visualisation; finally, *know* that what you want is on the way. Think of people who already achieved a similar goal—then raise your standards, improve your image, do the activities, and surround yourself with like-minded people. The moment your belief matches with any state you will activate the plans, conditions and circumstances which will bring about what you desire. When you combine a *clear intention* (act of the mind) with an *elevated emotion* (opening your heart) you will move into the future you desire.

Feel the strong emotions of having it now—see yourself living it and put yourself in the picture. You do not need to know how it will happen—detach from the current situation of lack and do not let the outside world control you. Doubt and worry are crippling vibrations which lead to fear so you must develop a stronger feeling of positive expectation. Open your imagination—we operate on vibrational frequencies, so let your desire influence your attitude and keep your conscious mind on your goal. Begin to live as though you already are the person you wish to be and have the things you wish to have.

To sum up the Law of Attraction, remember that it is only secondary to The Law of Vibration—we not only need to think good thoughts and assume we already are in possession of what we want, but we must *feel* good in order to attract such things. The heart and the mind will work together to inspire certain feelings and actions which bring us closer to the people and situations required.

Raise yourself to a higher vibration.

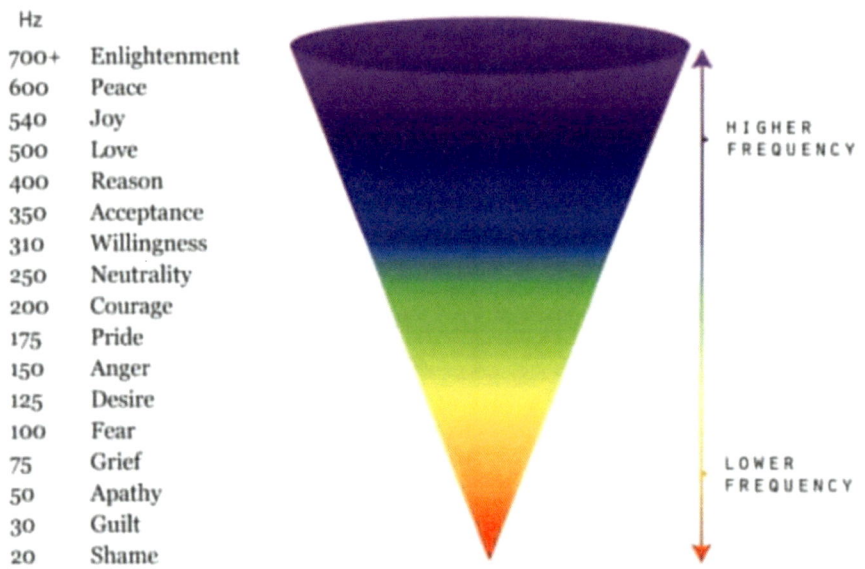

RENEWAL

By the time one has finished this book, many problems which aggravate depression will have been opened to solution. Many people reading this guide are undoubtedly on the right track—simply hoping to further improve their well-established lifestyles. Some individuals are merely starting out… and others still, may be in the midst of defeat. I would like to empathise with the latter group for a moment and share a time, when I too was in a desperate situation many years ago. Being young and naive, I did not know how to deal with my problems.

It was an excessive low with multiple-compounded troubles… to mention a few: an unsatisfactory personal relationship which had been dragging on for some time; employment in a vast methodical workplace where staff functioned solely for money rather than happiness, self-fulfilment and the betterment of others; I was surrounded by several negative influences with poor temperament and self-destructive compulsions; no extra cash, mediocre living conditions… on and on.

I would think of Shakespeare's word "When troubles come, they come not in single spies, but in battalions." Like the straw which broke the camel's back… one day in my mid-20s, it all seemed too much—life had become miserable.

Alone with a throbbing headache… I suffered the proverbial 'weeping and gnashing of teeth.' As I lay on the bed, overcome with anguish, I conveyed my grief to our Divine Creator and pleaded 'Please, please let my life get better, or let this end.'

If I had never believed in miracles before that episode… I surely did after. I soon fell back into a deep sleep, but it was not a troubled sleep, nor was it usual, but very profound. There was a spiritual guide present in my dream state and in my slumber, it was as though I had entered a beautiful place of paradise. Not only did I receive the ***knowledge*** that everything was going to get better, but I felt an extraordinary sense of ***euphoric bliss*** as I never had experienced before. I did not use any drugs /medication then or in my entire lifetime so there was no outside stimulus—it was truly a mystical moment of being completely and utterly filled with joy and in tune with the universe.

When I awoke, my emotional state was optimistic, peaceful, and exuberant… all rolled into one. The stressful physical symptoms had also disappeared—the trembling body, the pounding headache of mental overload… all the pain had vanished.

I knew that my words had been heard—that I was not meant to give up, but that a new life was about to unfold. More importantly, I understood that with the grace of God, all things are possible. I also became conscious of another strong realisation… that this miraculous recovery would require ***action*** as well as prayer.

As the saying goes 'When the student is ready… the teacher will appear.' Like magic certain things began to happen that very day. Books on creating happiness and positive mentality would literally fall into my hands from the truly good friends which I had. Following this lead… I began to increase my knowledge through reading, and listening to positive audio cassettes.

As my mind began to change and expand with information, circumstances altered incredibly. I brought the long unsatisfactory relationship to a swift, yet amicable end. I began more study and within a few months achieved another diploma and business licence. By becoming self-employed, I was able to work with enlightened, charitable people of my own choosing. I left a less than perfect neighbourhood and found an affordable flat in a very prestigious location.

I had finally driven myself out of that rutty road—more importantly, I became determined to steer clear of muddy trails in the future. Truly… it is adversity which creates faith—and when faith has saved us once, somehow, we know that at any time at all, we can call upon that faith to deliver us. Despair need not be disastrous, for it can lead to a new, radiant life—tomorrow can be a different type of day.

Many of us are familiar with the 'Lloyd's of London' story from the 90s when numerous investors lost everything and some took their own lives. Death for money?

Despair is not simply a loss of hope or confidence, but a deliberate action by which one refuses to recognise God's mercy and goodness. People must learn to ask themselves 'what's the worst possible scenario?' In a civilised country, if you end up destitute or bankrupt—will you be tortured? Will society let you starve to death on the street? I think not. If you begin to lose your faith—pray for our Heavenly Father to intervene. Put less emphasis on man-made circumstances—concentrate more on priceless qualities like love. Then remember that a ladder has many rungs and you must begin to move forward one step at a time by taking necessary actions. It is my greatest desire that what I've learned from my personal experiences will assist others to move along an easier path and keep true to their goals.

FEAR IS SEPARATION FROM LOVE

Nothing can kill the spirit swifter than the intimidation of fear. Some people fear for their relationships, others fear for their jobs, paying debts, whatever. True love is never present where fear exists—please see again the Hertz Vibrational Scale on page 32.

Once, while in a corner shop, I noticed a front page newspaper headline, it read: "Thousands have hands, ears cut off, reports say." The article informed readers of a country which apparently mutilated first time offenders for army evasion, or petty theft. What a complete disgrace it would be for any nation to turn away from love, and control others only by *fear.*

A business owner once told me how he controlled staff through fear: "Candy in one hand, a whip in the other!" That attitude is shameful—every action which purposely provokes pain is dysfunctional.

What about people on the receiving end of fear—those who actually place themselves in such turmoil by the temptation of money or security? 1st Cor: 10-13 reads: "May no temptation take hold of you but such as man is equal to. God is faithful and will not permit you to be tempted beyond your strength, but with the temptation will also give you a *way out* that you may be able to bear it." If you are in a situation which is dysfunctional you must remedy it or extricate yourself. Emotional pain is always an indication that improvement and changes need to be made.

You may have been cautioned about various fears: the one who constantly worries about theft, is one who has stolen or been fraudulent; the one who is jealous, is one who has been unfaithful; the one who is suspicious of gossip, is a tongue-wag too… and so on. This is why it is *not* wise to associate with jealous, fearful, or malicious people—more on this under "Associations" in Chapter 4.

FEAR OF FAILURE

Many people have a fear of failure—it might stem from low self-esteem, limiting beliefs or simply the unknown. We need to adopt curiosity and observe that nervous fear has a purpose to help us expand, grow stronger and remove self-defeating beliefs. Turn fear into fuel and remember that successful people make mistakes!

Another aspect of fear can occur when a person feels they must deal with "imposter syndrome". First coined in the 70s, it is loosely defined as doubting your abilities, and is most common with high-achievers who expect their accomplishments to be faultless. Please remember that "done beats perfect", and allow yourself to move forward with goals in knowing that all of our efforts are valid and to be appreciated.

Whether creating a business or a service, your main objective should be to share with and help others. If I were worried about how my book is received, it would mean that I am controlled by Ego rather than just being my authentic spiritual self. Fear of failure comes from Ego—worry of not being liked, etc., so relax, and go with the flow. I love complimenting others and I adore receiving compliments too—this is a beautiful form of increase and expansion; the problem only exists when a person is so insecure that they need validation.

ANXIOUS OR EAGER?

Anxiety occurs when one experiences trepidation pertaining to a situation which they fear or dislike. For example—writing exams might make one anxious. Eager is the anticipation of a happy event. Of course, they are both energetic behaviour which is a type of stress, although anxiety tends to be negative, while eagerness is positive. In the future when you speak to re-programme yourself, don't say "oh, I'm anxious about my dancing lesson or piano recital"—say "I'm eager to do it."

These two words have very different meanings, and it is what you want to distinguish for your brain. In the future, when you look at things, even though you feel a lot of energy, you want it to be positive energy, not a negative form. You don't want to be anxious anymore—you want to be eager. E.g.: Public speaking often makes people anxious, but consider ways of changing that emotion to eagerness. Use positive imagery to encourage your mind to look forward to the event. See the audience absorbed by your speech, and applauding vigorously afterwards. Don't pre-meditate standing on the stage with shaky knees or stammering voice —visualise good things only and break through the barrier of fear.

Conscious and Sub-Conscious

In order to work with the mind, one must have a clear understanding of the two states within. The conscious mind is controlled thought by which we have intellect, perception, education, intuition and can command ourselves to move, act, study, speak, reason, imagine and so forth—*it can accept or reject any ideas put to it.* Sight, sound, touch, taste and smell are physical senses of our environment which help us to see if we are going in the right direction and how best to use our higher faculties which were mentioned above.

The sub-conscious mind is emotional and contains information which exists on a separate level, but has great power and influence toward our conscious lives. Your sub-conscious mind has control over your health, bodily functions, sensations and physical conditions. The sub-conscious is strengthened through repetition, frequent action, visualisation, spoken or written words—all of which become a form of autosuggestion or self-programming. ***The sub-conscious mind cannot reject and will accept anything which you feed it—positive or negative, real or imagined.***

> You've probably heard all of the following maxims:
> 'We become what we think about—all day long'
> 'Whatever man believes—he can achieve'
> 'As man thinketh—so he shall become'

Believe it—sub-conscious mind doesn't reason why. Good or bad, whatever you continually declare, it will strive to bring about. As children our minds are wide open and are basically fed opinions from those around us. As adults, everything which happens is due to thoughts impressed on the sub-conscious mind through one's own belief systems. René Descartes said: 'I think, therefore, I am.'

The words you use and thoughts you think, are like prayers calling out to God's universe to be answered, and literally become your experience.

DREAMS

Before we further discuss re-programming the subconscious mind—I believe it is important to first determine what currently exists there-in ***Your present 'life' is a complete picture of your past 'thoughts.'*** But what is currently going on within your subconscious and how will this affect your future? Sigmund Freud said, "dreams are the royal road to the sub-conscious."

I once participated in a dream workshop based on Jung theory. We were taught that everything in a dream was pertinent, for dreams provided important information which one was not always consciously aware of. By attending these classes, my ability to recall dreams increased dramatically due to my desire and interest in them.

We were instructed to keep a microcassette or notepad at our bedside, and record dreams immediately upon receiving them. The following morning, they were to be transferred into a record journal. The images could then be examined either in the workshop, or with any close associate who possessed an educated understanding of dream study.

The following is a dream which I recorded during that time: I was in a building, near an elevator and there were several people around. We did not take the lift—we were all in the corridor of the ground floor, walking about, but getting nowhere. An older couple was at the end of the hall with their small pet dog at their feet. The dog began to run down the hall, and then it became a squirrel. Near the end of this gloomy grey hallway, large glass windows appeared. The windows conveniently became glass doors, so we let the squirrel outside to its freedom.

I too was also able to leave the confines of the claustrophobic building—it was at this point that the dream intensified, and I began to notice colour. It was incredible outside—the summer sun was shining brightly. There was green grass, rolling hills, shrubbery, colourful flowers, bees, and birds. It was freedom… a breath of fresh air!

This was a dream which marked one of the most significant turning points of my life. I had been very dissatisfied as a young wage-worker in a 'go nowhere' office position. The dream compelled me to wonder if one might be confined working for government or other big business and never get off the ground floor, i.e., reach the top level of freedom and ownership. This vision gave me the courage and inspiration to move on to greater things. Within three months, I became self-employed. I no longer spun on the methodical wheel going in circles—I was free at last. The dream was indeed the royal road of my sub-conscious desires.

What if we are purposely trying to change our consciousness, how will our dream-state respond? For example: if we were born into an ambience of poverty consciousness, but are determined to advance to prosperous thinking. In conscious life, one might begin by making changes or taking new actions: dressing differently, speech improvement, and better associations. Sometimes we become disheartened when we realise that progress can take a long time and a lot of energy.

To determine whether your sub-conscious is keeping up with your outer actions, one might observe their dream-state for clues. If you shift from disturbing dreams to brilliant and beautiful ones, then you will know that progress has begun on the inner level as well. Instead of dreaming of grey dreary places, you may see marvellous gardens and sunshine. When your consciousness has reached a more positive level, the dream-state may allow you to experience feelings of complete joy and being engulfed by love.

You will definitely know when you have achieved a sub-conscious level of prosperity; however, this does not mean that you will never again have dreams which are somewhat troubling. We will always have some less favourable dreams, but these are necessary to help us initiate required changes. For instance, if a particular person in your dreams is always avoiding you, moving away, untouchable, distant, or lost—perhaps this dream is trying to prepare you for detachment from that individual.

The dream-state is also a great place to work off past negative behaviour. For example—people, who have quit smoking, will often continue to dream that they are smoking. They become so frustrated in the dream-state wondering 'Why, why did I ever start again?' Then they awaken, and with enormous relief exclaim 'Oh—thank heavens I haven't really started up again, it was just a bad dream.' Ex-smokers may feel the denial through their sub-conscious for several years, depending how severe the addiction was.

The good news is that by experiencing discomfort in the inner state, we don't need to fulfil the action in the outer state. While we are working towards a conscious life-style change, we may ask ourselves—so why do I continue to dream of the past? This is natural because when you upgrade your image and identity it often takes time to accept your future plan as reality.

Another example might be an adult who has just replaced the use of their first name with their middle name. In regular life they have gotten associates to address them by their preferred name, but in the dream-state, people still refer to them by their childhood name. The previous years of sub-conscious programming will take some time to be revised. Another example: perhaps one has been actively studying elocution. In the dream-state they may be aware that they are still speaking with a poor accent, even though in real life, their English has already been cultivated.

Begin to analyse your sub-conscious. During sleep —what are you dreaming about? Has your dream-state changed in response to your actual lifestyle? When you are active in your own dreams—how do you appear, speak, and feel? What ambience is prevalent with your sub-conscious? Does it coincide or differ from your conscious life—is it better or worse?

Our dream-state does not always lag behind. Sometimes we are fortunate to have very positive futuristic dreams. You may currently live in a very small dreary place, but in the dream-state you may reside in a bright, grand house. If your dreams are like this, you have likely mastered prosperity consciousness.

When one really becomes successful in changing their life, so too will their dream-state improve.

Return to the example of the ex-smoker. After five years he may no longer dream of smoking, for he has totally overcome the desire on both the conscious and sub-conscious levels. You will see improvements in your subconscious. I point this out because it is good for one to become aware of how their inner mind is changing. We can easily change the exterior—our surroundings, the clothes we wear, the way we speak, our physical appearance, the people whom we associate with.

Monitor also how the sub-conscious has progressed. Keep your own mental record, as it is very beneficial for you to understand that the change is becoming a reality. ***What is prevalent in the sub-conscious mind will be easier to achieve in one's outer world.*** What your sub-conscious has thoroughly accepted, will become part of your conscious life as well.

PAST, PRESENT, FUTURE

When we do active mind work in the form of auto-suggestion, affirmations, or goal setting, we are concentrating on future desires which should one day become our present situation. Although it is important to shape our future, it is not necessary to become consumed by it. We must learn to live more in the present moment—today has 24 hours—make the most of them. Put your whole heart into your occupation, your hobbies, your studies, family, leisure time, and so on. Don't dread the rains coming in winter, while the sun shines in July.

Read Matthew 6:30-34… 'But if God so clothes the grass of the field, which flourishes today but tomorrow is thrown into the oven, how much more you, O you of little faith! Therefore, do not be anxious saying "What shall we eat?" or, "What shall we drink?" or, "What are we to put on?" For your father knows that you need all these things. But seek first the Kingdom of God and his justice, and all these things shall be given to you besides. Therefore, do not be anxious about tomorrow; for tomorrow will have anxieties of its own. 'Sufficient for the day is its own trouble.'

It is not enough to 'not worry' about the future, but we must also learn to appreciate the present. Have you ever met the type of person who says 'I'd love to travel' or 'I'd love to join the country club' or 'I'll golf and sail when I retire'... the 'when I retire' may never come to pass. To them I say, try a little golfing this week—learn to enjoy the present.

Now a word about the *PAST*. Everything that has happened in your life prior to this precise moment, is the past. All of our thoughts, words, and actions have put us exactly where we are today. We have made good decisions and bad ones. We have created peace, harmony, goodness, and we might have created despair and pain. In "Pride and Prejudice" one reads: 'Think only of the past as its remembrance gives you pleasure.'

The good moments should have been savoured as we experienced them. The mistakes should have taught us something and then been permanently dismissed. When thinking of your past, look at it from a positive perspective, as a school of learning where everything that has happened in your life thus far, has occurred to prepare you for the greater things you will accomplish and for the person you wish to become.

There are only two types of people who are not completely free to control each day—children, who are required to obey adults—and adults who are imprisoned. Every other person who lives in a *FREE* country should take total responsibility for their destiny. *THE PAST IS HISTORY—THE PRESENT AND FUTURE ARE DETERMINED BY CHOICE.*

I have lived in Canada, Italy, Norway and England and I truly thank God that I have been fortunate to reside in such free and civilised countries where one can do business, own land, engage in free speech and so forth. If you also have the good fortune to live in a land of freedom, count your blessings. Realise that not all people have the same opportunities which we have been given.

Many countries offer little freedom of choice, speech, or voting rights. Some nations are stricken with poverty or war and some people are tormented by violence, capital punishment and even torture. Do you have any idea what you are missing? Be grateful! Even if one has come from a rough background—if they are broke and currently without occupation ... in a civilised nation, they know that they will not have to starve to death in the street. Food and medical care are provided for those who are physically, mentally, or emotionally unable to care for themselves. A decent capitalist country will always have a social conscience.

There may also be others, who are not impaired, but simply believe that they have 'nothing' or no future. Some people, upon leaving the house of their parents, had less than nothing, and were actually already in debt with car loans, university tuition fees, etc. Where you come from should not determine where you are going—do not base what you can accomplish on what you currently have.

Take responsibility for your own life; it is said that "***we only complain about things we can change***." If you had a financially or scholastically inferior start, don't dwell—get on with things. Make the decision to become the person whom you were meant to be. This has no bearing on your current age, for it is never too late. Whether in your 20s, 40s, 60s, or 80s—the brain is always growing with knowledge "*Ancora Imparo*."

There are no excuses for those who live in a free and civilised country. The transition may not occur immediately—so be prepared, be steadfast and be committed. Read, study, learn from successful people—you must live, breathe, and dream the part. ***The way you think, speak, act and feel will determine your outcome***.

The world is filled with abundance from an unlimited supply—do not be afraid to claim your royal rights and privileges. One can create a world of paradise and believe in "life before death" as well as after! Leave all negative thoughts, resentments, and disappointments, where they belong—***in the past***.

TURN NEGATIVE INTO POSITIVE

There are often events in life which carry with them negative connotations for certain individuals. Most of us have faced various situations which make us feel sad, edgy, or uncomfortable. If there is something of this nature which currently is troublesome to you, try to devise a way of turning the negative into a positive. Some situations can be easily remedied. If one is discontent with their occupation, they will work at establishing a different one, i.e., increase their education, spread the word of what really interests them, and gradually become involved with something more suitable.

What about the things which we cannot control—like the weather? Many people suffer from SAD—Seasonal Affective Disorder. The grey weather and shorter days of winter reduce the amount of sunlight. Lack of sunshine can lower the production of serotonin, the brain chemical which is known for its calming effect. But the whole global population cannot pack up and move to the Mediterranean for more sunlight and more serotonin.

Find a substitute which pleases the brain: ***Love***—have you ever noticed how couples in love, stroll arm-in-arm under one large umbrella, totally oblivious to the rain? ***Activity***—create a pleasing ritual. Whenever it rains, put a log on the fireplace. Share the cosy evening with friends—sit in front of a blazing hearth, stoke the fire, enjoy good conversation, and perhaps a glass of fine wine. Keep busy with things which interest or bring pleasure and the weather will at least seem less significant.

AUTO-SUGGESTION —also called Visualisation, Imagery, Mental Practise.

The events you encounter are determined by your ***concept of yourself***. Therefore, create your desired situation first in your imagination—see yourself in your mind's eye—looking the way you wish to be.
- Your hair is the style and colour you prefer.
- Your weight coincides with the physical appearance you desire.
- You are wearing the clothing which makes you look and feel best.
- Your voice and accent are those of polished refinement.
- Your body language is relaxed, comforting and joyful.

Visualise an association or conversation which you are planning to have with someone—role-play in your mind. Practise this imaginative state in the evening, as you relax before falling asleep when your mind has entered the alpha state. Once the seeds are planted consciously, your sub-conscious will help them to grow. The sub-conscious does not recognise the difference between imagination and reality.

When visualising, do not merely envision a picture of something you desire, but add 'movement' to your vision. I would see myself in the 'Winner's Circle' being congratulated as my racehorse won, with pictures being taken and shaking the jockey's hand. You might see yourself entertaining guests for luncheon in your gorgeous new dining room, holding the crystal glass of champagne and making a toast… add the movement to anything you truly want—it worked for me and it can work for you too.

Also note that the time it takes for your assumption to become reality, is proportionate to the ***naturalness*** of already being it… do not consider it as the future, for that tells your mind that you **do not** have it yet, rather consider your vision as a current ***fact***.

By creating the situation in your conscious mind, your sub-conscious will eventually assume it to be correct. We have long heard stories of people being 'brainwashed' by others, but it is amazing that some individuals do not realise that they can actually re-programme their **own** minds. If one is an individual of strong character, they will be the **only** person who can influence their own mind. Other people's opinions will always remain 'outside' opinions. Persons of strong mind would be able to see a stage hypnotist, who is entertaining a huge crowd of people, but they will not become hypnotised—yet these same persons will easily be able to re-programme themselves, because they have personal power.

Become aware of your self-talk, and try to be cautious—keep sound integrity. Whenever you harbour a thought which is not conducive to a bright future, promptly replace it with more positive auto-suggestion.

Albert Einstein said, "Imagination is everything. It is the preview of life's coming attraction."

AFFIRMATIONS

To affirm something is to declare a positive assertion. By consciously affirming something, we are in effect programming our sub-conscious to bring it into being. Affirmations are thoughts and words, either spoken or written. Spoken words have been covered under a separate section—for now we will concentrate on words which we write and think about.

How does writing an affirmation actually provide auto-suggestion to our creative mind? In Shad Helmstetter's book 'What to Say When You Talk to Yourself' he explains it well, "The sub-conscious mind is a sponge—it will believe anything you tell it—it will even believe a lie—if you tell it often and strongly enough. The brain makes no moral judgments; it simply accepts what you tell it… the brain doesn't care."

If you have never written affirmations before, here are a few general guidelines:

* Always state your name, or "I am" ***in present tense acceptance***. Do not say 'I will be' as that would reinforce your thinking that you currently are not.

* Always *write in the positive* as opposed to negative e.g.: do not write "I don't have the bad habit of smoking" write instead "I breathe easily and lead a healthy lifestyle."
* *State precise details* e.g.: "I am certain that my best-selling book helps millions of people and that the Law of Prosperity operating through me blesses and enriches everyone I meet."
* Make the affirmation *as realistic as possible*—you will be more likely to attain results if you say that you earn a logical income, than if you hope to win a difficult lottery.
* *Carry the affirmation on a small card* so you can look at it throughout the day. I also have a 'book chair' and after writing my page of affirmations, I set the notebook opened on the stand, so that I can re-read whenever near it.
* *Write one full page of the affirmation every day for a month*—preferably upon waking and/or just before retiring at night.
* *Think emphatically or speak aloud* the words as you write them.
* *Feel how it would feel* having obtained your affirmation. Let your heart accept that today's self-talk is tomorrow's reality.

Create an affirmation for whatever it is that you desire to bring into being. Samples:

Success

I, your name, am enjoying total success in my business, and everything I do contributes to that perfect result.

Money

I, _____, now earn £10,000 or more each and every month doing what I love and loving what I do—money comes to me easily and effortlessly.

Personal

I, _____, am a calm, confident, strong, loving, secure person who deserves success and happiness.

Friendship

I, _____, am now attracting many friends who are honest, sincere, loyal, faithful, peaceful, happy and prosperous.

Or you may simply begin with ***"I am"*** and express gratitude with feeling, when you proclaim your desire. Examples: "I am so happy and grateful now that I own and live in a grand house with tall bright windows and huge beautiful gardens." "I am in excellent health—everything I eat, drink and do, keeps me in perfect condition." "I am surrounded by high vibrational people who positively impact my life."

If, after you choose an affirmation, negativity should creep up saying 'impossible'… purge yourself. E.g.: if you have chosen to write a money affirmation for the first month, and as you write the first page, many doubts plague your mind. Dispel all fears on the first day of your new affirmation. Deal with them by writing them down, for example: I can't earn £10,000 a month—I have never earned that much money, I don't deserve it. I can't work enough hours, I've always been broken, I have bills to pay…

Then immediately write a page of counter-attack: I can earn as much money as I like. Everything is possible. I deserve all that I desire—it comes to me from the infinite supply of the universe. I am attracting wonderful opportunities and creating new possibilities. I always pay my bills on time, and circulate money with joy—I give willingly and receive graciously. I am always connected to abundance and large sums of money come to me easily now. I receive more and more money through various sources on a continuous basis.

You should need to purge one time only on the first day of a new affirmation, and only ***if you feel strong resistance to it***. Once you have reasoned with yourself, the rest of the month should be smooth writing. Try not to skip any days, and not to change the affirmation or add others. It may take three weeks or more for the subconscious to accept this new idea. By the end of the month, you should feel more secure about it. Then you may choose to begin a different one for the next month.

One may not always see results after the first attempt at a new affirmation. Some people have absorbed negativity for so long, that it may take numerous undertakings to re-programme. Don't give up. If it has been three months since you last did a money affirmation, and you never noticed any financial improvement, perhaps it is time to choose another wealth affirmation for a month. Improved thoughts should eventually persuade one to take the necessary actions.

CLEAR OUT THE NEGATIVE

If affirmative new ideas didn't seep in, it may be because the mind is too cluttered with negative baggage. Sometimes we need to clear out the old to make room for the new. We cannot remove all negative ideas from the sub-conscious, but we can override them with new, more positive ideas. Say "discard" whenever poor thoughts crop up, nip them in the bud, then generate better thoughts and repeat those until they dominate. Say and feel "Something wonderful is happening to me!" We must have zero resistance to fulfilling our dreams.

In the book 'Psycho-Cybernetics' by Maxwell Maltz there is a chapter entitled: 'Dehypnotise Yourself from False Beliefs.' It reads, "but if you have accepted the idea—from yourself, your teachers, your parents, friends, advertisements—or from any other source, and further, if you are firmly convinced that idea is true, it has the same power over you as the hypnotist's words have over the hypnotised subject."

We all know the positive aspects of 'what we believe we achieve,' but it is also important for us to understand the negative side. This is why I stress the importance of avoiding negative programming. Whether it be violent films or news broadcasts, slanderous reading material, or paranoid associates. Pity the minds who are brainwashed into fearing 'black magic' and superstitions, what a pathetic existence that would be. If they listen to such concepts long enough, they may eventually come to live in fear. What's worse—their nervous system will accept the false beliefs and create 'real' physical or mental suffering. The best one can do is guard oneself, and not permit the effects of those who have been engulfed by superstitious delusional thinking.

If you do find yourself slipping into unwholesome attitudes on occasion… refresh your esteem by doing daily affirmations:
"I am the master of my destiny and manifest my highest good. Blessings flow to me in avalanches of abundance. I am a radiant being filled with love and healthful vitality."

PRAYER

Most humans presume that there is a source of infinite intelligence, a supreme creator—the alpha and omega, in which we as co-creators put our faith. Study metaphysical science which goes beyond physical laws like gravity, properties of waves, etc. and deals with energy, so you will understand that everything exists, moving into and out of form and how our vibrations create our reality.

A lot of people express that they are very spiritual and would like to use prayer, but are not certain how to do so. My only suggestion about religious prayer is that you must be genuine and sincere. Try to be positive, just as you would if you were doing affirmations. At mass, we often sing positive affirmations like the song "Ask and it shall be given unto you" and some say that singing is equivalent to praying twice! Also, we often ask God for help, but one should consider the importance of remembering to express gratitude.

The following are two prayer samples which may offer some guidance when praying for oneself:

TRADITIONAL MORNING PRAYER

O Dearest Father, most merciful God! Thou hast given me another day with renewed opportunity to faithfully comply with Thy holy will. I adore Thee and love Thee with all my heart and I thank Thee most sincerely for all Thy benefits, especially for having preserved me during the night. Please give me Thy grace that I may faithfully do Thy holy will in all things. Amen.

TRADITIONAL EVENING PRAYER

Heavenly Father, I thank Thee with my whole heart for all the favours which Thou hast bestowed upon me this day: for my food and drink, my health and all my powers of body and soul. I thank Thee for all Thy holy lights and inspirations, and for Thy care and protection, and for all other mercies. I thank Thee for them all, O Heavenly Father, through Jesus Christ Thy Son, our Lord. Amen.

If praying for someone other than yourself, you might ask "Heavenly Father, please keep <u>name of person</u> happy, healthy, holy and wealthy as long as they may live."

Like many, we also say a blessing before meals. Devout people might encourage this for religious reasons, but it is also in union spiritually with science; see "The Hidden Messages in Water" by Masuru Emoto. Cultures around the world equate water with healing energy and many believe is has the ability to absorb prayers.

THE OTHER SIDE OF THE COIN

If good thoughts and actions create positive results, would it not stand to reason that evil thinking or behaviours might bring about negative situations? I believe that it works both ways.

Scientists tell us that the human species came to live upon this earth long after the age of dinosaurs. It would then seem likely that the ambience here began as a virtual paradise, save for some dangerous tigers and such. So, what happened? Can we re-create that paradise, or will humans choose to manifest a living hell? We must be very careful to promote the beauty of this world, while avoiding thoughts and behaviour which cater to evil.

It is important to remember that **all things are divine** regardless of one's perception, for everything initially came either directly or indirectly from the source of infinite intelligence. Therefore, we need not struggle against what some perceive to be 'evil', but might rather ***accept*** it. Simply 'acknowledging' something is very different from 'focusing' upon it. ***If we focus on anything, either by promotion or rebellion, we are inviting it into our lives.***

Personally, I am very optimistic about the future—do not listen to the 'doomsayers' who try to tell you that the world is getting worse every day. This is simply not true. When was the last time that you witnessed a 'crucifixion', 'stoning' or 'burning-at-the-stake'? We have come a long way from the barbarisms of our tainted past. This brings us to a very serious point: unfortunately, sometimes the evil of the past is used to pollute the minds of our future's children. This is a dreadful mistake, and the consequences should be carefully considered. Some say: always remember history, so that we won't repeat the same mistakes. This is an incorrect method of thinking.

Whatever you dwell upon is more likely to come about. We are aware, that for many centuries, there have been grave mistakes throughout the world. Romans, putting people into the ring of lions. The horrible methods of torture used in England during the fifteenth century. The guillotine of the French Revolution. The horrors of American slavery and witch hunts. The Holocaust in Germany during World War II.

Atrocious acts like torture, war, and capital punishment actually exist in some countries this very day. To promote this type of thinking is a horrible mistake. It is all right if we read and become aware of history, but we mustn't dwell on it. To keep savage *memento mori* on display, to promote 'houses of torture' or 'dungeon museums' does more harm than good. As long as people continue to keep evil thoughts alive how will they ever die? Would our Creator want us to promote these haunting impressions upon the minds of our innocent children? Would infinite intelligence not prefer that we release the tokens of merciless behaviour?

It is far wiser to focus on the fabulous conditions of life. For example: most people will agree that music is a beautiful thing which delights and brings pleasure to all. Therefore, if one goes out and supports classical orchestras and choirs, they are actually creating more music, and more goodness in the world.

Those who predict disaster; however, promote the opposite of paradise, with their negative speech or actions. Have you ever heard a doomsayer speak about the coming of 'World War III' as though it were inevitable? Even worse are the 'doom-*doers*'—those who enter heinous museums, support detestable films, or participate in other abominable events. ***If a person spends even one penny on something which is dysfunctional, they become responsible for its contagion.***

I do not suggest that people exasperate their energy by trying to fight evil. Rather, I recommend that we strengthen our energy by promoting all things good and beautiful—this is a far more pleasant and effective method. Give your support to the kindest people, the highest quality service, and the best environmentally friendly products. Observe with purpose—go to see all of the finest places and things in the world. Focus on prosperity rather than poverty, excellent health rather than illness, peace instead of war, making the world a wonderful place as opposed to creating global flaws—and ***the good will increase***. When we learn to have pleasant thoughts, and practise heavenly behaviours, all of mankind can live in harmonious bliss.

HOW REPETITION AFFECTS BEHAVIOUR

A neighbour of mine once said in jest "People shouldn't worry about going to hell, because if they are there long enough, they will get used to it." It might sound facetious, but his words actually held some hidden meaning. ***Whatever one participates in long enough, may eventually become comfortable***.

Think of a blameless child, who takes up with a rough crowd. The first time the youth witnesses his/her peers shoplifting or committing some other crime, the innocent may be shocked and appalled. The next time the child may be nervous and apprehensive. Later, he/she may relax somewhat and consider the process. After several more trips out, the 'no-longer-innocent' may eagerly participate. The subject became accustomed to the idea, as the sub-conscious mind does with repetition, and later came to consider the actions as normal and acceptable.

Behaviour can be altered by surroundings, habits, thinking, associates, and so forth. Germans of the 1940s were not born Nazis as infants. In youth their innocence was reconditioned, by corrupt peers and elders. It is most regrettable that even today, the good can be manipulated into thoughts of hatred.

Some people do not actually participate in an action repeatedly, but simply view it on film, or read about it continually, thus producing the same results. Some psychologists have noticed that their patients re-enact situations which they previously absorbed repeatedly—everything from fearing murder to ideas of space abduction.

Perhaps this current millennium will become known as the age of the ***mind***. Humans have the option of using this powerful force to develop their full potential, or to wallow in absurdity.

You have probably heard the wise adage: "***Great minds discuss ideas, average minds discuss events, and small minds discuss people***."

Which brings us to…

THE POWER OF SPEECH

We know by now that what we most often ***think*** about, we ***bring about***. But what of ***speaking***? Does it not stand to reason then that whatever you **talk** about you are also inviting towards yourself? Do you speak positive words of kindness or negative derogatory phrases? Recall the wise saying "***if you cannot say something good, say nothing at all.***" Practise it! If you gossip or speak words in anger—be prepared for retribution. If you say to someone 'you are a failure', you are simply attracting failure to yourself. Matthew 12:37 says "For by thy words thou shalt be justified, and by thy words thou shalt be condemned."

If someone should say 'you have no class', they are only confirming their own impropriety at having spoken such ill-chosen words. The little children's rhyme 'I am rubber, you are glue—your words bounce off of me, and stick to you' might not be as elementary as it sounds. Fortunately, there is also a brighter side to this truth. If you speak words of a commendable nature, you will see admirable, deserving results. When civilised households speak of children, one may hear phrases such as "so well-mannered, an absolute angel, or an adorable child."

In less refined families, the offspring may over-hear words like "hell-cat, rug-rat, or little rascal", but notice how the children will usually ***mirror the comments***.

What incredible meaning and actions words can incur. It is also important never to take words out of context. Consider the following example of an order which an ancient king might have written to his court regarding a verdict – "Forgiveness —not necessary to chop off his head." What if the message had been erroneously re-punctuated and arrived like this "Forgiveness not—necessary to chop off his head." It would have caused the execution of a man who was to be pardoned.

In Betty J. Eadie's book 'Embraced by the Light', we are well warned about the power of our thoughts and words; she wrote: "Positive attracts positive, and negative attracts negative. Light cleaves to light, and darkness loves darkness." If we become mostly positive or mostly negative, we begin to associate with others like us. But WE have the choice to become positive or negative.

Simply by thinking positive thoughts and speaking positive words we attract positive energy… A person's words actually affect the energy field around him. The very words themselves—the vibrations in the air—attract one type of energy or another. A person's desires have a similar effect. There is power in our thoughts. We create our own surroundings by the thoughts we think.

Physically, this may take a period of time, but spiritually it is instantaneous. If we understood the power of our thoughts, we would guard them more closely. If we understood the awesome power of our words, we would prefer silence to almost anything negative. In our thoughts and words, we create our own weaknesses and our own strengths. Our limitations and joys begin in our hearts.

Every word you speak… every thought you think—will partially determine the pleasure or pain which falls upon you—it's your choice.

Education

Wisdom 6:13 "Wisdom is glorious, and never fadeth away, and is easily seen by them that love her, and is found by them that seek her."

A very important step to leading a full and successful life is education. It can be achieved in many different ways—through our parents, clergy and other mentors; by trial and error; via special courses or extension programmes; by attending seminars or watching them on YouTube; from private tutors or life coaches; by going to school or university; and by simply reading and studying material of an instructive nature. Education is unique to each individual—learn through the methods which you prefer, but always learn! Education does not begin with prep school, nor does it end with a degree. It is a continual process which starts at birth and should continue until death.

Education brightens and increases our natural intelligence. Even if a person has the extraordinary gift of common sense or was born a genius, there is still much one can learn. How are success and intelligence related? This is an interesting question because although the two of them seem to naturally go together, mankind's perception will occasionally change. In centuries past, one's success and intelligence were based upon their aptitudes, abilities, and accomplishments—we think of people like Leonardo da Vinci, Mozart and so on. By the 1900s much importance was put on academic titles or degrees.

Presently, success also seems to be determined by how much income one generates or other forms of merit. If a person has two or three degrees, but is unsuccessful at putting them to good cause, they are considered a professional student and nothing more. Is the bottom line on one's tax return more significant than the framed certificates which hang in their office? Personally, I would not base success on monetary profit or paper documents. ***Success is what one has***

contributed to the betterment of the world whether it be making a new discovery, inventing a product, creating a work of art or producing anything significant. Remember also that one can bring success to everything which we do as long as we enjoy life while fulfilling our purpose and complete each action in the best possible manner. An example might be caring for others: children, the elderly, the sick or the poor as Mother Teresa did.

A good education can be achieved in two ways: independently, or through the aid of an institution. In past decades as many as 80% of the population were considered to be 'followers' compared with 20% who were 'leaders', but times are changing, and the shepherds are gaining on the sheep.

An adult who is self-motivated and self-disciplined may easily become a success without a controlled education. Such persons automatically set aside time to study and read one or two enlightening books every week. No one has to push or encourage this group of people to become educated.

I am not suggesting that everyone quit going to school—I am only clarifying that 'true success' does not solely depend on formal education, and even if one has missed out on such, they need not suffer with regrets. Naturally the basics are still as important as ever—reading, writing, and arithmetic. How could one possibly handle their finances without arithmetic, or perform business without writing? Most significant of all: How difficult it would be for one to achieve great mental improvement without extensive reading.

Aside from live experience, reading is the foundation of most education, and best of all—it remains free and available to everyone. Even in this computer age, people can still make good use of public libraries. The American historian, Shelby Foote wrote, "A university is just a group of buildings gathered around a library."

Education is not just teaching people what they do not know, but leading them to behave as they do not behave. If you want to lead a successful life, learn how to make an educated first impression. Whenever one meets with a stranger, that vital 'first impression' is formed. Unless one has a renowned name or prominent title, this early-stage impression can usually be based on two apparent factors: the way you look and by the dialogue which is exchanged. See the chapters on clothing and speech to follow. When you speak to a new acquaintance, do you come across as being cultured, learned, creative, and accomplished?

What if that initial contact is not to be made in person, but rather, through introduction by written letter? Do you write in proper complete sentences? I prefer to spell in traditional English: aeroplane, cheque, colour, favourite, honour, neighbour, programme… although shortening these words into American form is not incorrect. However, some writers do worse than simply omitting letters, when they opt to take other short cuts like thru instead of through, nite for night, or thanx in place of thank you. Never advertise sloth, but demonstrate your aptitude, especially when writing professional letters. Education can be acquired by all, and will be an enormous factor on the road to living royally.

One of my early school masters wrote the following in my journal: 'Good, better, best… never let it rest, until the good is better and the better is best.' What an inspiring thought! As adults we are fortunate because we can choose to surround ourselves with people who motivate us with strong progressive ideas, high goals, and positive aspiration. This is not necessarily the case for children, whose educational fate lies in the hands of their guardians.

Granted, there are the fortunate ones who learn manners, etiquette, music, art, different languages, and diplomatic skills which might ensure their future success in life. Such privileges should be available for everyone. Whether you opt to give your child a state education or place them in an independent school, be sure to select a school of good repute. ***Only when people demand excellence, will excellence be achieved***.

Aside from self-education, there are three general types of learning: private tutors, independent schools, and government—for information about their various pros and cons, see Appendix #1 at the back of this book.

All of the above types of education may have good teachers; ergo, it will not really matter which form you choose, as long as you select one which puts great emphasis on learning and developing the talents of its students. Having said this; also remember that greatness can be achieved in various ways and one does not need to attend a superior college, if like the late Steve Jobs, you are capable of creating incredible things without the discipline of an institution.

In my late-20s, while self-employed as an estate agent, I would study goal setting, time management, positive attitude, motivation, public relations, and many other fascinating subjects. I developed a passion for seminars, small workshops, and private tutelage such as oil painting, piano, riding and golf lessons. I started a small thoroughbred company which was also a wonderful learning experience, and by the time I reached my mid-thirties, I sold the race-horses and was able to concentrate on writing, charitable works, becoming a goodwill ambassador, social hostess and director of our company.

The point is that learning, no matter what sort, is a vital part of living well. It need not be expensive, for one can always do an exchange of service or simply use the free range of library books, CDs and DVDs which cover everything from languages to business. In this computer age, much information can also be gathered from high quality Internet sites. If you want to progress in life, never place education on the shelf. Knowledge is a primary step towards success—one might travel to learn other languages and about different cultures or enrol in local educational programmes. At least be sure to read something instructive on a daily basis, for as the saying goes, "Readers are Leaders."

YOU ARE WHAT YOU READ

Aside from true life experience… reading may well be considered one of the greatest ways to enlighten the mind. Today there is a multitude of wonderful books available to choose from. 'How to' manuals, if one desires instruction on learning to accomplish or create something. Books which offer advice on financial matters, business, protocol, etiquette, etc. Autobiographies and authorised biographies in book, CD or video form that enable everyone to learn from the experience of others. Positive attitude self-help information, history, science, art, language, music and many other forms of non-fiction; as well as novels of captivating fiction such as beautiful romance, which encourage love and add sparkle to relationships.

Whether we read for entertainment or education, the intelligent mind will use fine judgement and discrimination to select material. These people shun books which are negative—slanderous ***un***authorised biographies, dictatorial propaganda, and anything which does not add to positive well-being.

Cultured people have another dictum about what ***not*** to read: ***refrain from everything which leaves ink on your fingertips.*** Muck-media, rag magazines, tabloids, gutter-press—whatever one chooses to call it, will wisely be avoided. Rubbish in—rubbish out… remember 'you are what you read.' If anyone suspects that you are interested in materials of that nature, you can say farewell to your cultured image.

So, what about newsprint? Aside from the health and well-being section; money or financial; or book, restaurant and theatre reviews, newspapers provide little education or entertainment. They can be laden with advertisements, and although they do mention some significant events—much tends to be local gossip. Classic FM or BBC radio generally satisfies my interest with their short world updates in the morning, but if you are a news enthusiast, consider subscribing to a weekly news magazine like The Economist. They generally avoid the petty 'other-people's-business' articles, and concentrate on more important global journalism—just avoid magazines where propaganda is known to creep in.

Magazines are beneficial then? It depends which ones you choose, as some are far superior to others. Remember that we are always in search of excellence—learning to expect quality. Therefore, if you wish to subscribe to magazines, try to select la crème de la crème; i.e.: if you want to read about your favourite sport —find the *best* magazine about yachting, golfing, or what interests you.

If you want to look at motorcars or real estate, try the 'Robb Report.' Satisfy your business tastes with Fortune, Forbes, or whatever pertains to your occupation. If you enjoy fashion, try 'Elle.' If heritage charm is your preference, consider 'Victoria.' For an aristocratic read… 'Royalty' offers the rare pleasure of no public advertising. I used to read Pacemaker, Spur, and The Blood Horse because I owned thoroughbreds for racing, but I also enjoy positive society magazines like 'Town and Country.' My husband and I are often featured in the society section of the Diplomat; established in 1947, it is one magazine where we can feel honoured to have personal pictures printed.

I purchase several periodicals every month, but do not retain them with my book collection. If, like myself, you do not wish to save your month-old magazines, take them to your local library and donate them to the 'free box,' or leave them in a public office or airport lounge where others might enjoy them.

Libraries are our greatest source of complimentary information, and many branches have expanded to provide free use of audio CDs and video DVDs, as well as books and magazines—the operating costs have become very high. If you are looking for a charitable tax donation, consider giving money towards this cause. *As long as libraries exist, every human being may have a source of free education.*

That brings us to your home library. When you read a fantastic book which you know will serve your family and guests for generations, be sure to purchase it for your personal library. Ours is full of the classics like Austen, Bronte, biographies and almost anything which the Folio Society has printed. We also keep many health and fitness, gardening, travel, self-education and other beneficial books available on our book shelves.

If possible, allocate an area of your abode for use as a personal library. Not only will it provide endless hours of gratification for you and your family, but if you open its doors to visiting house-guests, they will likely consider it a wonderful privilege as well. I adore browsing through people's literary collections, or watching them point out hidden treasures which I have never seen before.

What type of book is on the shelves? Fiction or non-fiction, from centuries old relics like Shakespeare to hot-off-the-press latest best-sellers, select anything which you consider in good taste. For extra appeal—books in leather bindings or high-quality cases like the Folio Society offers, as well as copies which are signed by the author, always rate highly.

Educational books or guides may also be found: Encyclopaedias, a good English dictionary, Roget's International Thesaurus, Berlitz—modern language self-teachers, an atlas—as current as possible, the Holy Bible—complete 73 book text with the words of Christ printed in red for quick reference, Debrett's guides, and of course—geographical books on various countries and cultures. To sum up: anything which may be considered to improve the mind.

This is not to say that lighter materials are avoided—magazines on business, sport, society, or fashion are often available. Some people also invest in acclaimed books which have been recorded on audio or video. If one's eyes are blurred from reading, they can relax and listen to classics on audio CD. Recordings also provide a marvellous way to master modern languages, work at self-educational programmes, or use motivational information.

If you want to extend your personal library to include DVD films, the secret to keeping it tasteful is to display mainly ***films which were originally classic books***. For example, one might include 'Pride and Prejudice' 'Sense and Sensibility' 'Jane Eyre' 'Wuthering Heights' 'Bleak House' 'Middlemarch' and many more; note that BBC has done a fabulous job of producing the classics on DVD—most bookstores will be able to order them for you.

Those with musical and artistic taste might enjoy productions such as 'My Fair Lady' 'The King and I' or 'Gigi.' Some private houses also stock documentaries, travel videos, and other educational films; or royal weddings which may become collectables, as well as films which received an Oscar for "best picture". Historical drama series like 'The Crown' or 'Downtown Abbey' are pleasing to watch and writers like Julian Fellowes have done a wonderful job in the research. Children can take delight in Louisa May Alcott's 'Little Women,' Lucy Maud Montgomery's 'Anne of Green Gables,' Frances Hodgson Burnett's 'The Secret Garden,' or some of the animated Disney classics.

Don't make the mistake of buying worthless TV-style 'hits-of-the-week' just because they are on sale. Libraries were designed for quality of an instructive, entertaining nature; anything less will diminish the character of your collection, so try to purchase only the best and it will continue to serve for generations.

Prosperity Consciousness

Prosperity consciousness—what is it, and how does one acquire it? Prosperity is defined as successful thriving which stems from the word prosperous: 'flourishing, enjoying vigorous and healthy growth.' Are we born with this mental attitude, or do we decide upon it? Considering that one's behaviour does not always correspond with their heredity or environment, I believe that we can choose this way of thinking. Throughout life we are all exposed to many different concepts.

Like most little children, I greatly enjoyed the fairy tales which portrayed a turn of luck or rags-to-riches: Cinderella, Sleeping Beauty, Snow White… In youth, we are presented with numerous and varying impressions, of which we have the option to envision our favourite selections. My childhood friends and I would play 'dress up' by donning a cape (blanket), a string of pearls (beads), and queenly tiaras (aluminium foil). At such a young age we did not own those material luxuries; but love was abundant, and my girlhood imagination was extremely prosperous.

Alas, as a teenager I left behind the 'childish' regal fantasies and chose to be part of the 'norm,' living a life where mediocre consciousness often ruled the day. Several years passed before my attitude made the turnabout back to its original belief in self-fulfilment. Good reason reminded me that we are free to determine our own destiny.

The people and circumstances which surround us influence our personal habits, and in effect, partially determine whether we choose faith, hope, and benevolence—or fear, worry, and malevolence. A major purpose of this book is to list various routes to a prosperous lifestyle and to encourage readers to remember the significance of their free-choice.

If, in this particular phase of your life, you are curious to know whether you lapse into 'poverty' thinking, or currently possess 'prosperity' consciousness, the following quiz may be helpful.

Prosperity/Poverty Quiz

* You own Baccarat crystal, silver cutlery and a set of fine bone china:
A. The adults in your house utilise these items on a daily basis.
B. You tuck away all expensive, high-quality tableware for 'special' days.
* You wear the hats which you own:
A. Whenever you feel like it.
B. Only to Royal Ascot or other obligatory occasion.
* You need to buy a pair of autumn trousers—you choose:
A. 100% wool, cut with pleats for style and comfort.
B. Torn denim blue jeans because they are the current fad.
* When you receive or invest a vast amount of money, you tell:
A. Possibly your financial planner, banker or tax accountant.
B. Your family, friends and anyone else who has ears.
* You have accumulated 75,000 (pounds or dollars) in cash, and also earn a consistent business income. Mortgage rates are very reasonable, and deciding to purchase a residence, you choose:
A. To use the 75K as a down payment to a mortgage on a superior property, in your favourite prestigious location.
B. To pay cash and have clear title to a small studio-flat or trailer in a less than desirable area, hoping that one day you can save more money and eventually move 'up.'
* You're going to travel abroad for the first time to a new destination on a holiday lasting at least a fortnight—you:
A. Do research, write query letters, read books, study locational videos and language; become aware of fine private restaurants, hotels, and events which will occur during your stay.
B. Couldn't be bothered with all the fuss, so you purchase a group tour.

* You're a young adult sharing a place with a compatible housemate and generally have some extra cash. The two of you agree to contribute 100 (pounds or dollars) per week towards:
A. A part-time house-keeper.
B. A carton of cigarettes or some cannabis.
* You would be more likely to say:
A. I'm going to my masseur/masseuse because I just adore a good massage.
B. I'm going to the physiotherapist because my back problem is killing me.
* We might find you listening to:
A. Classical music or opera on your symphonic quality, but discreetly out-of-sight Bang & Olufson.
B. Unrecognisable sounds which reverberate through giant size speakers.
* On the chimney-piece of your fireplace, sits a fine clock in the centre surrounded by functional candlesticks on each side. On the wall directly over the mantel, you decide to hang:
A. An original oil painting or a fine gilt framed looking glass.
B. A flat screen TV.
* Your jewellery:
A. Is available in your floor safe where you can easily access various items to wear daily at will.
B. Is stored in a safety deposit box at a bank or other secure location and very rarely, if ever, put to use.
* When out on the sea:
A. You will be on a friend's private yacht or perhaps on one of Cunard's luxurious Queens.
B. You rent a small boat or take a very cheap cruise.

QUIZ—CONCLUSION

If, in the past, you've studied the mind and how it operates, you will recognise that the 'A' answers represent 'Prosperity' consciousness, and the 'B' choices typify 'Poverty' thinking. The people who chose mostly 'A' answers automatically expect the best—they know that they deserve to lead lives with quality, freedom, and satisfaction. People who chose B answers, are frequently insecure, tend to feel less deserving and may not be convinced of the right to raise their standards.

Poverty thinkers come in extremes—if they do eventually accumulate something of value (like fine bone china), they may be reluctant to use it. Or, they will purchase something which is not created for artistic purposes (a huge and ghastly stereo or television) to display in a drawing room as though Michelangelo sculptured it.

Aside from the fine art upon their walls, **prosperous** people prefer to **use** their assets—rather than just look at them. Their motto is… if you don't appreciate and enjoy what you have—you didn't really need it in the first place. **Every day** one can experience the delight of eating from their best dishes, wearing quality apparel or jewellery and living in a terrific location. Fine dining and travelling in luxury will surely follow as the mind-set improves.

The only reason anything has manifested into physical form, is because someone has given thought and attention to its creation or making it so. Look around you at the many objects which were first only a thought. Original creation was complete with all materials long existing on our planet, but the world is now re-formed and further developed by human imagination.

One of the most prominent indicators which will determine whether or not a person has prosperity or poverty consciousness is their approach toward material objects. The affluent thinker will automatically expect the best. They will not stare for two hours at the painted ceilings of the Vatican because they're well accustomed to seeing beautiful art and architecture. Secondly, they will use objects rather than merely admire them, i.e.: they will stand upon their Persian rug, they will drink from their best crystal, use their silverware and eat with their fine bone china and silver cutlery daily.

The casual **use** of material objects, applies to other philosophies as well. **Action** is a similar word, for prosperous thinkers prefer to be participators as opposed to on-lookers. Consider their behaviour when travelling: rather than simply taking photographs of a cathedral, they will actually **attend** a mass. They will **swim** off the beaches, **dance** at the balls, **picnic** with the farmers, **drink** in the vineyards, but they will not join a public tour which stares at the Eiffel tower, while being told the number of beams used in its construction.

Prosperous thinkers would **never publicly discuss their financial affairs**— while poverty conscious people are pre-occupied by the thought of money, and their speech is often consumed by the subject. Also, with respect to speech, you will have noticed that affluent thinkers **always choose positive words, as opposed to negative**— 'adore a good massage' rather than 'my back is killing me.'

Frequently, from early childhood, one may be programmed to believe ***the misconception that life was meant to be a struggle.*** Some people assume that deprivation is natural, or that they are unworthy of comfort and gladness. Nonsense! Everyone deserves a pleasant life—the world is filled with abundance. There is fertile soil where fresh produce can easily grow; we have trees, flowers, green grass; water, blue sky, and sunshine—all things necessary of a virtual paradise on earth providing we remember to care for the environment.

Even if you chose all 'B' answers—do not despair. Our consciousness can be changed, and everyone can learn to accept-the-best. I earlier wrote about this renewal process following the section on 'mind.' At this point I simply wanted to clarify the difference between 'affluent' thinking and 'adversity' thinking.

STATUS

For those who enjoy classifying or categorising themselves or want to consider the general perception of social status, I shall oblige. Bear in mind that many people will fall into more than one category and one can certainly change. Although some items are based on intelligence, for example: wearing gold rather than tin, or buying property rather than renting… note that other samples printed are merely the 'general' perception.

A famous athlete from a lower background might shave his head and still get a nod from girls who are not normally attracted to bald men. If the uppers usually prefer seafood and T-bones, they might still indulge in the occasional hamburger. Also, consider that aristocrats might drive inexpensive little domestic cars just as readily as ride with their driver in the Bentley. The chart is simply a *perception* of various societal behaviours.

Questions regarding class, with sample answers from lowest ranking, to highest and best.

1. Where do you live?

Lower to Lower-middle: Rented apartment (flat), townhouse, maisonette or condo. Rented semi-detached house, or detached house. Mortgaged apartment as above; mortgaged semi-detached.

Upper-middle to Upper: Mortgaged detached house. Owned detached house with gardens; owned grand house with acreage or land.

2. What do you ride on/in?

Lower to Lower-middle: Tube (metro); buses; mopeds and motorcycles; low quality hatchback cars, trucks or vans; camper cars; small boats; second class rail; economy class air travel and cheap cruise lines.

Note: Walking and cycling have no class barriers, but it is preferable to do such for leisure rather than as transportation.

Upper-middle to Upper: Better motor-cars: Jaguar, BMW, Mercedes, etc. in sport or sedan styles; business class air travel; taxis or limousine with chauffer; thoroughbreds and polo ponies; Rolls, Bentley, etc. with one's live-in factotum to drive; fly first class or by private jet; sail on private yachts or best cruise ships.

3. What activities occupy your spare time?

Lower to Lower-middle: Watch free TV; play Bingo; casino, online gambling, etc.; watch cable or Pay TV; go to the cinema; watch competitive sports.

Upper-middle to Upper: Watch classic films on home screen like DVDs or YouTube; attend cinema – especially film premieres; attend live theatre, symphony, opera, ballet, polo matches, society races, top golf tournaments, gallery openings, museum previews, etc.

4. What do you read?

Lower to Lower-middle: Flyers and free papers; online social gossip; tabloids, yellow press; poor quality newspapers or magazines; books occasionally.

Upper-middle to Upper: Read front page headlines, stock column, obituaries etc. from best newspapers, but may prefer weekly global news like The Economist; select high quality magazines like Forbes, The Robb Report, Diplomat, Royalty, The Lady, Town & Country, Field, Country Life, etc.; read books often.

5. What sporting recreation do you engage in?

Lower to Lower-middle: Volleyball, bowling, stock cars, boxing or wrestling, basketball, baseball, soccer, hockey, football; swimming at public pools and beaches.

Upper-middle to Upper: Skiing, tennis, golf, fencing, English riding and hunt, boating, polo; swimming in private pools or beaches.

6. What type of music do you listen to?

Lower to Lower-middle: Heavy metal; country western; rap; hip hop; rock; jazz; blues.

Upper-middle to Upper: pop; easy listening; contemporary; classical.

7. How do you dine out with friends?

Lower to Lower-middle: Fast food franchise; pub or ordinary restaurant.

Upper-middle to Upper: High quality restaurant; in their private members' clubs.

8. Drinks anyone?

Lower to Lower-middle: Home-brewed; coolers; brandy; rum; malt liquor; cider; boxed or other cheap wine; beer; bourbon; liqueurs; cheap gin for tonic.

Upper-middle to Upper: Fine wines; sparkling wine including cava, sekt, prosecco; quality gin or vodka for martinis; aged whiskey or scotch; dry sherry; vintage or tawny port; best wines; champagne; cognac.

9. Coffee?

Lower: Regular – more than 3 cups per day; lower middle: Regular – less than 3 cups per day.

Upper-middle to Upper: Decaffeinated or specialty flavoured coffees; espresso/cappuccino before 11 a.m.

10. What kind of material is your clothing?

Lower to Lower-middle: Polyester, acrylic or other plastics; modal; rayon; blends of made-made with natural fabric.

Upper-middle to Upper: Pure cotton or linen; other 100% natural fabrics – virgin wool, silk, cashmere, camel, angora, etc. may be blended with each other.

11. What type of jewellery do you wear?

Lower to Lower-middle: Large plastic baubles; metals that turn green; wood, stones; some 9 kt gold or silver plated. * Often wear too much at once.

Upper-middle to Upper: 14 kt gold; Stirling silver; Semi-precious gems – garnet, turquoise, amber, etc.; fresh water pearls; 18 kt gold; platinum; pearls; precious gems – diamonds, emeralds, sapphires, rubies, etc. *Wear very little at the same time.

12. How's your hair?

Lower to Lower-middle: Permed, short frizzy, or long shag; extremely short pixies; wildly dyed like the colour green; skin head shaved on men; crew cuts on men.

Upper-middle to Upper: Colours may be highlighted or tinted in natural shades; unique fashion designs and chic styling for women; soft, shiny, smooth, classic cuts for women; classic left side part for men; individual style for men – never very short.

Class/Civility

Top quality, elegance, and similar words generally come to mind when we contemplate the definition of class. Then we have the many prerequisites. In order to acquire it, one must become civilised, cultured, and so forth. The good news is that these characteristics can be attained by everyone. The following is an excerpt from The Vancouver Sun printed one June during the prime racing season in England: "Ascot's pretensions to elitism have been swept away by a shoving horde of arrivistes who rent their morning suits," sniffed Ross Benson, the gossip columnist of the Daily Express newspaper.

Whatever it once was, however, this British social club, the class system, is today flexible enough to absorb many newcomers—as long as they are properly well-heeled. "The fascinating thing about the British class system," says historian Jacques, "is its ability to mutate, to reproduce itself in other forms, to attract outsiders and persuade them to be part of the act."

Adds social commentator Stephen Glover: "John Major is wrong if he thinks that our class system is particularly rigid. ***If you are rich or ambitious or forthright, you can always trade up, and if you are lazy or eccentric you can even trade down.***" Andrew Neil, editor of the Sunday Times, says, "The old Establishment has always preserved its position by not being too exclusive—it has been wily enough to absorb the up-and-coming and convert them to their attitudes and mannerisms." (My bold)

One can trade 'up' or 'down.' The article is most accurate in declaring that people can change status of their own free will. In order to live really well, I would suggest choosing 'up'—and the two basics for this, are culture and civility.

Culture

"… must have a thorough knowledge of music, singing, drawing, dancing, and the modern languages… manner of walking, tone of voice, address and expressions… improvement of mind by extensive reading." Indeed, the meaning of accomplished has not changed much since those famous lines were written in Jane Austen's "Pride and Prejudice" published in 1813.

If one cannot identify the difference between a Rembrandt and a Picasso, or distinguish Chopin from Beethoven—make haste, and get thee educated! Aside from private study, one might register for art, language, or dance classes, at a community association. Select a centre in a sophisticated neighbourhood, where you will be able to study with people of cultivated taste. Just as one would avoid shopping on evenings or weekends, so it is wise not to take classes at these times for they may be overcrowded. Weekday mornings generally provide an ideal setting where one can associate with other independent people.

Perhaps most important of all—remember that the best education is experience. Attend symphonies, operas, art galleries, museums, and so forth. Avoid being 'provincial' and unsophisticated with narrow vision, restricted interests, untravelled, or capable of speaking only one language. Associate with others of refined taste—people who search for the best in everything.

Learn social graces: politeness to everyone despite their status; kind speech and sincere interest in the conversation of others; honesty; temperance; charity, and love for your fellow man. Go to a quality book dealer, and see if you can locate a traditional work on manners. Sometimes older items such as Barbara Cartland's Book of Etiquette or its reprint called Etiquette Handbook, can still be quite useful today. If you have additional questions, please see "Tradition, Etiquette and Advice" on our website. A wonderful saying goes: there is nothing in the world so attractive as gentleness and good manners.

Many of us are familiar with Nancy Mitford's essay from the 1950s, which coined the expressions 'U' referring to upper class and 'non-U' meaning not characteristic of the upper classes. These abbreviations have become common usage; however, I should like to create an additional term: C and un-C.

In this case the C does not merely stand for 'class' or 'cultured.' I want people to move beyond the narrowness of the class system and have a broader vision. C or un-C mentioned hereinafter will also refer to CIVILISED and UNCIVILISED. This is required, because on some occasions in life you might actually meet someone who is 'U' but 'un-C,' and vice versa. This removes all barriers like class/royalty, or money/millionaires. A few aristocrats and far too many rich people behave in an un-C fashion, living rather undignified lives. It is important that we *do not group money and status in the same category*. ONE CAN BE RICH WITHOUT CLASS just as ONE CAN HAVE CLASS WITHOUT MONEY… I have observed numerous examples of both.

CIVILISED **does not** refer to rank or fortune. If you check a good thesaurus, you will find it synonymous with many other words: advanced, cultured, developed, educated, gracious, improved, polished, refined, and sophisticated.

C-people are those who continually contribute to making the world a more beautiful, harmonious, and pleasant place to live in. Now compare the definitions for UNCIVIL: not civilised; barbarous; lacking in courtesy; ill-mannered; impolite; not conducive to civic harmony and welfare.

What might one consider to be civilised, cultured, classic or not so?

UN-C	C
* War, killing, terrorism	* Peace, harmony, safety

* Tabloids, yellow press, radio commercials, television	* Books, art galleries, theatre, cinema, symphony, opera
* Intemperance, drugs	* Moderation, strength of character
* Crime, gossip, lack of charity	* Probity, generosity, philanthropy
* Lies, deceit, deception	* Honesty, loyalty
* Hitler, Stalin, Bin Laden and other leaders who promoted cruelty, evil, death and destruction	* Jesus, Mother Teresa, Buddha John Paul II—and others who encouraged forgiveness, life, love
* Fear, superstition, hatred	* Faith, hope, trust, love
* Political or government control	* Noblesse Oblige, freedom
* Zoos, circuses, bull fights, battery caged animals	* Huge natural wildlife reserves, free-range farms
* Physical, verbal, or emotional abuse	* Manners, etiquette, gentle kindness

If we truly desire success and want to live the good life, we must first be sound in morals, mind, and actions—we must be CIVILISED. If anyone has an aversion to the word CIVIL, consider this: If everyone in the world were truly civilised, in every sense of the word, there would be no criminals, no prisons, no need for police, no wars, no famine… no misery. The word literally equates to paradise on earth—who could possibly not be in favour of that?

Two "Un-C" characteristics to be avoided are:

*Prejudice. People have long blamed apparent distinctions for causing the problems of bias. Human differences such as colour, race, and religion are frequently used to determine whether someone is liked or disliked. Negroid, Caucasoid, or Mongoloid; socialist, liberal, or capitalist; catholic, protestant or Jew… these are external categories. How dull this world would be if everyone was identical and unvarying in opinion.

Variation and open-mindedness are human blessings. I understand more than one language; my pedigree is western European; my religion is Roman; I have property in Italy; I have lived in Norway; I have done business in the US; I have visited the six continents and have friends in all of them; my passports are Canadian and British… and I feel so fortunate to possess parts of different cultures and be able to avoid *nationalism*. We all share this earth and must not pre-judge people by outer categories… get to know the 'real' person. If one is truly 'C': kind, honest, forgiving and charitable… who could possibly dislike them?

*Primitive Actions. I was fortunate to spend my youth in a very civilised country where the military was non-aggressive, serving as global peace keepers who would also handle search and rescue, avalanche control, etc. Torture and capital punishment did not exist and we had excellent role models: Our head of government the Prime Minister, our head of state the Sovereign and the head of our majority church the Pope.

C-people show their gratitude for the love and freedom which they possess by working hard to promote civility throughout the world.

Character/Charisma

CHARISMA IS CONTAGIOUS

Those who have that inborn ability to bestow approval and radiate cheer naturally, will always be blessed with well-deserved reciprocal benefits. Recall and envision some past occasion when you met a person with a wholesome, sincere, and irresistible smile. Did you not find yourself compelled by intercommunication to reflect the likeness which you saw? The person on the receiving end may be compared to a looking glass, for they act as a reflector. The sender may be likened to a boomerang—for whatever signal they convey, will generally be returned.

Charisma is so contagious, that sometimes one's face will beam impulsively at a mere image—like a photograph, or a cinema character who smiles on screen. The intoxicating power of gaiety and grace are immense.

Naturally, this does not include insincerity. A laugh can be vulgar, or a smirk can be rude, but a truly earnest smile, is always charming. Who could resist smiling back at an innocent smiling baby?

One might think that those in the public spotlight would become fatigued at so much smiling, but it need not be overdone. A subtle glow and sparkling eyes radiate good spirit and are always 'très elegant.'

So, too, a negative look will almost always incite an adverse impression, and induce an unfavourable mirror response. I once asked a fellow for his opinion of what made a woman appear either adorable or unattractive. He offered a long list of endearing qualities, but provided only one negative characteristic as to what would detract from handsomeness. He replied 'a woman can only look unpleasant when she displays a glaring frown, rolls her eyes or reveals a scowling face.' Touché for men.

For those who are not naturally blessed with a charismatic disposition, how difficult can it be to smile? In some of the more frustrating situations, it can be quite bothersome indeed. These are generally the moments when we most need to have a light heart. Let me relate a couple of examples.

While occupied as an estate agent during my younger years, I had just bought my first brand-new motorcar. It was expensive for my budget, and I had to borrow extra cash to make the purchase. I was motoring with a client in my new possession enroute to view a property, when a speedy truck slid against us. Fortunately, all people involved were well enough, but… yes… my new, unpaid possession was a disaster. I was not amused.

My irritation smouldered within, and I feared an impending eruption. The offender approached us wearing an enormous smile on his face. My client and I looked at one another, thinking perhaps that this strange fellow was inebriated. He was not. He just happened to be one of the happiest, most pleasant personalities imaginable. After five minutes of conversation with this man, one could not help but like him.

A charming smile and friendly disposition can rescue one from the most unfavourable circumstances. P.S.—we did not vent our spleens because his charisma was contagious—and a good thing too, because I later learned that he was a great friend to one of my other valued clients. It's a small world, and what goes around comes around.

The incredible quality of charisma is so powerful that it is not solely limited to homo-sapiens. Anyone who has ever owned a dog, or loved a pet, will understand what I refer to. Here is an example of this sort. Once, as I came in from the garden, I heard a shuffling noise coming from the sitting room. At that time, I kept three uncaged parakeets and no other pets inside the house.

To my horror, a neighbouring cat had entered and decided to amuse itself by scurrying about, frightening the birds out of their wits. My protective instincts surfaced immediately, and I lifted my voice in protest, ready to have a go at the furry foe. To my complete surprise, the culprit took no fear of me. On the contrary, it sauntered up to my side and began to purr and nuzzle its body affectionately against my own. One can easily foresee the end of the episode.

I certainly could not harm such a tender creature. I carried it back outside, petting it along the way. Once again, my initial response had been transformed completely to assume a looking-glass reaction.

Personal magnetism is important—charisma **is** contagious. Allow these endearing qualities to become part of your essence. ***Grace is like a boomerang***—when you send it forth, civilised beings will always return it. Remembering this, will pave the road to the 'good life.'

Avoiding Extremities

In my youth I was somewhat rigid in my ideas. It was day or it was night—I never considered the time on the other side of the planet. There was good and there was bad—who could appreciate that some concepts contain a bit of both? It was black or it was white—didn't dullards live in shades of grey? As I grew older, the narrow vision gradually became wider and more understanding.

Of course, we should all honour our principal beliefs... my only suggestion is to avoid ***extremities.*** As a sample only, I will use a political chart to illustrate:

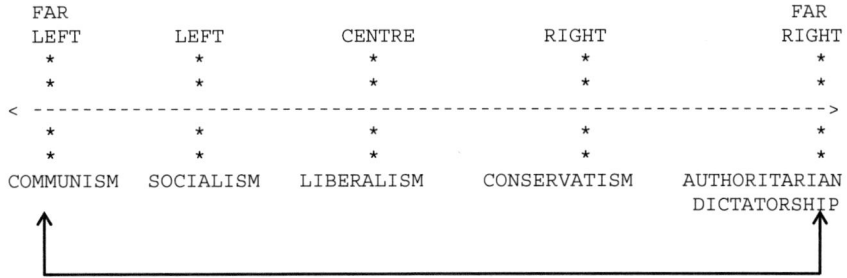

Left, right, and centre may have secure reliable reputations, but the two extremes at the far ends are both equally precarious and if you draw the line into a circle – you will note that they are basically one and the same. Stalin and Hitler were both very dangerous and destructive to society. Extremists may abhor each other, but in actuality, they are one familiar fanatical entity.

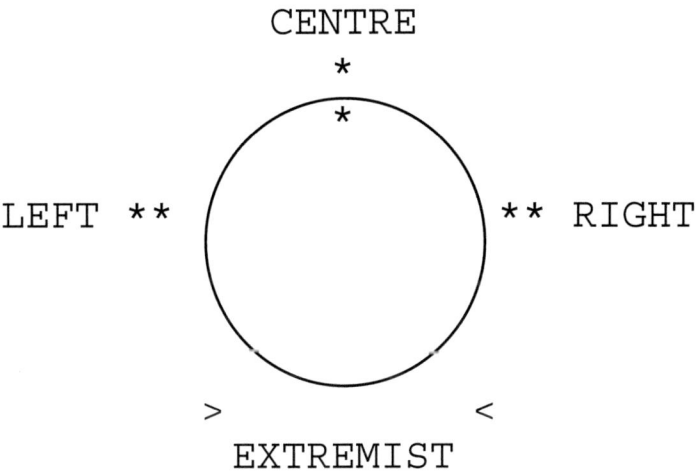

Radicals, fundamentalists, activists—in politics, religion, and sex respectively—are wisely avoided. Hetero or gay, protestant or catholic, capitalist or socialist—we do not need to hear the arguments from people making public spectacles of themselves. There are many opinions in written form where people have the option of reading whatever their heart desires. Nearly every country which suffers serious anti-libertarian ailments does so as a result of extremists. A wise philosophy is:

In a free country, be what you want, but don't antagonise anyone else. High society and high-strung do not mix—benevolent gentlefolk will seldom befriend irritating, opinionated brutes.

Manners/Morality

MORALS

Why should I burden the reader by writing on morality? Skip it if you like—but consider the next sentence first. **People who have a clear sense of morals and actually practise them, tend to receive a greater portion of success and happiness.**

We all know that this is true—take any simple example. Would you hire a thief to work in your retail store? Would you want a gossiping liar to write your biography? Would you hire the philandering husband to give your wife tennis lessons? How could someone be loyal to you if they are not even faithful to their own? Morality is important... perhaps it is true, that we all get what we deserve, so let's be sure to merit the best.

How do we determine what is morally decent and avoid what is deemed to be dishonourable? Whether you have studied the 4000-year-old Judaism, the 2000-year-old Roman Catholicism, or a more modern Christian faith, you will notice that each of these religions utilise the moral law which was given by God to Moses.... and so, we list the famous guideline, known as:

THE TEN COMMANDMENTS

1. I am the Lord thy God; thou shalt not have strange gods before me.
2. Thou shalt not take the name of the Lord thy God in vain.
3. Remember thou keep holy the Lord's Day.
4. Honour thy father and thy mother.
5. Thou shalt not kill.
6. Thou shalt not commit adultery.
7. Thou shalt not steal.
8. Thou shalt not bear false witness against thy neighbour.
9. Thou shalt not covet thy neighbour's wife.
10. Thou shalt not covet thy neighbour's goods.

What perfect teachings. Imagine for a moment, how wonderful this planet would be if everyone followed these simple guidelines… fabulous I should think.

Stealing… one would never buy theft insurance if there were no thieves. Adultery… (the act of copulating with a married person, who is married to someone other than yourself) … surely there would be fewer divorces and less sexually transmitted diseases if people kept this commandment. The 4th commandment… show us a child, and we'll describe their parents. What we think of our own parents often resembles what our children will think of us.

The 5th commandment… sometimes considered to be the most serious of all is easier to camouflage, than to obey. Remember the saying 'a rose, is a rose, is a rose… no matter what you call it, it always smells the same.' Likewise, the fifth commandment—infanticide, abortion, capital punishment, euthanasia, homicide, murder, suicide, war… no matter what we call it, 'killing, is killing, is killing… one can change the name, but the outcome remains the same.'

What about the eighth commandment? Lying and cheating are disastrous habits to get into. Some people reason that they must lie to protect others, or to 'keep the waters calm.' If those around them are in such a desperate condition, they require counselling… not lies. If you are subjected to impertinent curiosity simply reply: 'I'm sorry, but that is a private matter;' we should speak the truth, but it is not necessary to become a tattler and tell all. Neither gossipmongers nor liars ever hold a place of respect amidst civilised society. Finally, giving false witness, i.e.: accusing an innocent person of something which they did not do, is the worst lie of all.

I cannot even imagine why anyone would break the final two commandments by being covetous. Nothing pleases me more than to see a couple in a very happy marriage or with an abundance of personal possessions—rather than envy them, I would pray that everyone acquires such blessings!

In conclusion, Jesus Christ summed up the first three very well in the New Testament (Mat: 22: 37–40) "Thou shalt love the Lord thy God with thy whole heart, and with thy whole soul, and with thy whole mind. This is the greatest and first commandment." Then He summed up the last seven "And the second is like it, 'Thou shalt love thy neighbour as thyself.' On these two commandments depend the whole Law and the Prophets."

If you have broken commandments in the past—don't punish yourself emotionally. The **Lord** is merciful and forgiving, and all *civilised* humans are forgiving, so the only person left to pardon you… is yourself. ***Forgive yourself—do not repeat the same errors—then get on with a better life.***

FINDING PEACE

*Associates. How far should one go for the sake of being a good person? Sometimes one may end up in association with an individual who is so wicked that it becomes impossible to deal with them. Of course, it is only fair to give everyone a second chance, and sometimes we give them dozens for good measure, because all souls are upon the earth to experience goodness.

Thus, we care for our associates as we would care for anything precious to us—like our teeth. When a tooth goes bad, we have the poison removed by root canal, and spend time and money on repairing the tooth with a beautiful crown, until it shines perfectly and comfortably like the others. This reparation can be done in the majority of cases, although at rare times you will find a tooth that has been rotten or cracked for so long—the only course of action is to 'pull it out.'

We have to make a similar decision when dealing with those around us. One may turn the other cheek as long as we are able, but even the Holy Bible warns that we withdraw from bad company: (II Thessalonians 3:6 and 3:14) (II Corinthians 6: 14-16) (I Corinthians 5: 9-13).

In Catherine Ponder's book "Open Your Mind to Receive" she writes of how troubled people affect us: 'If we resent problem people, fight with them, or criticise them, we just hold them in our lives by our own strong negative emotions.' She offers a solution by recommending that we say to them mentally 'I freely give you my blessing and I now release you to your highest good elsewhere.'

*Other influence. Many of us follow one of the main mono-religions, while others though non-baptised, also believe and have faith in one infinite intelligence. As adults we often become more ecumenical and begin to read about the different philosophies. Each individual must search for what is right for them, and brings them the most harmony, joy and goodness.

Look around for a suitable influence who is well educated, enthusiastic, and stresses the more positive aspects of your religion. For example, if you are a protestant, attend several protestant churches to find the most suitable minister and parish. If you are Roman Catholic, go to all of the RC churches nearest you, and determine which has the best priest. You have the right to select holy guidance, just as you would choose your favourite banker, broker, doctor, etc.

Avoid all negative preachers who speak of hell. How could anyone be happy in heaven, knowing that others may be suffering in hell? Also avoid those who speak of evil—for evil is a product of human thinking—if one fans the flames, how shall the fire ever go out? Do we take the old teachings literally—would you cut off hands for stealing, or stone people to death for adultery? Jesus taught us more than 2000 years ago, *not to be fundamentalist, but to be forgiving*, and Buddha said, "Only forgiveness will make our soul peaceful."

Ignore the dysfunctional fear-spreaders, and war-mongers—show respect for the peacekeepers. If we listen to speeches of our religious or royal ambassadors, we must hear messages of kindness, love, charity, and forgiveness.

People have spoken of good and evil entities for thousands of years—angels and fallen angels. If your beliefs are positive and your actions are full of kindness and love, *you can only be surrounded by the presence of goodness*. Search for the positive.

We create our own destiny and shape our future through strength in thought and action; but do not forget the power of our creator—from where this *strength* comes. Mat. 6:33 'Seek first the kingdom of God and His justice, and all these things shall be given you besides.'

I can remember attending masses back in the eighties when the church was only crowded at Easter and Christmas. Now I have to arrive ten minutes early on Sunday if I want to find space in a pew. It seems as though the baby-boom generation has matured, and begun to think more about the meaning of life. The late Dr Wayne Dyer's words seem very appropriate: 'We are not *bodies* which have a soul—we are *souls* which have a body.'

After we get our priorities straight, the fear goes away. One begins again, to reach beyond the man-made items which we enjoy. Like a child, we explore the *supernatural* creations—the stars, moon, trees, grass, rivers, sunshine. Rediscover the ultimate sources of pleasure. Take some time to consider the universe and its infinite creator—suddenly the worries of the world will seem petty indeed… as you experience an inner road to happiness.

Chapter 3
Outer Appearance

Cary Grant famously said, "I pretended to be somebody I wanted to be until finally I became that person. Or that person became me."

Dress, talk, and act like the person you want to Be. Do and then you will Have.

Physiology

This is a topic somewhere between inner improvement and outer appearance which will be covered next. In order to enter a higher vibration where the mind will be able to attract all the goodness desired, one should first improve the way the body works and get into alignment by 'feeling good.' I have often heard the wonderful speaker Tony Robbins say that one of the best methods to accomplish this quickly and easily is by improving our physiology, for example: Stand straight and with your hands on your hips—hold your chin up with shoulders back which is part of naturally good posture. Now breathe more deeply and put a large smile on your face—do you notice how your feelings begin to change? Move your body—dance to music, clap your hands, take a brisk walk in the fresh air and sunshine, etc.

If you want to feel like a winner, you must look and act like a winner—live as though it's already done. ***Embrace the 'higher' emotion before the desired event occurs***—learn to feel good! Dr Joe Dispenza said, "Your personality creates your personal reality" and "How we think, act and feel creates our state of being." He provides a lot of excellent information in his book called "Breaking the Habit of Being Yourself."

Expression of Self

When one considers the meaning of success, we quickly realise how much appearances count. If one is a sophisticated, professional person—how would new acquaintances immediately become aware of such, if we allowed a negative first impression? When a stranger in the street requires information or directions, notice how they will usually approach a man or woman who projects an 'established' image. Why is this? The answer is simple—when you come across as being accomplished, people will automatically assume that you have the answers.

Likewise, it will be easier to reach one's goals if those around you can see that you are already well on the way. The secret to success is not only learning to think rich, but also to establish a look and feel of affluence. Your attire should make you feel phenomenal—consider that today's self-image will become tomorrow's reality. With this thought in mind, we begin with...

Apparel

It is important to make a fine impression; however, this does not mean that everyone must go out and buy exactly the same business attire. The last thing we want to see are a lot of clones running around, like in the 70s when it was a denim world. We are all individuals with different preferences and taste. One can dress beautifully and comfortably regardless of whether they have a classic personality and favour traditional apparel, or if they are casual by nature. There is information available which identifies very different personality types and how each can be attractive. Women might enjoy "It's You" by Emily Cho; for male and female readers I recommend "Dressing to Win" by Robert Panté originally published in 1984 but still valuable if you can find a copy.

For various occupations, events, and personalities, clothing becomes an expression of oneself. Flamboyant people wear flashy clothes; classic society prefers timeless conservative apparel; jet-setters may look chic; active people dress appropriately for various sporting events... and so on. This concept could be summed up in saying "You Are What You Wear."

There may not be 100% accuracy in determining one's lifestyle by their choice of clothing; however, I have noticed that much of the time ***clothing is a serious reflection of one's true nature***. A person soliciting their body in the streets will wear costume very different from that of a sovereign addressing parliament. We not only dress for the occasion, but we also use apparel as 'freedom of expression' to let people know 'this is who I am.'

Each person's wardrobe will consist of various ratios which are suitable for their own individual needs. The clothing which I wore as a child was quite different from what currently reflects my lifestyle, e.g.: my present percentages resemble the following:

* Lingerie and sleepwear 5%
* Formal black tie 20%
* Sports casual—walking shorts for golf, bathing dress for beach, jacket and trousers for riding, etc. 25%
* The remaining 50% of my wardrobe is daily business wear : two-piece suits of jacket with skirt as well as tailored dresses which take me from my home office, to a luncheon, to church, to events, and almost everywhere that I might consider going during the normal course of any day.

If you rarely perform or attend sports for more than 20% of the week. you wouldn't require more sporting clothes. However, if you were famous golfers like Jack Nicklaus or Tiger Woods, perhaps 50% of your wardrobe may consist of sporting apparel. One's closet generally caters to the majority of their activities—thus strangers often estimate our vocations by the clothes we choose to wear.

If you spend very little time at a particular activity, it will not be necessary to spend a lot of money on a closet change. When I took up oil painting as a hobby, there was no need to change my whole wardrobe into cotton shirts, trousers, and coveralls. It was simply a pastime, and merely required that I purchase one painter's smock. This lab style coat could be worn over all of my regular day clothes, eliminating extra expense.

Women have the opportunity to wear a wide variety of clothing—everything from dresses, skirts, trousers, or shorts. The important factor for women to remember is that choice of item makes an immediate statement about who they appear to be, and what they appear to be doing. A female donning a suit of jacket and skirt, may give the impression that she is very professional and 'prepared to talk business.'

Day dresses, woollen fashion trousers, and skirts can be dressed up for going out, or left basic for household wear. Cotton trousers or walking shorts may suggest that one is about to do some gardening, sailing, golfing, riding or just walking the dog.

Men and women alike should both remember that they are constantly making a statement. What do *you* want your clothing to suggest about yourself?

COLOURS COUNT

Many of us are aware of the importance in choosing between *warm* or *cool* colours to match our physical appearance. The colour of our skin, eyes and hair can determine if warm tints such as cream and gold are better suited to one's natural colouring, or if cool tones like white and silver are preferable.

Sit in front of a looking-glass and hold various cool and warm coloured fabric swatches below your neck to reflect towards your hair and face. If one should find it difficult to determine whether they are complemented by warm or cool, there are many professionals available who specialise in colour coding.

Although I realised years ago that my shading was warm, I only discovered later that there was another factor equally as important, which I refer to as '*strong* or *soft*.' My dark eyes allowed me to look good in strong, jewel colours, but I could not carry soft, pastel colours very well, as people with light eyes like the late Queen Mother always wore.

Examples of strong/bright colours and soft/subdued colours:

STRONG	SOFT
Black	shades of grey
deep yellow, marigold	pastel, lemon yellow
turquoise, royal blue-sapphire	robin egg, tender blues
emerald, dark hunter green	soft greens
Fuchsia	powder pink
imperial purple	mauve
bright coral	delicate salmon
scarlet, vermilion	dusty rose, soft reds

Do the swatch test one more time to determine whether bright or subdued tints are most flattering to your complexion.

Often one has a favourite colour but may have been told that they cannot wear it—a person can wear every colour, if they choose the right shade. Let's use **pink** as an example: first find out whether you are suited to brights or pastels—hold both varieties across your body up to the flesh of your neck. The pastel may give you a radiant glow or it may make you look pale. If you have determined that bright pink is best for you, you must then choose between a cool or warm hue.

First try bright fuchsia (cool) and then try bright coral (warm). You should be able to easily determine which shade of pink is best for you. If you want to wear wine—warms can choose maroon and cools can select burgundy.

It is important to remember that you can wear *all* colours and look terrific. E.g.: If I really want to wear a pastel yellow dress, but fear that it will cast a sallow hue against my skin, I can always brighten the area around my face by adding a scarf of bright autumn colours. Vice versa: if a strong brown doesn't suit one well, perhaps they could soften it with a cream or white patterned scarf (cream if they are warm tint/white if they are cool shade). Everything is wearable if accessorised properly.

Contrary to popular opinion, everyone can wear the non-colour **black**. Granted it may look slightly better on certain people. If that is the case, decorate the neckline with another shade—try a coloured silk scarf, or depending on whether one is suited to cool or warm shades—add a wrap of silver or gold[1].

Black is simple—what about whites? Whites generally look best on swarthy or tanned complexions including people who have dark hair and eyes—the 'cools.' In cold winter climates like Canada, many people follow the tradition of only wearing snow white clothing between Victoria and Labour Day. While cream and ivory whites are considered fashionable throughout the whole year—very handy for the 'warms.' Pearl and cream-coloured shoes can be worn, but *pure* white shoes are generally avoided except for sports, such as tennis, running, golf or croquet.

---

[1] Note: avoid glittery tones on classically traditional occasions—flashy tends to indicate déclassé. Classic formal colours include: black, navy, cream, and beige. Classic casuals include white, khaki, loden green, and brown.

HATS AND GLOVES

One may notice people wearing hats or gloves on many occasions—while out shopping, at garden parties, race tracks or polo matches. Although they are generally worn outdoors, there are exceptions. Women ***do not*** remove their hats in church, restaurants or while visiting a friend's house. Men ***should*** remove their hats in church, elevator lifts and when greeting people.

Ladies' hats are usually made of natural materials: cotton, wool, or straw, and are sometimes decorated with feathers or silk flowers. Note: the brim of your hat should not exceed the width of your shoulders.

Millinery can make an average outfit look extraordinary—a minor investment, with major rewards. Today, hats can be found in all shapes, sizes, and colours, so there is definitely one to suit every individual. They can also be very practical on a cold winter's day.

For women who absolutely do not feel comfortable wearing any design of hat, there is an option. Gloves demand equal consideration as a fashion accessory, and offer the added benefit of keeping hands in beautiful condition. During the Covid pandemic, my hands lived in gloves when out and about, because I did not want to dry them out with alcohol hand gels.

Although gloves are ultra-stylish when they accompany millinery, they also look splendid on their own. While summer hats are not used after dark, gloves can be worn 24 hours a day.

If a woman attends a stately 'white tie' affair wearing a sleeveless evening dress, she should also wear long, above the elbow, cream/white kid gloves. No hats are worn at gala balls, but hair ornaments are frequently seen, and tiaras appear at certain grand functions.

It is correct for ladies to wear gloves in church, but they must be removed before receiving Holy Communion. Gloves must also be taken off prior to eating, drinking, or Smoking. Note—although women may leave their gloves on to shake hands, men prefer to remove theirs. Also, men do not generally wear gloves indoors, unless they are working as a formal waiter.

Gloves are chic and easy to coordinate. Unlike belts, which are often colour matched with footwear, gloves may be a totally different shade from shoes, providing they work well with the general ensemble. For example: with black shoes and dress one may wear white, yellow, red, or other coloured gloves to add some pizzazz. Some women prefer quieter colours like cream, beige, or navy… men often wear neutrals like black, brown, or grey when outdoors.

Lavish yourself in style throughout the year and dress your hands for all seasons. Ladies summer gloves are generally made of white cotton. Winter gloves are made of leather and lined with cashmere. Spring and autumn offer gorgeous leathers, including suede, lined with silk.

MEN

Although few men don hats on a daily basis—I must say that on the right occasion, they still make them look irresistibly handsome, especially when they take the hat in the dip of its crown and do a gentle doff when greeting females.

The basic dark coloured, fur felt hat—sported so often in the forties, still looks terrific on businessmen, diplomats and speculators from the race track to financial districts like Bay Street, Wall Street or the City of London—my husband looks dashing in his navy-coloured fedora. In summer, he wears a light straw Panama hat—to Henley Royal Regatta, at garden parties and many other sunny outdoor occasions; his black top hat is worn to Royal Ascot and daytime weddings.

Many men also look dapper in various casual designs: a yachting cap for boating; the tweed shooting cap for golf, fishing or walking the dog; a cotton 'Tilley' hat for nature safaris or other outdoor pursuits.

Baseball caps are best for when you're actually playing "out in the pitch" but gentlemen, if you do like using them as commonplace, please do not even consider wearing one backwards!

TIES FOR MEN

Sophisticatedly chic men and those involved with an artistic occupation frequently choose a European silk foulard which is tucked in at the collar around one's neck. For conservative business wear, choose regular design long silk ties. They are to be tightly knotted and should be of length to reach the top of your belt. More formal occasions, such as a wedding, may find men sporting an 'ascot' to go with their morning suit. Black tie affairs require a black silk bow, tied by hand rather than clipped.

BAGS AND BILLFOLDS

I've been informed by men that they sometimes draw impressions of women by the contents of the ladies' bags. Now this is interesting… picture two women: #1 carries a small neat handbag of sturdy leather, perhaps a simple envelope style or maybe a designer type like Chanel or Cartier. Inside there are: a silver comb and compact, lipstick in a silk case, a folding fan, a passport, a lace handkerchief, a tiny French perfume, opera glasses, a Waterman pen and a leather notecase with Gold or Platinum credit cards.

Woman #2 carries a huge zippered patch sack which has a tendency to flop over and spill the following contents: three rings laden with keys, a bottle opener, small packages of ketchup, sugar and other fast-food tokens, a wrapped pork chop for Prince, paper tissues, a cheque book with plastic Bic pen, and a vinyl wallet with loose change.

I think the picture is clear. Can you describe the probable lifestyles and tastes of these two women? A bag is a very personal item—whatever you remove from it will give away many secrets, much like the items on a man's dressing table.

Speaking of men… the sophisticated ones will carry a silver money clip or a leather billfold for paper cash and credit cards in the inside pocket of their jacket. Wallets which bulge with change and are stuck in the back pocket of a fellow's blue jeans or chained to the front are definitely déclassé. Cheque books are rare now, but in the past if you saw someone carrying one outside of the house, the action would shout to the world 'I don't have any cash and I cannot get credit either!'

SHOES

Just as one takes inventory of their clothing, so too should we gather all of our footwear, and make an assessment. Create three lots:

Save	for shoes which are high quality and in excellent condition
Repair	for quality shoes which are in less than perfect condition
Discard	for any footwear of poor design, little comfort, or worn out

Remember to look at your feet when wearing shoes—the same as one observes their clothing profile in a full length looking-glass. Shoes that are in poor condition, lack style, or simply do not compliment one's foot size, should not be worn. Many varieties can look terrific providing that the design, quality, and fit are good. Golf shoes can look attractive; even trainers can look fine when you clean the leather on them.

Purchase practical designs—this is especially important for women. Consider the poor shopper who wears cheap very high-heeled spike shoes which need the little tips replaced bi-weekly at a cost of about £20.00. By the end of a six-month period, the inexpensive £50.00 non-leather shoes will likely be worn out and the total investment will have reached well over £200.00.

The wise buyer will spend £200.00 or more (depending on sales) for a pair of classic quality leather Italian pumps with low to medium, solid heels. These will look fabulous and last for years with some regular £3.00 tins of shoe polish, and perhaps a heel repair every couple of years.

Classic Court shoe, Ballerina flats, and Patent Pump samples;

Quality… quality… demand it! Yes, we often do get what we pay for. If one needs to conserve money, they can become a *quality*-sale-shopper. I have purchased £300.00 Gucci flats which were reduced to £200.00… and £600 Ferragamo shoes for 40% off. A single pair of black pumps can carry off almost every outfit. Queen Elizabeth II wore the same style of black, low-heeled shoes for decades; and why not, when you find what works best there is little need to change, so she always had new shoes handmade in the same design. Pumps should never have heels which exceed 2½ inches and even this height is more appropriate for soirees or the ballroom. Lower heeled executive styles are preferable for business and daily comfort.

It is easy to stick with the basics—bright coordinating colours are an unnecessary expense—only neutrals are required. A woman might buy black, brown, and cream. Navy, grey, or beige can also be used quite easily depending on one's wardrobe. Men might choose black, brown, burgundy and grey.

Men and women should own at least five quality pair of shoes (even if all the same like the late Queen's) so they can be rotated and never used two days in a row. It is a good idea to alternate for durability and hygienic reasons. The inside of footwear will also remain fresher if one remembers to always use some form of stockings inside of 'closed' shoes—bare feet are only suitable in sandals where they can breathe.

Never go shoeless, even indoors—this is very unhygienic, as one is at risk of picking up dirt, germs, fungus and parasites. Your daily business footwear should be comfortable enough for inside your house; if not, keep a pair of loafers, sandals or slippers handy to put on.

To keep the exterior of shoes in good condition, make a habit of having all of the shoes which have been worn polished on a weekly basis. Once a week should not take an unreasonable amount of you or your helper's time. It will be well worth it for durability, and most importantly, for daily attractiveness. Some people say you can judge a person's character by the condition of their shoes—think about it. Don't let yourself be seen wearing shoes with scuff marks or poor heels.

Light cream-coloured shoes should have scuffs removed and cream polish added after *every* wearing. Shoe care products are not extremely expensive to use. An initial spray with leather protector and subsequent buffing with shoe cream or polish will keep quality footwear looking marvellous.

As a general rule, women should always buy the best shoes and handbags which they can afford and men should buy the best shoes and silk ties that they can afford—these will be very prominent and individualistic statements of 'who you are.'

BELTS

Women have a wide variety of belt choices and can improve the look of a plain dress or shirt with a simple belt or a colourful long scarf tied at the waist; or you might see a white silk sash around a ball gown to match gloves.

As a rule, the colour of women's or men's trouser belts will match the colour of their shoes. Medium width 1″ or 1¼″ belts to fit in the loops, are the most classic and should be made of quality material: leather, suede, or reptile.

Men of sophistication will sometimes choose braces instead of a belt. They may be black which is the norm, or a more daring design or colour, but they must be of high quality with leather button loops—never clip on!

OTHER ITEMS FOR MEN AND WOMEN

Socks—short white, nearest to 100% cotton for sports/casual.

Both formal and regular trousers should have longer calf to knee length in cotton, wool, or silk (fabrics alone or blended together). In formal wear, the colour should match or blend with the trousers' hem: e.g. dark socks with dark trousers. For a more flamboyant mood, brighter colours may be worn.

Stockings (women)—thick, black tights are ideal for winter months. For the dignified look, choose high quality sheers with lycra to provide a good fit and stick with neutral shades—suntan to complement brown shoes, night shade to wear with black shoes, sheer natural (no colour) to wear with cream. Avoid bright colours, tacky patterns, spots, lines, and once past junior school—permanently retire white hose. Always be sure that stockings are free of holes or ladders.

UNDERGARMENTS

100% silk boxers are great for both men and women.

Women will often wear 100% cotton 'French cut' or bikini knickers, but men do best to stick with 100% cotton boxers as opposed to tight underwear. No one should ever use synthetic, non-breathable undergarments.

UMBRELLAS

Whenever men or women wear quality apparel, it is appropriate for them to protect the clothing from getting wet or dirty. For some women the umbrella also becomes a fashion accessory, although not to the extent that cotton sun parasols once were. Look for a sturdy umbrella with natural curved wooden handle. The less expensive plastic and tin compact designs lack finesse.

SCENT

Rather than buying a bargain cologne and splashing it on, purchase a quality perfume, where a single drop will last for hours. Do try to avoid cheap imitation brands which tend to induce nasal congestion and sneezing.

Like our clothing and accessories, scent is also a personal reflection of who we are. Soft feminine florals, exotic orientals, sensual musks, sporty fruit or spices and so on, all identify the type of image we wish to convey. When one discovers a scent which always feels right, they never need to change it. Humans take comfort in recognising people not only by their look and voice, but also by familiar scent.

JEWELLERY

In the same fashion as one would choose high quality naturals for clothing, shoes and belts, select also genuine jewellery: pearl, diamond, gems, gold, silver, coral, etc. Choiceness can be affordable provided that one stays with basic essentials.

WOMEN

My personal preference has always been a pearl necklace with matching earrings. Like the clothes I wear, pearls are suitable for business, socialising and almost everything that I do throughout the day. Jewellery of precious metal or gem stones also make splendid earrings, bracelets, or necklaces for daytime, while diamonds are superb for formal evening wear.

Avoid faux jewels, especially the type which are designed to imitate the real thing. A strand of artificial pearls, no matter how expensive or pretty, will never possess lasting value. The highest quality are the completely natural 'fine' ocean pearls. 'Cultured' pearls are also authentic, although they are mass produced by live oysters in breeding farms.

To determine whether pearls are real, rub them lightly between your teeth. If they are very smooth like plastic, that is probably what they are. If they are gritty like the mother of pearl coating which live oysters create, they should be genuine. Always ask for a guarantee of authenticity, especially if you buy from a small antique shop. These private dealers are splendid places to shop because one can find quality at fair prices. Pearls vary in price according to thickness (years of growth), type, shape, colour, lustre or defects. Fresh water pearls are too common for women of discriminating taste, but are fine for youth and teens, as they are economical to replace.

MEN

Men with refined taste generally keep jewellery to a bare minimum—one ring and one high quality watch. If married, a simple platinum or gold band (no diamonds) on the left ring finger. If single, a signet on the right little finger will do. One classic watch—Rolex, Patek Phillippe, or my personal favourite, a Cartier Tank, always exudes good taste. Men of great distinction are so averse to jewellery that often their wrists will be bare and you may need to search their jackets for the traditional pocket watch.

They do however, prefer wearing shirts with French cuffs, so naturally a good pair of links is required. Choose a small set of solid gold, silver, mother-of-pearl or other high-quality item in traditional style; i.e., two identical sides joined by a chain shank. Avoid clip-ons and everything which is fake, too large or ostentatious.

QUALITY MATERIAL

What type of fabric do those who live like royalty prefer? Only the best, *naturally*. Garments with even a small content of polyester or other synthetic material are generally avoided. The traditional preference is 100% natural in wool, silk, cotton, linen, cashmere, etc. Not only is the quality superior (I still wear wool dresses that I had tailor made 25 years ago) but natural fibres are a renewable resource which is important for sustainable living.

Leather and fur are also natural quality products; however, fur creates controversy due to animal suffering previously involved with trapping, so people today usually choose not to wear it. With respect to leather, there is an established saying "the aristocracy has long considered leather suitable only for accessories and saddlery." Refined people will sport leather belts, gloves, handbags, shoes and such, but will never wear leather as a form of clothing.

NOTE: Myself and others concerned with animal rights have often discussed the question of whether it is acceptable to use leather. I have been informed that leather is a by-product of animals which are used for food; in other words, it is a secondary item produced by the remains of the major item.

This implies that animals are not slaughtered to make a pair of shoes, but are butchered to provide meat for carnivorous humans. In this case, using the leather for accessories is less wasteful than throwing it away. As people continue to eat red meat leather will remain a by-product to be used.

Getting back to quality material—some people have a serious misconception about choosing quantity over quality. One superb outfit is worth a dozen of poor fabric or design. The price of the excellent choice may be ten times greater—but so too will be the: prestige, durability, style and longevity of the item.

Don't be afraid to spend money on priority items. If you live in a cool region where a winter coat is required for several months of the year, spend what is required to purchase a premium wool or cashmere of classic cut, colour and design—for this is what the public will frequently see you wearing.

A wise shopper will be able to purchase high quality at reasonable cost. Remember 'if you don't enjoy shopping, you're using the wrong shops.' Frequent the better personal service boutiques only—the trend is beginning to see the smaller shops gaining market share over the large franchise department stores.

After visiting the specialty stores on a regular basis, one will become familiar with the pricing systems. Many shops have bi-annual sales, usually in January and July, so you will be able to purchase the best garments at the best prices. Always try to support the best in everything you purchase—by doing this we increase beauty and quality in the world. Why would anyone want to support or promote poor grade anything? The universe will be far more pleasant if we utilise the best that it has to offer and stop promoting the manufacture and use of rubbish.

Gentlemen, is your tie 100% silk—ladies, your scarves? Are your casual golf shirts and walking shorts 100% cotton or linen? In the future when you go shopping, remember to always check the labels and buy items of quality. Women, instead of buying three cheap poly dresses which may end up in a shapeless, throw away condition a few months down the road, invest the money in one good quality silk dress or wool suit.

The item of premium quality will retain its shape, look classic, and last for many years to come. In Alex Doulis' book "Take Your Money and Run" he wrote, "have a few top-quality outfits that always look 'rich.' The wealthy can't afford to buy cheap things over and over again. But the poor always do, and therefore, remain poor."

Buy whatever suits your current needs—perhaps a summer silk dress, or an autumn wool jacket and skirt.

Cotton is very comfortable in hot summer climates and can be easily laundered and pressed by yourself or your helper. Many good cotton dresses, if hung whilst still damp, will dry into perfect shape without any ironing required.

Wool and silk tend to be considered best quality, although some people think that they are expensive to care for due to the dry-cleaning costs. I beg to differ, unless all of one's suits happen to be white. Dark wool jackets, trousers, and skirts need dry-cleaning less frequently as a spot can often be wiped away with a clean wet cloth. Changing our undergarments daily should keep outer clothes fresh.

Still, do search for a good dry-cleaner—larger cities usually offer plenty of competition. I have had the same silk shirt dry-cleaned for £11.99 at one shop, and £5.99 at another—with the latter doing a superior job and using safety pins rather than staples in the label tag.

When one considers that the synthetic non-breathable fabrics like acrylic or polyester need to be washed after every wearing due to odour, the cost of detergent, plus the ineffective use of time, will likely make the 'cheap' laundry costs far more expensive than dry-cleaning. This fact generally comes to the surprise and detriment of those who thought they were saving money by purchasing poor material. Madame Dariaux who said "Elegance is the privilege of age" also said "I cannot afford to buy cheaply." We would do well to remember her words.

CASUAL WEAR

Much of the populace is notorious for another misconception that to be comfortable, one must be dressed unattractively. Really! One can wear extremely comfortable casual attire that *looks* and *feels* fabulous. People who work privately out of their own house could easily fall into a habit of wearing a 'jogging suit' day in and day out. I met someone who started living in pyjamas, but imagine how psychologically damaging this could be to their prosperity consciousness and inspiration.

Some people will allow themselves to lounge around in sweat pants or a worn-out housecoat whenever they are not planning to go out. They actually have the notion that it is all right to look a mess at home in front of their consort. Instead, one could look terrific in a comfortable polo-neck jersey with wide-leg trousers. How fortunate is the man whose wife dresses especially elegant when she is alone with him. A beautiful peignoir or silk lounge outfit will do far more for a marriage than a cheap jogging suit. Never associate comfort with ugliness—*apparel can be both extremely comfortable and attractive at the same time*.

Jogging suits are for jogging—blue jeans are for mucking out the horse stable—*sport clothes and work clothes should not be confused with casual wear*. Naturally people may wear tough cotton trousers for gardening, or a mechanic might wear denim coveralls to change the oil in the car.

Of course, when it comes to sports, most people dress appropriately—tennis clothing for tennis, boating apparel for yachting, whites for croquet, Jodhpur breeches and riding boots for hacking. If one is going on a nature safari, they might don a Tilley hat, bush shirt, cotton trousers and gum or leather boots. To stroll your hound—cotton walking shorts and a Lacoste shirt looks well enough. Actually, everyone can do just fine with a few *classic, comfortable, casuals*:

BASICS—WARM CLIMATE

A classic cool white Lacoste short-sleeved shirt, with a pair of pleated, comfortable fitting, light cotton trousers or walking shorts is all any man or woman will require for golfing, sailing, tennis, or simple walkabouts. Complete the outfit with a tan coloured belt and loafers—opt for Gucci, or other high quality leather products for these are often what will make or break the total look.

BASICS—COOL SEASON

Men and women should both invest in a 100% wool blazer, trousers and a good quality cotton, silk, wool or cashmere polo-neck jersey; i.e., a long roll neck sweater—not to be confused with the shorter turtleneck. Some classic colour combinations for women are: navy trousers and jersey with cream jacket; black trousers and jersey with red jacket; khaki (camel) trousers and jersey with brown jacket.

Autumn fashion colours which men might try include: navy, grey, burgundy, or tweed.

Once again, top off the outfit with a high-quality pair of flat heeled leather shoes, in black or other winter shade. Naturally there are dozens of other casual clothing combinations, especially for women who will want to invest in more colours, comfortable skirts, dresses and so on. The 'casuals' which were listed are simply the classic basics, which make an excellent initial investment.

Unless one is stuck in a denim seventies time warp or the grunge fad of the early nineties, we should recognise a lack of taste and individuality for the dinosaur it is. Blue jeans continue to project left-wing, poverty conscious connotations of 'sameness' for all. They may be appropriate for growing teenagers who require economy with durability and are yet to develop any sense of fashion, but if one is over 20 and not in a labour job, why would they even consider them? If you do like sturdy cotton trousers, at least try some different colours like black, navy, tan, etc. so you can avoid common blue denim.

When I attended a ladies' finishing school, our wise female teacher suggested we wear more comfortable loose dresses instead of tight trousers. I later admitted in a report that not only was it more comfortable, but it made me feel more feminine, and therefore behave more like a lady; ergo, clothing can also change the way one feels inside and greatly increase one's confidence.

It is most unfortunate that envy is sometimes exhibited towards those who have good taste. One may hear something negative like "must you always dress so well—it makes me feel self-conscious." Wonderful people will not covet, but would congratulate your success by saying "you look fabulous as always!" It all comes back to that important word 'conscious' poverty or prosperity thinking. Which type of person would you prefer to associate with?

Have you ever prepared for a luncheon party, business meeting, or date and had a companion ask if you were going to dress up? One can't help but wonder what that question implies. We are, who we are. It doesn't matter where one is going—taste is reflective of one's individual personality. Maintain integrity—don't just enjoy life when you are in front of a crowd—pamper yourself! You deserve to look and feel marvellous all of the time.

Why do some people insist on dressing poor? Lack of money is no excuse. A pair of quality wool trousers at a 50% off sale might cost less than torn blue jeans. Do they lack a sense of fashion, or are there underlying reasons like poverty consciousness? People have actually dressed poor to acquire sympathy from others by pretending that they are in an impecunious state. Recall the words in "Pride and Prejudice" *'Nothing is more deceitful than the appearance of humility.'* Even people affecting to be rich are more tolerable than those who pretend to be poor.

Still others dress in labour clothes because they feel guilty about having arrived. This notion is ridiculous in modern society where nearly every youth begins with little money of their own, and must establish themselves through intelligence or talent. One needn't do penance for becoming successful—reward your merits.

If you are an adult with children of your own, realise that you influence much of their environment and have a great obligation. Consider if parents tell their teenage daughter not to wear blue jeans because it is considered déclassé and unladylike. Yet they enrol her in a high school where all of the youth wear denim. Naturally, being young and insecure, the girl will probably follow the crowd, since children do succumb to peer pressure.

The girl might continue to dress poorly until completing high school and being able to choose her own surroundings. But what is the moral of the story? Their child might have been more than happy to dress in classic clothing, had she been sent to a more traditional school. Parents must realise that they play a large role in creating their children's environment. One cannot expect to get back more than they put forward.

BUSINESS—SEMI-FORMAL

Casual wear was discussed at length to alleviate any misconceptions as to its reference. *Sports*wear is self-explanatory: *swim* suits, *ski* pants, *tennis* shorts, *golf* shoes, *riding* boots, *jogging* suits and so forth.

During the middle stage of life, the majority of clothes worn will generally fall under 'business' apparel. Since many of the Millennials, Generation X and the tail end of Baby Boomers fall into this category of being out and about in the business world, it is a good idea to dress appropriately.

I won't get into fashion details because there are already many excellent books on the subject. The only piece of advice that I would mention, is to keep business wear as classic as possible. Picture the traditional look for men: a dark suit with flower buttonhole on the left lapel, and real buttons which actually close at the sleeve's cuffs.

There could be a bit of white handkerchief showing from his breast pocket. His shirt may be bold striped or plain white and his tie, fashionable, but not faddish. If this man's photograph were taken today, or decades ago, you wouldn't be able to date it. Avoidance of time fads is essential for the semi-formal look.

Women especially should not become too pre-occupied with the current rage. Some women are designed for short skirts, and others look best in calf length. If you're 5'10" with firm thighs and ballerina breasts, many clothes will be easy to wear, but this is not always the case. Women with zaftig figures may need to be more selective when choosing a wardrobe. Actually, there are several different body shapes. To find out which fashion designs coincide with one's figure, study books like 'The Diana Look' by Sue James.

When women dress for business, they needn't feel that they must give up their femininity. A wool jacket with matching pencil skirt looks far more executive than trousers. There is no reason why legs cannot be showing, and with a moderately heeled pair of classic pumps, the look is very professional. Adding a string of pearls or a Hermès scarf, serves not only to beautify a woman, but will add richness and make her appear more successful as well.

Hints: *Never buy a skirt or dress unless it offers a built-in colour coordinated slip (preferably in silk). *Shawls excluded, be sure that the length of your over coat exceeds the length of your skirt or dress hemline.

SKELETONS IN THE CLOSET

Once we have decided to accept only excellence in clothing, there is one vital exercise which needs to be carried out: remove the regrettable mistakes. It is important to choose a period when you have plenty of time—a day off alone; or a long evening with nothing to do and no interruptions. It needs to be a moment when one feels optimistic about the betterment of life. Set aside one of these occasions of privacy, spare time and enthusiasm to deal with your clothing.

If you don't own a full-length mirror, please take a moment before this project to invest in one. Many hardware stores carry them for a low cost and they are narrow and easy to transport. For those who can afford, a full '3-way' design is far better and will provide vision of one's complete profile. It is not a large cash investment, but it is one which offers huge benefits.

Finally—you're organised, eager, and ready to start. This could be a several hour project, so make sure that you've selected a choice interval. One need never experience frustration, but should enjoy every task which they endeavour. Put on your favourite music and dive right in. To begin: go through your existing wardrobe—all drawers and closets. Set aside every item of clothing to be dealt with piece by piece. If you are female you may begin with a dress, or jacket and skirt. Put on your first outfit—stand in front of your full-length looking glass and *honestly* use your judgement while asking yourself—does this make me look terrific?

Don't concentrate on your makeup, weight, hair style, or other physical features. Look at the garment on your body—is it your colour? Does it fit properly? Is the outfit very becoming? Professional? Classic? Does it coincide with what you do, who you are—and most importantly, how you would picture yourself in your ideal future? If it does *not*, lay it on top of your bed. If it fits well, is attractive, and you are absolutely certain that it makes you look handsome with little effort, put it back into the empty closet or drawer. Go on to the next item of clothing—hold the colour in front of you—put it on—what is your *first impression*… does it make you look especially wonderful? Does the image reflect the person you desire to be? Would you admire and respect a person who looks this way?

One may remove something from their closet which has been hanging there for years—perhaps it is unnatural material—covered in poly fuzz-balls; it may have a tear in an area which cannot be mended; it may have been poor quality which has lost its shape—if so, lay it aside on the bed. Continue to go through everything. Remember that you are only saving the items which are of good taste, good quality and make you look and feel outstanding. You are re-hanging only the excellent clothing which you can wear *any day* with pride.

Gentlemen, begin by checking your jackets. Determining their fit, fashion, quality and look should be quite simple. Next, while wearing a plain white shirt, move on to your silk tie collection. If you put on a tie which is two inches wider than the fashion—you might have it narrowed, or wait until the style returns; but, if it has a huge gaudy image on the front of it, that is another matter. Sentimental gifts from your children may be stored away in the attic, otherwise if you come across such a relic, which you know that your preference would never permit, set it aside on the bed. The clothes which are decidedly inappropriate for your lifestyle must then be sorted through. Throw out items which are useless; give pleasant but outgrown clothing to charity; tear up old cotton tee shirts for dust cloths.

After one has gone over everything, they will likely find that the apparel in the closet has been reduced to half… maybe less. The drawers may have a lot of surplus room, after discarding shrunken wool polo-neck jerseys or worn-out sportswear. Closets may be half bare after removing suits of poor taste. Remember however, the law of attraction relating to clutter—we must remove the drab and dingy in order to make room for the new and wonderful which will arrive sooner, once the space becomes available. William Morris said, "***Have nothing in your house that you do not know to be useful, or believe to be beautiful.***"

Next, if possible, narrow it down one more step—material quality. If you don't have enough clothing left to wear, you may need to delay this action until after you have restocked with some quality clothing. If, however, you still have a sufficient amount of tasteful clothing left in your wardrobe, go through the tags and check the material to see if the item is 100% natural. Is your coat 100% wool? Is your tie/scarf 100% silk? Are your walking shorts and golf shirts 100% cotton or linen? Combinations of ***pure natural fabrics*** are fine – a shawl might be 40% cashmere and 60% virgin wool – excellent. Try to eliminate all plastic or man-made materials such as polyester, acrylic, or rayon.

Now that your wardrobe has been dramatically improved, remember in the future: every time you shop, try on the apparel and observe yourself in a three-way full-length looking-glass. The items may be comfortable and within your budget, but one still must ask the vital questions—does this make me look attractive? Professional? Distinguished? Pleasing? Or does this look drab, common, mediocre, third-class? Whether the garment is on sale or not makes no difference—only purchase it if it passes the 'excellence' test. If the item is not good quality and 100% natural fabric, don't even waste time trying it on.

You've gone through your clothing; you go through your footwear... one can continue on and on. Deal with your hats, gloves, scarves, and belts. What you are looking for *every* time you stand in front of the looking-glass is choice apparel, attractive and in good condition. Concentrate on your profile and feet—turn around to observe all angles—what do you see? A well-tailored suit with shoes in perfect repair? Or scuffed shoes with poor heels, creased trousers, and a shapeless shirt of poor colour or quality?

Under the section on shoes, we mentioned the importance of keeping footwear in good repair, but let us not forget our apparel. A hanging thread, a loose button, laddered stockings, or a hole in your socks are circumstances to avoid. A common mistake which people sometimes tend to overlook is the lining in their coat. Although the sturdy wool exterior of the coat may be in perfect condition, thin linings tend to tear and develop holes.

Now that you associate in the upper circles of manners and politeness—hosts, or servants will be helping you put on, remove, or hang up your coat. Go to your tailor and have faulty linings re-sewn. Also, keep clothing altered to fit properly—check waists, shoulders, and hemlines. Gentlemen, be sure that your trousers are the correct length, and that your shirt cuffs are approximately one centimetre beyond your jacket sleeve.

The last, but most obvious point about clothing, is to keep it clean—have the wool suits and silk items dry-cleaned when necessary. You or your housekeeper can easily launder and press the items which are cotton or linen.

Jim Rohn said, "Don't work hard on your job – work hard on yourself," We can never outperform our self-image, so make it a seven figure one! Lasting change requires an upgrade of identity because we stay consistent with how we define ourselves.

Appearance

There are so many stereotypes attached to appearance. Men are to be tall, dark, and handsome with broad shoulders, narrow hips, and firm biceps. Classic  women are expected to be thin with taut abdomens, well-formed derrieres, teenage breasts, and long shapely legs. Not to mention the human face, where the ideal is to have flawless pure complexions and soft silky hair.

I doubt if anyone was created with the whole package. Who's to say what handsome or classic is anyway? Hundreds of years ago, Rubenesque women were considered more attractive as they were well rounded, but today one might think the corpulent look is considerably overweight. Our bodies can be physically changed to a certain degree—see chapters on diet and exercise. Also consider that we can be made to ***appear*** differently depending on what we choose to wear, as noted under the section on clothing. All we really have left to cover under appearance is hair, complexion, posture, and such—so let us take it from the top…

Hair

At one time I had a shoulder-length hairstyle with very dark colour similar to the late Jacqueline Kennedy Onassis. I also favoured shift dresses with pearls and everywhere I went, people would say "You look just like Madame Kennedy or Jackie O." Later I changed my hairstyle (colour and length) plus make-up, and when out at a reception, fellow guests kept telling me, "You really resemble Celine Dione." Now for an ordinary woman to temporarily look like a famous lady is one thing, but consider also how extremely different in appearance the two were. This means that with the help of hair dyes, cosmetics, clothing styles, etc. one can basically look however we choose—now that is a fabulous thing!

Getting back to hair, pleasing appearance begins with an attractive haircut. If you notice an acquaintance that always has terrific looking hair, you might wish to be directed to the stylist. Once you have found a professional, accomplished designer, make an appointment and discuss the look that *you* want to achieve—pictures usually help to provide clarity. Do you prefer a classic style, sophisticated, chic, or latest fashion? Be conscious not only about the design of your hair, but also about the texture.

It is ideal if one can attain a great look, while avoiding too many chemicals, permanent waves and dyes. Some people have an aversion to a greying look which can be aging, so they prefer to use colour when white hairs appear, but wave-perms are always unnecessary and considered somewhat déclassé.

Men also have to give consideration to the design of their hair. Do you want the 'left side part swept over' which is a classic traditional look, or perhaps one of the more modern designs which are chic in appearance 'horizontal short near the ears—long over the top.' Artistically stylish men sometimes opt for the 'shoulder length ponytail.' Whatever you decide—remember that it should reflect who *YOU* are. Boris Johnson exudes his Etonian confidence and is expert at this. Make a clear statement of what you feel, or wish to represent, rather than simply following a trend. I recommend that men avoid the skin-head look which often has neo-Nazi connotations.

Women's styles generally have more versatility. A simple cut of soft straight hair can easily be worn brushed away from the face, or held back with a hair band for daytime. If the hair reaches beyond shoulder length, the basic cut can be worn in a chignon or fastened with a nape of neck bow tail for business wear. To transform into elegant evening, have it loosely swept up, and adorned with a diamond brooch, tortoiseshell barrette or pearl combs.

Other women prefer very sophisticated short designs, which needn't be put up to look glamorous. A neat style which is suitable for daytime business can easily be tossed to give a chic casual look. For evening, short fashion cuts may not support the wearing of hair accessories, but they will provide an ideal opportunity to display gorgeous drop earrings of pearl, fine gemstones or gold.

Once you have established the right cut, be sure to keep it trimmed as often as required to maintain the look. Aside from this… proper diet, hair conditioning, the avoidance of strong chemicals and hot styling irons, should keep your design looking fabulous.

COLOUR AND CONDITION

If your hair is 100% natural—untreated, unpermed, not artificially dyed—you will be able to enhance it without using chemicals. The natural colour of my hair is fair to light brown. When I felt the urge for golden highlights, I would shampoo with camomile, or else I would comb fresh-squeezed lemon juice through my hair before sunbathing—either method would significantly brighten the hue. When my taste moved towards a darker look, I chose natural henna plant with indigo to produce a rich strong colour. Before one's hair goes white, we can easily use botanical products to tint and revitalise it. Later in life, if one does not care for greying hair, there are special formulas available to reverse the process.

Those who prefer a colour totally unlike their own may need to use an artificial dye, but be careful—remember that permanent dyes, like permanent waves, can be very damaging to the hair. Also, if choosing a colour of great contrast from your own, there will be the need for occasional root touch-ups. Once again—try to avoid chemicals, hot-irons, and other items which can cause damage. It may be difficult to escape from the blow-dryer, but one can invest in a quality unit, with lower speeds and cooler temperatures. The goal is to achieve smooth, soft, silky, shiny, 'healthy' hair.

Today there are many natural and sulphate free shampoos and conditioners available on the market. Some people experiment with items from the refrigerator—beer, eggs, mayonnaise and such for conditioning. Rather than simply soaking in food products, remember that what we consume ***internally*** will largely determine the health of hair and nails… follow a sound nutritional diet for best results.

Nails

I once was interviewed by a woman who was a major shareholder of a company. Upon our introduction, I felt overshadowed and more than a little intimidated by her assertive and professional appearance. She had gorgeous hair in a classic style; wore a well-tailored beige jacket and skirt; and sat behind a large desk in her private office. Like many people, I tend to observe new acquaintances and mentally record first impressions. The woman had a clear voice and calm yet powerful disposition. I was thinking to myself 'this formidable woman has definitely arrived.' The glitter of an incredible diamond cluster ring drew my attention to one of her hands which rested upon the desk. Just as the insecurities of my unseasoned age were about to get the best of me, I noticed it… the dirt under her fingernails. This little anecdote brings us to the importance of…

THE MANICURE

Classic nails are smooth in front with neatly rounded corners, and will always be clean, without chips or hangnails. Gentlemen's nails should be buffed only—ladies may opt for French manicured, clear enamel, or coloured to match lipstick. Go to a salon, have a friend give you a manicure—or do it yourself:

* Use a cotton pad to wipe away old nail colour with a non-acetone polish remover.
* Trim nails with an emery board or crystal file. I use Leighton Denny. Keep nails a moderate length, not short to the quick, nor too long, and never pointed.
* Soak nails in warm water with oil treatment… or for problem cuticles, use a conditioning cuticle remover. Wash and dry thoroughly.
* Use an orange-stick to gently push back cuticles and clean under nails.
* Buff nails for a natural shine, or choose a French manicure, clear nail enamel, or a polish which coordinates with the lip colour you use.
* After nail varnish has dried properly, use an effective skin lotion to condition finger tips and hands.

Grooming

We've all been instructed upon the merits of cleanliness, and personal grooming certainly has significant value. It is difficult to feel completely at ease around someone who permits foul breath, body odours or unwashed hair. Have you ever experienced walking in a city with pollution, or sitting in a room clouded by cigarette smoke? Not only do we breathe in these noisome odours, but the foul smells are also absorbed by our skin, hair, and clothing. Fortunately, in current times, most people have become very conscientious about cleanliness. Objectionable surroundings are avoided when possible, or at least followed up with a trip to the cleaners and a bath.

Every morning should begin with the habit of good grooming. Take care of your teeth and achieve fresh breath. Many of us start each new day with a body bath, hair wash, and invigorating rinse under the shower—what a wonderful way to set forth! Men and women should allow a sufficient amount of time for shaving and hair grooming. Be sure to have immaculate clothing and clean undergarments laid out to wear every day. Your personal lavatory should have a bidet or 'wet wipes' for freshening up. If it's been a stifling hot day—try a cool foot wash in the tub during the afternoon. Don't forget to take time out for weekly rituals, like a good massage or facial, and most women will need to epilate once every fortnight.

THE BATH

People who live life in the fast-lane often have less time for life's leisurely luxuries, and by falling into the morning shower routine tend to forget how soothing a lengthy soak in the tub can be. Choose an evening when you are free from engagements to relax in a bath. Illuminate the room with candlelight, maybe bring a glass of wine, set the intercom to classical music—invite your consort if you wish. Enrich the bath water—add a quart of whole milk and scent with a natural essential oil of frankincense, lavender, rose or other essence which can be purchased in health food stores. Avoid using commercial bubble baths and other non-botanical chemical products—you might try Epsom salts.

There are additional advantages to an evening bath as opposed to the rushed morning shower. One needn't blow-dry hair, for it will have time to dry naturally. Also, lotions can be applied to the body with all night to absorb, thus one can wake up with soft hair and satiny skin. This brings us to a final note about grooming… maintaining a fresh scent.

Antiperspirants reduce perspiration and may or may not be scented, while deodorants only mask odour. Antiperspirants are usually the preference for underarms where uncontrolled wetness could permeate clothing. For other areas which are prone to sweat, such as the soles of feet and centre of back, one can use a natural deodorant stone. It resembles a small chunk of mineral salt, and when dampened, can be smoothed against the skin to leave its beneficial deposits. This will not hinder natural perspiration, yet it will reduce bacteria and can prevent fungus which usually manifests as blemishes on the back, and odour of the feet.

COSMETOLOGY —Women and Beauty

Women can't help but notice how rapidly fashions change in both clothing and cosmetic lines. Apparel designers and make-up consultants are well aware that if we lay aside old items, we will be more likely to spend money on new acquisitions.

Look at photographs from various decades—thin eyebrows to bushy; narrow lips, full lips… remember the heavily lined 'cat eyes' of the sixties and their bright blue shadows?

Fortunately, the cosmetic market, like the fashion industry, has acknowledged a certain 'classic' look which is timeless on photographs and in everyday life. For a traditional look, one simply avoids extremes. We wouldn't choose pencil thin eyebrows with a curvy moon arch, nor would we wear our eyebrows bushy and straight as a board across the bridge of our nose. One would opt for a moderate arch and width which does not cater to the latest rage.

A significant and positive new trend of recent years, pertains to the *type* of facial products which are being used. Women who once chose to use foundations and powders to cover up spots and blemishes, today prefer to invest in products which will **correct problem skin rather than disguise it**. The trend has moved towards radiant, natural, healthy looking—as opposed to heavily concealed. Glamour cosmetics may still be necessary for certain occasions like photo sessions, filming, or modelling. At such times, makeup can be used to help contour facial shape, and hide marks which are exaggerated by camera lighting; but, when not on the catwalk, or doing a shoot, it's more important to consider how we look up close in real life.

Who wants to be seen wearing pasty foundations or dusted in powder? We now have products available which are actually skin conditioners, lightly tinted for transparent coverage. Remember… when projecting an image of class, one always avoids cheap, gaudy or extreme. We don't want oily skin which looks acne prone… nor do we want the matte, flaky powder look that can emphasise wrinkles and make us appear much older than we are. The middle ground for a youthful, healthy appearance is a **natural, moist, dewy look**—fresh as opposed to fake.

WRINKLES

They may initially occur due to our heredity, but wrinkles become intensified by certain external elements—cold dry winds, overexposure to the sun's rays, pollution, smoking and heavy makeup are all common culprits. Severe facial expressions can also worsen the problem. I had developed two noticeable horizontal lines running across my forehead, when a friend suggested that I stop raising my eyebrows so frequently—I took the advice, and after a few weeks, my skin was practically smooth.

Instead of getting "crow's feet" from squinting while in the sunlight, invest in a good pair of sun-specs. Squinting, frowning, puckering to smoke and ear to ear grins can turn a fresh face into a road map. One needn't stop expressing emotion—rather, consider more elegant ways to do so with simple charm and sparkling eyes.

FACIAL CARE

Morning—Freshen face with tepid water and pat dry. People under 40 might apply a lotion/gel eye wrinkle defence to any dry and lined areas, plus use a light day cream if desired. For those of us who are older: I start with a good serum like Niacinamide, Vitamin C, or Hyaluronic Acid followed by a super day cream to moisturise. For lips, balm or lipstick is beneficial for protection against the elements.

Daytime—Skin can be periodically moistened by a mist prepared with distilled water and witch hazel. Touch up lips or makeup as required.

Evening—Before Bed

* Remove makeup with a tender cream cleanser or micellar cleansing water with disposable cotton wipe-offs.
* Rinse off film with tepid water and dry with a clean cotton face cloth. Cleanse inner eyes with saline drops to remove any film or traces of makeup. Note: saline is similar to one's natural tears and is used to rinse contact lenses prior to insertion. Read the bottle carefully before purchasing, as there are many other harsh solutions on the market.
* Apply a light firming facial serum. Retinol is often preferred by people with deeper wrinkles but should only be used before bed and never in the sunlight. Follow with a heavier night cream if skin is exceedingly dry.

Weekly—Twice a week, remove dead cells with a peel-off gel mask or natural exfoliating scrub (mine is made with crushed walnut shells), then rinse.

Physical beauty in youth is an act of nature, but if you are older and attractive, you've earned it!

Makeup—Always use quality makeup and professional sable brushes (which should be washed in shampoo regularly); or, if preferred, use sponge eyeshadow applicators, but change them every month. Experiment through consultations with the various cosmetic chains to determine which products you prefer and which counsellors offer the best advice. The classic look for women can be summed up in one word: **RADIANCE**. We have replaced the pasty foundations and dry powdery look for a natural glow which is achieved by a good replenishing gel/lotion. As foundations become passé, lightweight anti-wrinkle serums and tinted moisturisers become the norm.

I have often heard men speak of women saying "She doesn't need makeup, that's a plus." But those 'natural beauties,' subject of male admiration, are generally wearing some light makeup. Perhaps a beige shadow over eyelids, and smoky brown or grey along the lashes, a touch of mascara, a hint of blush or cheekbone highlighter… and few women go without the protection of lipstick. Gone are the bright blue and green eye shadows, as well as the contour look of artificially created cheekbones. These methods are still used for photography sessions and fashion shows, but the business woman's look is fresher and more natural.

One's lipstick should neither be too pale nor too dark – the classic shade is a light to medium which will be derived from either a pink or orange undertone. The tint will depend on your personal features i.e.: colour of eyes and complexion. Blush must correspond with a similar coral or rose tint, i.e.: we wouldn't wear pink lipstick with apricot blush. Check the shade when you have a natural glow, also notice that the colour rises to the 'apples' of our cheeks—applying blush should simulate the real thing in a very mild way. In order to achieve the classic look of using very little makeup, take the following 'morning test' and see if you can improve on some features 'naturally.'

Upon arising in the morning, wash your face and take a good look before applying any cosmetics.

* Do your eyebrows or lashes appear too light without pencil or mascara? There are kits available for tinting them – I use RefectoCil. The oxidant liquid and tube of colour last for numerous applications. Semi-

permanent tattooing can be a longer-term option for colouring sparse or light eyebrows.

* Do your lips feel dry and cracked? Use a quality lip balm every morning and night.
* Is your skin pale or sallow? Perhaps you need more natural sunshine. Note: enjoy the sun, but also respect it—overexposure during peak hours will encourage wrinkles, and may cause more serious skin problems. You might want to try a self-tanning mousse like St.Moriz.
* Are the whites of your eyes yellow or bloodshot? Reduce alcohol; eliminate drugs.
* Do you have dark circles beneath your eyes? Drink plenty of water and get ample sleep.
* Are you creating pucker wrinkles or yellow teeth? Don't smoke.
* Do you have 'crow's feet'? Use sun-specs to stop squinting when in direct sunlight, and apply a good anti-wrinkle product every day.
* How's your hair? A professional cut will look attractive with little effort.
* Does your skin have blemishes? Consider what you are eating/drinking; also avoid dirty face syndrome – wash skin with a pure glycerine soap.

Keep health in mind and begin from the inside out. Consume fresh berries, fruits, vegetables and plenty of water. Eat quality protein—nuts, seeds, wild seafood and only free-range eggs, poultry or meat. Avoid condiments, preserves, and refined sugars which may increase blemishes and cause worse ailments. If one must eat processed food, remember: the fewer ingredients the better, but try to avoid packaged edibles. Also, limit caffeine and alcohol, for these substances are often responsible for red facial blotching and broken capillaries.

Now that your hair and eyebrows look permanently terrific, and skin has improved to a healthy colour and radiance—give yourself the 'morning test' once again. Notice the natural improvement… can you get by with less makeup? A youthful, fresh dewy look can be achieved—work at it!

Posture

It is much easier to portray an image of elegant sophistication, if one has first mastered correct posture and carriage. Do you carry your body with confidence, or are head and shoulders slumped with eyes downcast, generating a troubled appearance? Do you walk gracefully from the hips, or does the majority of movement originate with your knees, creating an awkward stride? If your posture needs improvement, there are personal development courses and plenty of books available on the subject to help one progress. Posture may seem of little significance, but the impact on one's image is extraordinary—so take poise seriously. Even more important are the psychological effects, for good carriage helps one to feel more secure and self-confident as I mentioned under physiology.

Walking—Choose any room with a reasonable length of floor to exercise an effective natural pace. Practise a graceful step to the classical sounds of royal march music. Keep your back and derrière straight (no swaying) with your head raised—balance a book atop if that's what is necessary to achieve the correct position. The walking motion begins at the thigh (not the knees). When taking a step, transfer weight from the heel to the ball of your foot.

In a Nutshell:

* Chins are worn high i.e.: neck erect and face forward—the eyes will handle required motion.
* Keep a straight plumb line (vertical spine) with shoulders back and down.
* Concentrate on movement from the hip. Avoid swinging arms or bending knees too severely—they should have a relaxed, slight movement only.
* Walk gracefully with a slow to moderate pace in a smooth natural glide. Running across the street, rushing through corridors, and constant dashing about are inelegant.

Climbing Steps—Retain a straight plumb line. Avoid bobbing the head up and down to view the stairs—learn to move the eyes rather than the neck. Place ball of foot first on each step—maintain slightly flexed knees, like when golfing.

Sitting—Choose straight backed chairs for attractive posture and comfortable support. Place your derrière slightly away from the back of the chair, and relax your spine against the support. Many chairs are not designed properly—they should be lower in the legs and higher in the back, so that feet can easily rest upon the floor, and the back has ample support.

Never fidget—learn to sit gracefully with body straight, and feet together on the ground. If you must cross your legs, cross them at the ankles rather than at the knees.

Sleeping—Buy a high-quality mattress and to improve spinal posture, lie on your back, then stretch from the top of your head to the tip of your toes to elongate the body. Note: pillows often do as much good under one's knees as under one's neck, for this can flatten the back and alleviate pains. You probably also like something soft to rest your head upon, so choose a pillow containing loose, free-moving down, and cover it with a mulberry silk pillowcase—your neck, hair and facial skin will thank you. Unless one is allergic to feathers, or has a medical condition requiring elevation, it's best to avoid high, uncomfortable, stiff cushions like the artificial foam varieties.

Standing—Maintain the good posture discussed under walking, i.e.: keep a straight vertical line with no slouching. I have scoliosis, but since my crippled spine's curvature is a sideways *S*—shape, most people cannot tell since it creates a balance. If I stand up straight, I almost look normal except that the top half of my body is two inches shorter than it should be, making my legs and arms look long.

Aside from posture, learn how to occupy your hands and control your facial expressions. Women frequently clutch a handbag, but when not doing so, it is appropriate for a woman or a man to simply clasp the hands together in front of oneself or behind one's back.

Other important points to remember while standing and at *ALL* times:

* Keep hands out of pockets—if they're cold, wear gloves.
* Don't scratch, rub or pick.
* Keep your finger nails away from your mouth, and avoid touching your face.
* Try not to point or speak excessively with your hands.
* Don't twirl your hair, twist your lips, whisper, roll your eyes, etc.

Speech

The famous play 'My Fair Lady' was not an exaggeration when it implied that elocution is a key to the 'good life.' Today there are many steps towards success, and impeccable speech is one of them. When a person decides to improve their vocabulary and pronunciation, it is not an affectation. Speech education merely ascertains that we are not lazy or averse to self-improvement.

Learning is a process—it does not end after leaving school. If a person comes from a past which provided limited enlightenment, they can change their status, and work at personal improvement throughout their adult life.

It would appear much easier to avoid this apparently nonessential form of linguistic study, but what does our speech relate about us to strangers?

It may indicate:

* The type of environment we currently participate in.
* What sort of people we presently associate/communicate with.
* The extent of public, private or self-education.
* Whether or not we are well travelled and so on…

Speech can literally turn your life into an open book, as breeding, cultivation, education, and current lifestyle become readily apparent. In the long term, speech could indeed be very significant on one's road to success.

THE PROCESS

Be sure to purchase and regularly consult a good English dictionary. Another useful book to own is the hard cover, 'Roget's International Thesaurus.'

How will most adults go about the business of vocabulary and pronunciation improvement? If we could holiday for a season with the king, one would be very likely to pick up a proper accent. Unfortunately, our choices are more limited. One can hire a private tutor/elocutionist, if they possess the money to do so.

A less expensive suggestion is to borrow books and BBC CDs/DVD videos free of charge. ***Reading is vital to vocabulary education, and listening is a major factor in pronunciation development***. If one does decide on self-education, the most convenient and economical method is to use their local library, which will be invaluable as we begin with:

Voice/Pronunciation

Watch YouTube or borrow some DVDs which contain royal speeches of the King, late Queen, etc.

I have heard it said that Julie Andrews is considered to have a perfect English accent. This honour is befitting, for she exhibits both a charming voice and exemplary pronunciation. Obtain a CD book or a film which has lengthy dialogue by Julie Andrews—perhaps 'The Sound of Music.' Many classic films had polished speech. Most ladies admire the voice of Deborah Kerr in 'The King and I'—and Grace Kelly, though not of continental birth, spoke with aristocratic elegance in 'The Swan.'

Gather BBC films—Shakespeare, Elizabeth Gaskell's novels, and especially the Jane Austen series 'Pride and Prejudice,' 'Sense and Sensibility,' etc. Listen to what classic English sounds like. You can record famous speeches and select highborn dialogue of male or female articulation. Listen to the recording every day, until you are able to assimilate a similar sounding accent.

It is essential that you only study from expert material. This is especially important for English language beginners—don't make the mistake of learning dialect from unskilled sources, such as lower-middle class TV programming. A CD and DVD player or laptop computer are very good investments and will allow you to select the highest quality.

If you would prefer to buy your own famous writer classic films, they can often be purchased through quality book stores, online, etc. Today, I have a very well stocked collection at home, which I'm certain will be passed on for generations.

The voice for success is clear, easily understood, mellifluous and exuberant. One's voice can make words sound interesting, refreshing, and vibrant. People will actually want to hear what you have to say, because they can sense the emphasis in your speech. Find out what kind of voice you really possess—listen to it on recording or have a professional elocution instructor assist you.

If it turns out that you have trouble in sounding wonderful, find out what the shortcoming is: Too loud? Too quiet? Mumbling? Shrill? Monotone? Croaky? (Often the result of smoking, overuse of alcohol or drinking beverages while they are too hot). If an obvious problem exists, work hard at solving it. Practice reading aloud on micro-cassette, IPhone, etc. Study books which deal with the subject of vocal effectiveness. Create the pleasant, perfect voice that you desire to become a permanent quality of your being, as you journey through the good life.

HIGH SOCIETY

If you would like to come upon a successful lifestyle with more ease and less struggle, it is recommended that you practise using 'high' rather than 'low' dialect. Try to study the formal language, as it will be more easily understood by the general populace. For the moment we will concentrate on English. It may sound very unfair, but the fact remains, that people will feel that you are more intelligent, cultured, and generally more pleasing to listen to if you converse in RP (received pronunciation); that is, Standard, BBC, King's English. London East-end cockney, Brooklynese, American Southern drawls and other dialects, although we love to hear the charming sounds, can be very difficult for some people to decipher and such can make the listener feel uncomfortable. On the contrary—the crisp, clear, enunciated words of classic English are a simple pleasure to comprehend.

Also, practise speaking at a relaxed moderate pace—not only does this make comprehension easier for the international audience whose mother tongue might not be English, but it also prevents the negative impression of nervousness which is frequently associated with very fast speech.

FOREIGN SPEECH

Our primary language may be English, but it is vital that we also educate ourselves in commonly known foreign speech. Not only will this intellectual acquirement display a certain level of culture, but it will demonstrate good manners towards our foreign associates. The four most widely spoken languages in Western Europe are: German, French, English and Italian.

If you have ever studied art or music, you will recall that Italian is often the language of reference: 'impasto' from painting, 'largo' and 'pianissimo' in music, and many more examples.

When exercising our culinary tastes, one will note that French is the language required to order in many fine restaurants; it was also the language of the Diplomatic Corps. French is very popular in school and we learn how to correctly pronounce universally recognised words like bouquet (boo kay), encore (ahn kor), en route (ahn root), etc.

What if, however, one does not possess this basic knowledge? For example: one goes to breakfast at a French bistro (bees troh) and wants to order 'cafe &

croissant' (ka fay & krwah sahn) but does not have the experience to pronounce the words properly. What should they do? In such situations there are two options:

1. You may ask how a particular word is to be spoken. Never be embarrassed—people love to instruct, and they respect those who are humble enough to enquire.

2. Play it safe and request in English—order 'coffee and a crescent roll.' This approach is less favourable than the first, but is sometimes necessary. E.g.: if you absolutely cannot pronounce 'Monsieur' (muhs yuh), perhaps you should just say 'Mister.'

If you would like more information on speech habits of high society, I have included a supplement consisting of: Status Enunciation, Foreign Words, and Classic Speech in Appendix #3 at the back of this book.

ACCENTS

There is no need for a foreigner to be embarrassed if they carry the accent of their ancestral nationality. An accent can be a beautiful, unique, and attractive part of one's presence and personality. An accent is when someone says a word like 'lovely' and it sounds like 'luv' lee.' The word is unchanged, but merely has some added pizzazz.

An accent is not when a major deformation occurs—for example:
>'Whaja wanna do afterdat es-school?'
>'What do you want to do after school?'

Using a non-existent term like 'whaja' to replace three correct words is not considered an accent, but more like unlearned English.

Even proper English can have more than one dialect. You may recognise: Australian, Irish, Scottish or American enunciation. In the UK, those who take residence in upper neighbourhoods, associate with aristocratic people, receive private education, listen to BBC radio and so on, are generally inclined to speak RP English. Like a computer, the brain will turn out whatever is continually programmed into it. The people we most often communicate with will also play a major part in determining whether our speech exemplifies the King's English, or takes on a somewhat removed dialect.

WORDS FOR THE WISE

If someone had never met you in person, but was initially introduced to you via the telephone, how would they picture you? What kind of impression would you present? Would they hear a well-versed intellectual with an impeccably clear, upper class, mellifluous voice? Or would they hear one emit incomplete sentences filled with slang and self-conscious pauses? If you are not sure what you actually sound like, record yourself… be natural during the communication and then play it back. You will understand what image is conveyed by your speech. Practise improving your language by reading cultivated prose orally and recording it at the same time. Continue this exercise until the results are optimal.

To master top-drawer conversation, practise these straightforward "do's & don'ts" in your everyday communication, whether you talk by telephone/Skype or in person:

1. **DO** speak in complete sentences; i.e., don't leave anything ambiguous. For example—your neighbour speaks over the garden fence and says: 'I sure did a lot of carrots today.' You don't know if she planted them, weeded them, pulled them or cooked them. Say exactly what you mean.

2. **DO** elaborate the message. Very similar to number one above—if you want someone to see a picture, describe it in detail. For example: don't say 'The weather is going to be frightful!' If it's going to be frightfully hot you may want to bring lotion and a bathing dress, but if there is going to be a frightful storm, you may decide to bring an umbrella or remain indoors.

3. **DON'T** destroy the King's English and don't use any slang. There is nothing respectable or professional about either jargon or mispronunciation. It is worth taking some time to think before speaking.

4. **DO** articulate in a clear and relaxed tone. Too loud, too soft, or too fast are all inadequate.

5. **DO** put life and expression into your speech. It is not only important to say something intelligent, but 'how' you say it is also significant. Lifeless, boring, monotones can soon lose the listener's attention.

6. **DON'T** be reduced to gibberish and gestures. Have you ever been baffled by an utterance which sounds like this: 'You know eh, what I mean huh, you know eh, huh you know… eh' The words are generally accompanied by the

waving of arms. Unfortunately, the hand movement does not facilitate one's comprehension of the speech. Learn to communicate well.

7. **DON'T** use counterproductive word replacements. Realise what is really being said to others as well as to your own subconscious, e.g.: it can sound common to associate wildlife (birds and deer) with money. "A couple of loonies or a few bucks" as you might hear in North America. You wouldn't hear one say "Last year I earned 80,000 loonies." The appropriate word 'dollars' seems to work like an affirmation. Perhaps that is why those who say 'dollars' usually have more of them.

8. **DO** use dialogue instead of monologue. Those who master positive speaking habits, will soon notice that more people tend to gather around them at public engagements. Once you've achieved this social privilege, one must remember not to abuse their talents. Using dialogue rather than monologue means to create an equal verbal exchange. Take turns listening and speaking… ask for feedback from those around you—this is what makes good conversation.

SPEAKING BY TELEPHONE

Whether you are making a social call or using the telephone for business purposes, there is a certain telephone etiquette that should be observed. The following are some suggestions:

1. Identify yourself— 'Hello, this is Dr Adams calling, may I speak with Victoria Bradford please?'

2. Identify the receivers allotted time— 'Hello Victoria (if a friend) or Ms Bradford (if a patient), do you have five minutes to chat, or am I interrupting your dinner hour?' N.B. If the receiver is busy or has guests, ask him/her to call back when they are free—or if you have a very short message (one minute or less) proceed to make your announcement and then say good-bye.

3. Speak pleasantly—use proper vocabulary. Don't whisper, shout, eat or chew gum. A good exercise is to set a looking-glass on your desk and watch yourself as you speak on the telephone. Also, remember to answer the telephone with a smile—the person at the other end of the line will hear your expression.

4. Do not monopolise time—if the receiver says that she/he is free to speak, that does not mean for a whole hour. If the message is that time consuming, consider sending a letter, email or better yet, meet with your associate in person to participate in such detailed conversation.

5. Exchange dialogue—avoid one-sided speeches. Listening to someone who insists on doing all of the talking and does not exchange proper conversation can be a dreadful bore. Good dialogue means to speak *with* a person rather than *at* them.

6. Remember to check global time zones—both personal and business calls should occur between 9:00 am and 5:00 pm—only intimate associates and emergencies are exempt from this social code.

POSITIVE SPEECH —I VERSUS YOU

We already understand that it is very important how we speak—the tone of voice, vocabulary and pronunciation. But what about our manner of speaking? Consider every sentence which leaves your lips—make this observation for a complete day. Did most of the phrases sound negative or positive? If you've noticed too much negativity toward others, I recommend this simple exercise. For one week, replace all *you* sentences with *I* sentences. For example:

A lady would not say to her consort: '*You* never bring me flowers anymore.' She would change the *you* sentence to an *I* sentence: '*I* just love when *I* receive beautiful bouquets.' Negative becomes positive. 'You' can be blaming someone other than yourself. Change your words—change your reality.

Remember: **POSITIVE SPEECH ATTRACTS POSITIVE RESULTS**.

Another example: Teachers and guardians must be very careful with young people: don't say   '*Your* tardiness and idleness are abhorrent—*you'll* never amount to anything.' Say: 'I admire punctuality and love to see motivation—well done!' This will inspire better results and make an incredible difference.

Third example: An employer to a member of his staff: don't say— '*You're* never responsible, *you* can't be trusted to do a decent job without constant supervision.' Say '*I* admire a self-starter who is capable of working independently.'

When around other people, speak with energy and enthusiasm. Say positive things like: I adore what I do and helping others! I am always lucky! This is a wonderful day! I am so happily married! People like to be around people whose vibrancy is contagious because it helps them to feel better too.

Speak joyful words about yourself, but also compliment and encourage others. Leave every person you come in contact with, feeling an impression of *increase*. Make them feel important—you can always find something to compliment others on with sincerity. People will feel: I like myself better when I am with you and I want to see more of you.

If you constantly repeat positive phrases to the people who surround you, you should notice vast improvement in your life and theirs!

Part II
Lifestyles

When life begins to progress due to your own hard efforts—don't be surprised if you hear people refer to you as being 'lucky.' Does luck really exist? Happenchance rarely occurs; in fact, nearly all 'surprise forces', whether bringing adversity or good fortune, are premeditated.

Consider the threatening saying "If you lie down with dogs, you wake up with fleas." Or examine the more auspicious advice "You can be in the right place at the right time."

Isn't it amazing that individuals who are determined to associate with kind, intelligent people and circulate in respectable places, always become so lucky? Why do they get all the personal success and career breaks? While those who prefer to keep company with mean characters in disreputable districts attract so much trouble and "bad luck." Magical fortune is easily found when one learns where to search and takes the initiative for opportunities to present themselves.

Does luck exist? Apparently… enlightened people *create* it every day. The wiser you work, the luckier you will become. This brings us to the second section entitled 'Lifestyles,' which is designed to assist readers in choosing personal and tangible surroundings that will increase their prosperity consciousness, improve chances for success, and allow them to live royally in the process.

Chapter 4 will discuss association, entertainment and occupation i.e., our personal surroundings. Chapter 5 deals with property, house, and other palpable possessions, which may affect our present sense of worth, and thus aid in determining our future success.

Chapter 4
Personal Surroundings

Associations

THE PEOPLE AROUND US

Why would a chapter on personal associations be significant in determining whether or not we live a pleasant lifestyle? In Dr Robert Anthony's book "The Ultimate Secrets of Total Self-Confidence" he wrote: "be aware that ***YOU TAKE ON A DEFINITE PORTION OF EVERY PERSON WITH WHOM YOU ASSOCIATE***. So, be *very* careful of the company you keep." How often have we heard similar words from parents, teachers, and advisors who cautioned us? Choosing one's associates wisely does not merely represent advice for the young, but can be a serious success/fail factor in our adult lives as well.

You have likely noticed already how the people whom you associate with will have a serious effect on your own life. Jim Rohn said: "You are the average of the five people you spend the most time with." Search out positive, uplifting people who will inspire and motivate you to become the best that you can be.

What type of people presently surround you? Are they vibrant, honest, optimistic companions—or do you attract negative, gossipy, complainers? Remember: ***YOU ATTRACT WHATEVER YOU PROTRACT***. We cannot expect wonderful people to associate with us, unless we ourselves live wholesomely. You must first *become* the person whom you wish to associate with, marry, etc. One has the right to surround oneself with civilised, intelligent, honest people. Be selective—you deserve the best, but you must also ***live up to the standards which you set***.

Will the people with whom you associate, also increase your chances for financial success? Absolutely. Someone once told me, "If you want to live rich… observe the poor… and do exactly the opposite!" If the less fortunate spend time in shady bars, casinos or bingo halls, perhaps this is a clue about where **not** to earn money.

If the disadvantaged spend a great deal of time in front of the television or looking at their smart phones, rather than participating in life through sport, exercise, or occupation as the successful do, then perhaps idleness is something to avoid. If the poor spend their time smoking cigarettes, taking drugs and reading tabloids, while the affluent spend time on health and higher education—who should we imitate?

Let's look at a strictly monetary example: If one was to associate with **only** millionaires for the next ten years of their life; what sort of financial state do you imagine you would find that person in at the end of the decade? Do you think that they would be in an impecunious position, or would you expect to see them becoming more financially established? Whatever one surrounds oneself with has a greater likelihood of occurring.

In Catherine Ponder's book "Open Your Mind to Receive" she warns: *"Whatever you notice, you are inviting into your life. Whatever you talk about, you are inviting into your life. Whatever you identify with in your thoughts, words and actions, you are inviting into your life."* So, be careful! I used to keep that message taped on the wall to remind me every day, just how important all forms of association are.

What if one finds oneself stuck in a situation where they are surrounded by less than wholesome people. Most frequently, this problem occurs because of location or work. The world is ours—remember that you can live in many different places. The other problem of being stuck in a group of negative people might occur when one is employed by government or some other large institution. Since the wage-worker does not actually do the hiring, they have absolutely no control over whom their fellow employees are.

If one should find oneself in this situation, surrounded by a large group of negative people, often the best recourse is to leave that particular work scenario. Try to work for a very small business, where there are only one or two others—thus reducing the odds of being grouped with incompatibles; or better still, try to become self-employed, where you will be completely free to choose associates.

I was blessed to be born to very happy, generally optimistic parents. Unfortunately, not everyone is so fortunate. Another situation where one may find themselves amidst people whom they do not get on with is family. Consider the saying: "You can choose your friends, but you can't choose your family."

Aside from selecting a 'Godparent' or adopting a child, this statement is basically true. Try to get on as best you can with your biological siblings and other relations; if it is truly an unbearable situation, one may eventually need to distance themselves.

PEOPLE IN TRANSITION

True 'movers and shakers' are constantly involved with change. Perhaps one is leaving the location where they grew up, or maybe they are planning to get into their own business venture; whatever the new path may be, sometimes obstacles will appear. The disappointing truth is that these 'obstacles' are often the people whom they care about the most. It may be your relations or circle of friends, and the negative feedback is simply a reluctance to let you go. One might hear phrases like: 'Don't leave that secure wage job you have' or 'Don't invest in that business—it's too risky.' 'Don't leave our community, the place where you were born.'

The pessimists may not intentionally want to curtail your success—so what are their real reasons for trying to stop you? Picture a person who has a lot of energy; one who is prepared to make innovative change—to really 'go for it' and create an incredible life. Chances are that they were the 'rock foundation' of their social group, or perhaps they were the spirit and joy of their family.

Relations and friends do not want to lose the maverick—they depend on this person's courage, enthusiasm, and support. Thus, when one hears negative feedback coming from the worrier, we should not become cross... they are not doing it out of jealousy or spite. They try to hold you back because they really care for you and they don't want to lose you. Now—contrarily, I am not saying that you should listen to them either. Life will be far more rewarding when you follow your own heart and your dreams.

If these people truly respect and admire you, in a short period of time, they will come to understand and accept your goals and do everything they can to promote your success. Sometimes the people who are ***extremely*** close to you, perhaps your consort or very best friend, will choose to move onward and upwards with you, starting a business or new venture together.

With maturity, many will find themselves going through very similar changes. We do not need to lose touch with those whom we continue to share ideas in common with. This world is small enough, that no matter where one relocates geographically, we can always maintain contact with our acquaintances. Indeed, the most successful people are those who know a close friend or relative living on every continent. We should have associates around the world because the spirit of friendship and love travels wherever we go.

Don't expect, however, to drag along the whole lot of your family or original circle of friends. A few people might even choose roads which lead in the *opposite* direction of your own, and you cannot expect to change them. If you feel that you've outgrown certain companions, simply release them. You can't pull them along if they don't want to travel.

If they *do* want to make positive changes, that is another matter—give advice and assistance when it is *asked* for. Take care to realise your own divine plan and don't allow anyone to discourage you.

On a positive note, remember that whenever you lose something, you make room to gain. Let go of things of a lower nature in order to receive something of a higher nature. One may distance oneself from those with negativity and fear, but there will also be many new relationships developing as you begin to attract others who share the kindred spirit of love and faith. Go positively and wholeheartedly into your new order. Don't cry about an imperfect past; just be grateful for the transition and marvellous present.

FRIENDSHIPS CREATE SUCCESS

Ecclesiasticus 9:15 "A new friend is as new wine: it shall grow old, and thou shalt drink it with pleasure." Every time we make a new friend of good character, we are inviting more happiness into our lives. I was very sad once, because a wonderfully positive and inspiring priest was leaving our church. My eyes grew misty as I told him how dreadfully we would all miss his presence, and he comforted me by saying "but this is our purpose—to move about, always creating new friends, and sharing goodwill with the multitudes." I understood then, that my attachment was selfish, and that other parishes also deserved some piece of this incredible man's time. His words also encouraged me to travel more, and to increase my own personal friendships.

Why are good friends so important? The obvious reasons are:
* Love—the wonderful bond which is the centre of all happiness.

* Social pleasures—the privilege of participating in sport or recreation together.

* Emotional support—the peace and comfort of simply 'having someone to talk to.'

Such are the fundamental reasons for friendship, but are friends also necessary on our road to occupational success? Yes indeed, let me give an example.

When I was young and had just become self-employed as a real estate agent, it was my friends and relations who helped me enormously by giving me their personal business—buying, selling, and equally as important 'referrals' i.e., introducing me to their associates who required my services. There is no easier road to success than the road paved by **loyal** companions.

One of the greatest privileges of getting into business is the enlightenment of discovering who *really* cares about you. Those who do, will always try to help out. A true friend or devoted mate will possess the characteristics of *honesty* and *charity*. Anyone who is deceitful or ungenerous does not really love. Those who attribute your success to luck, or do not support you, have not yet learned that success stems from kindness and friendships.

How can we ever repay these loyal friends? Pave *their* road to success. For me it was easy, because nearly 90% of my associates are self-employed, freelance or self-contracting. Some own restaurants, or retail shops—others have their own service industry like insurance, legal attorneys, accounting, dentistry, photography, etc. When someone sent business to me, I would try to reciprocate by sending referrals their way.

This is a marvellous experience, because you and your loyal friends will eventually become successful and enjoy life's rewards together. The motto at my daughter's school is: *Confident, Capable,* ***Connected***—so wonderful to learn this at an early age.

What if some of your friends are not self-employed and you cannot send them any business? Reward them in some other way. Send flowers or presents—take them out for luncheon… always express your appreciation and gratitude.

Supporting friends can bring us vast amounts of pleasure in ways other than reciprocal business. If your acquaintance is a musician in a symphonic orchestra, or author of an interesting manuscript… you can support them by attending the concert, or buying the book. These actions automatically bring pleasure to yourself as well, for you will most likely enjoy the marvellous music, or the interesting read. Indeed, true friendships create *royal living*.

ASSOCIATES AND TRAVEL

It may not be the wisest idea to travel or take long holidays with one's companions, as too much time spent together, can breed disquiet. How then can our friends make travel better?

Consider utilising the flair for hospitality. If for example, one person resides in London, and their good friend lives in Paris… when they have the urge to make a shopping expedition, sample a new famous restaurant, or simply view a change of scenery, they can visit at their friend's place for two or three days. Note on etiquette:

1. Never stay for more than three days—your hosts *do* have other things to do and you should largely be able to amuse yourself while you are a guest.
2. Only go *where* and *when* you have been *invited*, i.e., do not invite yourself.
3. Always invite your host back to be a *guest at your house* within the same year—otherwise do not expect to receive future invitations.

If you do wish to travel with friends or relations together on a holiday – I would recommend selecting a way where independence can be maintained, such as a luxury cruise with Cunard. Everyone on the ship is completely free to spend their day as they desire: whether going on shore to walk about an interesting port; staying on board to relax by the pool; getting a spa treatment or attending one of the fascinating seminars or other activities.

When evening dawns, one might attend a reception or ball; see a theatre performance, and so forth. A nice idea is to meet up with your group over dinner, where everyone can tell each other what they saw and how they enjoyed spending the day. There will be more than enough time to visit together at your designated dining table – you could meet up for breakfast, luncheon or afternoon tea if you wanted to. Finally, you may decide to participate in some delightful activities with others but you'll always know that privacy is an option.

Mentors/Role Models

Take a moment to think of people whom you admire, whether living or deceased and ask yourself, why are they very special people? Were they kind, generous, considerate, loyal, successful, intelligent, spiritual, energetic, compassionate? If you admire them, you probably already possess some of their quality characteristics—or you certainly would like to. Model yourself after their highest attributes and repeat them in your mind, for example "I am graceful, I am generous, I am confident, I am affluent," etc.

The way you see yourself subconsciously, is the quality that others will begin to see in you, and as you begin to behave as your ideal self, others will begin to treat you accordingly. Love and respect yourself in order to attract love and respect—never dwell on the imperfections of self or others.

Of all the people whom we associate with, it is very beneficial to choose at least one mentor. This role model must be someone for whom you have an enormous amount of respect. It may be a relation, teacher, friend, business associate—it really makes no difference, as long as they are worthy of a protégé.

If one truly cannot think of a close associate whose standards and life-style they admire, they might instead choose a world renowned figure. Great mentors are often those who fulfil the obligation of Noblesse Oblige, i.e., noble people who behave in an honourable, charitable and respectable manner.

Whenever an issue arises which challenges your decision making, pretend that you are the role model and compare the situation with *__their standards__*. For example: If someone asked you to appear on one of those embarrassing talk shows, one should first contemplate the damage to their reputation. A lady might ask herself 'would the late Queen have done it?'

Gentlemen, if you were tempted to swear during your business conference, you may first question, would 'Our King speak like that?' If someone offers to sell you drugs or stolen merchandise... consider, 'would our Pope or Prime Minister accept?' In all of these cases, the answer would likely be 'No.'

Bear in mind, that not all questions would be answered in the negative. If one is wondering whether it is a good idea to join a volunteer organisation or begin some charity work and asks, 'would members of the aristocracy participate in this cause?' The answer may well be affirmative. If you want to be a well-respected person, learn how great people make decisions.

Choose a mentor with fine taste and high reputation... then raise your own standards. Maintain integrity... there is no need to lose your individuality—be the best that *you* can be. We tend to become much like the company which we keep. After you have chosen good role models, you may begin to observe their behaviour: how they speak, what they wear, what they do, and the way they think. Keep your individual personality but **add the characteristics which you desire to add, and discard old behaviour patterns which you no longer feel comfortable with**.

An incredibly wise female mentor of mine once informed me that the most tolerant and charitable people could usually be found in the most noble and eminent positions. She said, "If you desire attention to your requests, do not waste your time at the iron-bulwarks, i.e., reception guards—but find a way to speak with the person in charge… go straight to the top."

Individuals of proven worth should be chosen as mentors to guide and instruct us. Look to the people who have demonstrated success, whether in business, personal, or spiritual—preferably in all three. If you want advice on how to have a good marriage—don't ask someone who is twice divorced because obviously they didn't learn the first time. If you want advice about how to make money—don't ask someone who is always broke. If you want to know how to live a happy life, don't ask someone who is frequently miserable.

Always go to the people who are living examples of success. Ask *these* people how they came to achieve their goals. The person who is happily married might actually be able to give you some sound advice on how to have a good relationship. The person who has a profitable business might teach you how to earn more money. These established people should become your mentors and role models. Most top-drawer people often feel complemented and happy to help someone who has a desire to learn from them. Don't be too proud to ask them to share a part of their wisdom.

What about trial and error… can't we also learn from making mistakes? Of course, one can, providing we learn not to repeat them. I am only saying that instead of wasting so much time, it can be more pleasant to get on board early. Otto von Bismarck said, "The wise man learns from the mistakes of others."

Your Consort

For those of you who are still single, but would like to develop a serious relationship—this section is for you. ***Our consort is the most important associate we will ever have and should be considered our greatest asset.*** This is the person who should love, motivate and inspire us to become the best we can be.

One probably makes no personal decision in life which is more vital to their ultimate happiness than choosing their spouse. The old saying 'behind every great man is a great woman' can also be reversed, for behind great women, there are often great men. For those who prefer to remain bachelors or bachelorettes, that is fine and good. One can take love and support from the multitudes of people around us—marriage is certainly not a requirement of a happy or successful life. But for those of you who are unmatched, and would prefer to be otherwise... read on.

Your consort will become the most significant person in your life. Aside from the will of God and your own destiny, put your consort above all else. The person you marry must take priority over family, friends and associates. Most of us adore our parents and children, but the former usually pass away before us, and the latter, when grown, may leave the family estate one day.

Our consort remains 'til death us do part.' They are our 'life' partner—to be with us always, well into old age and hopefully until we transition from this world. Your consort must be your confidante, the one whom you are most devoted to and confiding in—more so than any best friend. Your husband or wife should be top priority—they become our pillar of strength.

When two highly compatible, very loving people mate for life, they have a special power to reach incredible heights of success and self-fulfilment. On the negative side of this coin—if you choose the wrong person, you might actually curtail your ability for achievement and happiness. If you desire a worthy relationship but have not yet attained one, don't settle—you would be far better off to remain single. Never marry just to conform to the status quo; indeed, do not even date an unsuitable person just to have a partner.

CHOOSING A CONSORT

Why is it that top-drawer people rarely seem to have any trouble meeting worthy consorts? The answer is understandable: because they are *social* people. They know all of the single members at their golf club, country club and church as well as their business associates. They do not have the need to ever begin a relationship with a total stranger. This is where a lot of unsocial people mess up.

They want a relationship, and will pick up someone from the Internet, a nightclub or any *public* place where people may have little in common.

They meet a complete stranger, and hope beyond hope, that this may be 'the one', but the odds of finding compatibility when approaching a total stranger are very low. Whereas, circles of influence can encourage people to know each other well—how they behave, their habits, what business they are in, their religion, whether they enjoy similar sports… and if they are really 'single.' It is an extreme advantage to know whether one is compatible—this is the edge and reason why social people are much more successful in choosing consorts.

How can one tell if a person whom they've only dated for a short while could be pleasant to develop a relationship with? The answer: determine whether they show respect towards everyone, and that includes any former girlfriends or boyfriends. A good partner will speak ill of no one. If they resent someone from their past… they are likely to end up showing little respect for you too. Also try to choose someone who is kind with good humour and a love of laughter.

If you are having difficulty in meeting someone of your taste, what should you do? One could go to a dating agency; however, it would likely be less costly and more intriguing to simply *become more social*. Like attracts like: common agencies for the bored and lonely will attract similar, unsocial people. The well-adjusted movers and shakers not only know dozens of interesting others, but will become acquainted with new faces at places of *mutual* interest.

They meet their dates at: * the golf course * luncheon parties or receptions * sailing or yacht clubs * the theatre * gallery exhibit openings * polo and riding clubs * charity balls * the races * fashion galas * health or beauty spas * travel resorts * business conferences * film premieres * garden parties * wine tasting events * in their parish * on luxury cruises * at the opera * through their occupation * while doing volunteer work * through friends or relations… and dozens of other places, where they may at least share some common interest.

If someone says 'I never meet anybody'… one might be concerned about their social behaviour—are they couch-potatoes, or perhaps even sociopathic? Most people eventually end up with a clone of themselves i.e.: ***Whatever you are—is what you will attract***. Which brings us to the next issue:

COMPATIBILITY

Birds of a feather—fly together. The marital success ratio becomes much greater when people pay attention to the wise formula: ***Opposites might attract, but compatibles stay together***. People are attracted to opposites only to satisfy that which they lack, for example: the calmly boring and the overly dramatic might seek comfort or amusement in each other, because neither is well balanced. True soul-mates are similar in temperament. Life is generally much easier on those who choose a partner with whom they share common ideas. This is especially important regarding the big three: sex, politics, and religion… better to be alike in such opinions and leave less to row about.

Class and money are also factors which can cause problems, i.e., when a husband and wife have vastly different manners or fortune. If one person's taste is champagne and caviar, while the other's is beer and meatloaf… trouble in paradise could become imminent. Perhaps this is why the royal and rich still prefer endogamous marriages, i.e., union with their own kind, or matches of equal rank and fortune.

Although sometimes, there will be marital mixes for certain benefits. For example, a newly rich person who lacks refinement may choose to wed cash-poor nobility in order to gain status or a title in exchange for wealth. There are three different prospects (aside from love) which people tend to take into consideration before uniting. They are: better *class*, *attractiveness* and greater *financial* estate. One may not find a person who has all three of the aforementioned, but chances are that one will not wish to settle for a person who has 'non-of-the-above.'

You may be the wise cultured person of civility and grace… or one who possesses a bloodline of excellent health and striking handsomeness… or be the sophisticated business talent with fortune and success. This is why we sometimes see a person of class and handsomeness, but short allowance, marry one who is not so fair, but has acquired fortune. Become a successful entrepreneur and establish great wealth, or cultivate your mannerisms and raise your rank to a high-society level. In either case, you may become a much sought after consort.

Even though people may desire to choose a consort with one or all of the three benefits… please do remember that the most important reason for choosing a partner should be based on love and intimacy.

LOVE AND INTIMACY

The ultimate goal is to *love* someone, and be *in love* with that person, at the same time. *Love* is an everlasting commitment of true loyalty, respect and caring for another individual. E.g.: one usually loves their parents, children, close relations or best friend. To be *in love* is a passionate enamoured emotion, as one usually feels toward a romantic partner. Alas, some people *love* their spouse, but are *in love* with a paramour. They have an illicit affair to provide temporary excitement, but might remain with the wedded spouse for other reasons. This needn't be. The ideal, as I mentioned before—is to ***choose a person whom you can love and be in love with at the same time***.

Similarly, there are two types of sexual activity—divine and carnal. The first form is a heavenly sort of love-making that is romantic, compassionate, loving, spiritual, giving, sensuous, and highly gratifying. The second type is of the flesh: earth bound, self-serving, unemotional, and strictly performed for physical reasons.

One can have carnal sex with oneself, anybody, or anything, for that matter. It may bring temporary pleasure, but it tends to leave the participants feeling empty, bitter, or confused. On the other hand, if one is intimate with a soul-mate in a totally loving, euphoric way, they will experience the true magnificence of elated ecstasy. Love and sex can be wonderful human attributes, providing that we make the right decisions with respect to both.

COMMITMENT

Once you've found someone who is highly compatible, and that you feel seriously in love with… you will likely involve yourself in a relationship, and may eventually enter into marriage.

We hear so many different viewpoints about creating a good relationship. One advisor will say 'you have to work at it' and the next will say 'never analyse the relationship or you will destroy it.' Perhaps we need to be realistic. Even though we may have found someone compatible, there will be things which we simply adore about them, and things which annoy us.

They will have similar feelings towards us—attitudes which they love, and behaviours which they could do without. The logical key to a successful union is to concentrate on the mannerisms which endear us to each other—this will strengthen the bond. If we analyse and pick at our consort's negative characteristics it will only serve to weaken the relationship.

PREVENT DIVORCE BEFORE MARRIAGE

I will begin with two popular sayings: "Marry in haste, repent at leisure" and "There are the desperate who marry at once, and the wise who marry at last."

Personally, I think you should know your partner for at least five years before you can say "I *really* know this person." More and more people are waiting until later in life to make a permanent commitment. This is likely so because people want to avoid the pains and price of divorce. Most divorces occur between couples where one or both partners were under 30 years of age at the time of wedlock. Many people go through dramatic life changes during their twenties. They often change their location, friends, occupation, financial status, and complete life-style.

What are the chances of remaining compatible, for two young people who are going through rapid growing changes? Example: A young lady and fellow in their twenties meet and share an attraction for each other. They enjoy each other's company, and consequently decide to become flat-mates. They believe themselves to be in love, and soon marry. After a year or two, the serious realities of life begin to surface.

This young lady has chosen to start a business, earns plenty of money, and makes many fine friends. Her young spouse lacks similar ambition—prefers the security of being a low-income wage-worker, and does not enjoy public socialising. Their twenties, 'the decade of change', have seen these two young adults choose to travel down very different paths. A few years later, they realise that they are complete and total opposites, for life has become most inharmonious.

The teens and twenties are very formative years, where we gradually decide which roads we are going to follow. If we were to settle down *after* this volatile age, chances are that we would have already established a certain direction, and could choose a truly compatible partner. Our behaviour and customs will be well decided upon… our path well plotted. If you are compatible *after* the age of 30— you have a greater chance of remaining so.

The spouse you choose may well determine whether you will live in a rented flat or own a villa, have gambling debts or holidays in the Mediterranean, mingle with dullards or the intelligentsia. You will be marrying not just a person, but their potential way of life.

You have likely noticed that in current times, high society is not generally in a terrible hurry to make a permanent match. You may have wondered why they prefer to marry when they are in their thirties or forties. C-people would never purposely bring children into the world until they were established enough that they could afford to give them the best care and education, an adequate home and nutritious diet, and much *quality* time. The success oriented demand so much from life that they are not prepared to settle for less, hence they often marry and procreate much later on.

As I earlier mentioned, the vast majority of divorces occur when either the bride, groom or both parties marry before the age of 30. 'Until death us do part' can be quite a long time—there is no need to rush. Charles, as the Prince of Wales, was 32 years of age, an acceptable time for marriage. Unfortunately, he made the mistake of proposing to a teenager. Had he married someone more compatible in age and manner, his first marriage may have been successful.

The current Prince and Princess of Wales (William and Catherine) were just under 30 when they wed, but fortunately they had dated for seven years and knew each other well enough to plan their future. To live like royalty—consider additional wise couples who have married, only *after* the age of 30 as in this list below:

Sophie Countess of Wessex, born 20/January/1965, married 19/June/1999 to Prince Edward, born 10/March/1964 Ages: (34 & 35).

Princess Maxima of the Netherlands, born 17/May/1971, married 2/February/2002 to Willem-Alexander, Prince of Orange, born 27/April/1967 (30 & 34).

Crown Princess Mary of Denmark, born 5/February/1972, married 14/May/2004 to Crown Prince Frederick, born 26/May/1968 (32 & 35).

Crown Princess Letizia of Spain, born 15/September/1972, married 22/May/2004 to Felipe, Prince of Asturias born 30/January/1968 (31 & 36).

Princess Marie of Denmark, born 6/February/1976, married 24/May/2008 to Prince Joachim, born 7/June/1969 (32 & 38).

Crown Princess Victoria of Sweden, born 14/July/1977, married 19/June/2010 to Prince Daniel, born 15/September/1973 (32 & 36).

Prince Nikolaos of Greece, born 1/October/1969, married 25/August/2010 to Tatiana Blatnik, born 28/August/1980 (40 & 30).

Prince Carlos of Bourbon-Parma, born 27/January/1970, married 20/November/2010 to Princess Anne Marie Gaulterie van Weezel, born 18/December/1977 (40 & 32).

HSH Prince Albert II of Monaco, born 14/March/1958, married 1/July/2011 to Charlene Wittstock, born 25/January/1978 (53 & 33).

Zara Phillips, born 15/May/1981, married 30/July/2011 to Mike Tindall, born 18/October/1978 (30 & 32).

Prince Georg Friedrich of Prussia, born 10/June/1976, married 27/August/2011 to Princess Sophie of Isenburg, born 7/March/1978 (35 & 33).

Princess Maria Carolina of Bourbon-Parma (niece of Queen Beatrix—Netherlands), born 23/June/1974 was almost 38 when she married Mr Albert Brenninkmeijer on 16/June/2012.

Princess Madeleine of Sweden, born 10/June/1982, married 8/June/2013 to Christopher O'Neil born 27/June/1974 (30 & 38).

Lady Gabriella Windsor, born 23/April/1981, married 18/May 2019 was 38 when she wed Thomas Kingston.

Princess Maria Laura of Belgium, born 26/August/1988 was 34 when she married William Isvy 10/September/2022.

C-PEOPLE ARE TANTALISING

During the young adult years, twenties to thirties, we have observed that many upper-class people tend to remain unwed. The main reason for this is their strong sense of prosperity consciousness… the search for a sound future. C-people will generally spend more than a decade dating: socialising, attending the arts, participating in sports, wining and dining, and so forth. They use the skill of flirtation in true romantic sense as Oscar Wilde described it **'attention without intention.'**

They are very selective and very tantalising—they may go out on dates with dozens of people, but the individuals with whom they will actually become 'intimate' are few and far between. C-people are not 'easy'… they consider this pastime for hard-up folks who have little to offer. This tantalising behaviour is what makes them so alluring. Cleopatra, celibate for much of her life, was regarded as the greatest seductress of all time. Every man may have desired her, but she reserved herself for only the select—like Caesar and Anthony.

When these special individuals finally do settle down, they are normally prepared to practise fidelity and commitment. They know that *love is a decision as well as a feeling.* I've never yet met a highly respected philanderer. Why be loyal? Call it class, call it civility, call it integrity… eagles are monogamous birds—turkeys are not.

C-people truly know how to keep love alive. They practise the intense, mysterious and exciting art of romance. They live rich continually: candlelight dinners, romantic music, fresh flowers, fragrant scents, herbal baths, captivating apparel, traditional chivalry, endearing manners, blissful strokes and delightful words as often as possible. One cannot possibly tire of love and romance. This bond between two people will create a force of energy and strength like nothing imaginable!

Together you can rise to the high echelons. Work side by side, encourage each other, help your consort to realise their true potential. Goethe said: *"If you treat an individual as he is, he will remain that way, but if you treat him as if he were what he could be—he will become what he could be."* Treat your wife like a queen—treat your husband like a king—as the saying goes, '*give the person a fine reputation to live up to.*' Unite in success… experience the glory of love. Together you will create your destinies—make them the best they can be!

BROADEN THE SPHERE OF INFLUENCE

Fortunate are countries with a *shared system of responsibility*. They have a Monarchy which represents security, stability, and fair judgement. They have the church, whose duty is to promote peace and charity on a global level. There is a Prime Minister who is chosen by the people, and may serve as long as the majority of citizens desire. With royal ambassadors, Christian messengers, and parliamentary representation all combined and working together, they have continuous peace and harmony.

Now observe countries where all responsibility is put on *one individual*—perhaps a religious fundamentalist, or a dictator. How many *solitary* rulers and presidents have been targeted? History has indicated time and again that *sole responsibility does not work*. "Heavy is the head which bears the crown"—a saying from earlier centuries when monarchs had absolute authority. The chances for success and harmony are always increased when numerous parties work together providing balance.

Getting back to our sphere of influence, consider the above example carefully on your personal road to success. Learn to work with others, even those who do not always share your views, for this will reduce narrow vision. Every person has something to offer, and can help to broaden our knowledge. When you become an unbiased goodwill ambassador with an apolitical stance like our Sovereign; when you enjoy dining with socialists and capitalists at the same table; when you learn to avoid extremities, and love all of your fellow men—then you have broadened your vision and are truly on the road to royal associations.

SOCIALISING

The Dalai Lama said in an interview, "Happiness comes from meeting, serving and mixing with other people."

I once read about problems which tend to aggravate depression—they were: substance abuse, poverty, occupational discontent, and *social isolation*. Getting out and being with people is so important. When I owned race horses people used to ask me if I went to the track, to watch them or to bet, and I would answer 'neither.' For me, going to the races tends to be a social occasion to see good friends and enjoy drinks or lunch.

As a child, I had absolutely no idea what loneliness was, having lived near so many relations and classmates. But if one has ever moved to a new city, or country where you do not have any friends or family residing, that person will soon understand what loneliness is.

Fortunately, there are many immediate ways to alleviate it—join a church or clubs, do business, volunteer for non-profit organisations, etc. These activities are splendid; but to truly eradicate loneliness, one must establish ***true***, ***close*** friendships which often take time.

When meeting a new person, always try to see the best in them – concentrate on what is interesting and pleasant about them, so you will both immediately rise to a higher vibration. Some of the people whom you meet will like and admire you straight away—these will generally be people who have something in common with your personality, opinions, ambitions, or lifestyle. However, don't expect all new acquaintances to appreciate you.

Accept the fact that a percentage of people will not understand or care for you—and it is usually better to just be pleasant when meeting and then release them to their own environment. There is never reason to get involved with the 'whisper, point, and gossip crowd' nor the negative 'let's sing the blues' group.

Socialising is undoubtedly an important step on the road to royal living, for the greatest pleasures in life generally arise from association with interesting people. If you feel that you are not meeting enough of the right people, perhaps you are not serving enough people. Hopefully your vocation or avocation will put you in contact. But aside from *occupation*, we should also find reasons to socialise on an *entertainment* level. The next section will offer some ideas of how to get out and mix with the positive crowd who partake in the 'joie de vivre.'

Entertainment

MUSICAL MOMENTS

What could resound more perfectly of royal living, than the mellifluous notes of music? I have included music under entertainment, because it so often serves as an activity for gathering people in merriment. We may be out listening to a symphonic orchestra playing baroque or other classical sounds... Bach, Beethoven, Brahms, Chopin, Debussy, Liszt, Mozart, Puccini, Schumann, Strauss, Tchaikovsky, Vivaldi... or any of the other great composers. Perhaps we are in attendance at the opera house, listening to the outstanding voice of Placido Domingo or a romantic solo by Andrea Bocelli.

On other occasions we will hear the pleasing sounds of contemporary and modern music, showering down to us through speakers as we are out and about in public places. From the European sounds of Il Divo, to the peaceful sounds of Enya, and the energetic tunes of Elton John. It doesn't matter what type of music one prefers—naturally, that is their choice.

I would only caution people to avoid music which contains negative lyrics; indeed, music without lyrics is probably best of all. The instruments which are used, and how they are played, also affect us. Studies have shown that certain types of sound actually expand our positive energy, while other sounds stir negative feelings and behaviour. Music can have an enormous effect on how we think and feel, and will also influence the way others feel toward us. The 'Beautiful People' tend to love *beautiful* music.

If you can afford, invest in one good quality music system—perhaps a 'Bang and Olufson.' Be sure to choose a design which is compact and can be placed discreetly out of sight. Recorded music is to be *heard* only—live music is *seen* e.g.: someone playing the piano in your sitting room.

In present times, with the various seating arrangements and sampler packages available, public music entertainment has become much more affordable. Attend the local symphony and opera house—you will have a marvellous time and meet many fabulous people. If you have any spare time, be sure to volunteer your services as well. These committees generally organise many exciting functions and fund-raisers—charity balls, fashion shows, wine tasting events, and other festivities which you can become a part of, simply by volunteering to help out.

Try also to support private musicians whenever the occasion arises. Hire a pianist for an evening soiree, or contract a private string quartet for your next party. Enjoy!

PRIVATE DINNERS

Although most people who partake in the fine art of royal living are very social, and have no aversion to large public receptions, I think that there is nothing they truly enjoy more, than the smaller private dinner party. What a wonderful way of sharing our blessings and friendships with one another. Indeed, when one has been invited to dine at the home of another, that is when they truly understand that they are considered a 'close' friend. Perhaps this intimacy stems from the fact that 'family' dines together, but whatever the reason, dining has been a most popular form of both past and present-day socialising.

If you are already well acquainted with this practise, feel free to move along to another subject; however, if the thought of hosting a dinner party is new to you, the following is a list of very basic guidelines, which of course, can be rearranged to suit your personal tastes:

Guests may be invited by telephone, email or on more formal occasions, by written RSVP note. One generally dresses for dinner in basic business type of apparel (lounge suit) unless special formal wear (black tie) has been requested. A party of six, eight, or 10 people should provide for an interesting group, while still maintaining an intimate ambience. Allow time for an aperitif, by asking guests to arrive half an hour prior to the designated meal time—for instance, one might state the time as 6.30 for 7 p.m.; or if hosting a luncheon which is more popular these days—I might suggest 12.30 for one o'clock.

It's always best to hire a helper, so that as host, you can mingle with your guests or introduce them to one another if necessary. Your staff will pour champagne or sherry for yourself and guests to enjoy while visiting in the drawing room or outdoor patio if a sunny day. When the meal has been prepared, the party will move into the dining room, where the food will be served one course at a time by your helper/cook.

At rectangular tables for 10, the host and hostess will be seated at each end of the table, with guests of honour to their right, and others proceeding onward. Round tables are more intimate, ideal for smaller groups of guests, and an odd number of people will make no difference. The table should be nicely laid out with a white table cloth or fine placemats, and perhaps a low centrepiece of candles, ornament or unscented fresh flowers. Fine bone china, crystal, silverware, and folded white linen napkins will add a touch of refinement.

In times past, there were six courses at *formal* luncheons or dinners: soup, seafood, meat with vegetables, salad, desert, and savoury, but in current times, a three or four course meal is more than sufficient. At our house, we tend to serve hors d'ouvres with the champagne, so we can skip having a starter at the table. When seated, we go straight to the main course, followed by a pudding and finally a savoury of cheese varieties with biscuits.

Mineral water and wine should be served with the meal and port may be passed around with the cheese. When all courses of the meal have been completed, it is the modern custom that the whole party, both men and women, retire to the drawing room where the helper will offer herbal teas, more champagne, cognac, etc. The complete duration of the evening lasts not more than three hours, with luncheons tending to be somewhat shorter. Avoid party games or over drinking, and reserve dancing for the charity balls.

This is the basic procedure for the formal meal. Of course, there are many other types of very enjoyable occasions: outdoor sporting, pool parties, garden parties, drink receptions, picnics, etc.

There are also a variety of less sophisticated gatherings such as fancy dress, stag and hen parties, etc. If one should be invited to such an event—do feel free to graciously decline.

THE GARDEN PARTY

The garden party is a most spectacular way of entertaining; indeed, this is one custom which royalty partakes in every year. One may not have the good fortune of being invited to all of these grand affairs at Buckingham Palace, but if you have access to a garden, you can certainly host your own and hopefully attend many which are held by your associates.

Since most modern dining rooms are designed to accommodate 12 or fewer guests, the garden party is an ideal way to arrange larger gatherings for more than a dozen people. These splendid outdoor events are frequently hosted for special occasions: weddings, anniversaries, birthdays, re-unions, visiting foreign guests, or simply to provide one with the opportunity of inviting many friends or relations all at the same time.

The guests will generally dress in a summery fashion of light suits, filmy dresses, whites and bright colours, flat comfortable shoes, with spring-like hats for the women and Panamas for the men. If in doubt, one can get good ideas from the Royal Ascot website and look at their dress codes. Garden parties can be held anytime between spring and autumn, and in countries of suitable climate, all year round.

The invitation will usually state the precise duration of the gathering, for example: 1 to 3 p.m. or 2 to 4 p.m. When we lived in Ascot, we always hosted our mid-June garden party from 11.30 a.m. until 1.30 p.m., so that we could all enter the Royal Enclosure next door to us by 2 o'clock in order to see the Queen arrive by coach in the Parade Ring for the start of the races.

Arrange that the kitchen staff arrive early to prepare canapes, sandwiches and such in advance. Since garden parties are larger affairs, you should also hire one person as waiter/waitress to serve the food platters and at times to circulate with bottles of champagne and sparkling mineral water like Perrier to 'top up' flutes which are getting low.

The cook should prepare about a dozen varieties of finger foods and make enough so that each guest gets to taste an item of each. We serve foods where paper napkins suffice and no china or silverware needs be brought outside.

Consider: finger sandwiches, stuffed baked mushroom caps, shrimp in wrap, spring rolls, mini-Wellingtons, mini quiche or other little tartlets, cocktail sausages, scallops, teriyaki chicken cubes, etc., the latter items would be served with wooden cocktail sticks. On our outdoor patio table, we would also have some platters arranged with various cheeses and biscuits, crudité vegetables with dip, etc.

Garden chairs are sometimes set up in shady areas for elderly guests to rest, but many gardens are basically an expanse of trimmed lawn for standing since guests would generally be in attendance for a maximum of two hours. Much as lawns benefit from free aeration, hopefully ladies will remember ***not*** to wear any spike heeled shoes which tend to sink into the turf and would damage their footwear.

AFTERNOON TEA

Apparently, the late Queen's favourite meal, and one of the greatest ways for others to socialise with friends, patrons, fellow volunteers, or business associates is through the ritual of afternoon tea. It can also be a fantastic way to meet charming new acquaintances as luxury cruise ships offer the finest white-glove service. This delightful tradition has resurged with full vigour, as we see many fine restaurants and hotels now providing it. If one prefers not to go out, they might consider the pleasure of hosting at their own residence and here are some suggestions:

Invite your guests to arrive at 3:00, 3:30 or 4 o'clock—whatever time suits. Ambience is of major importance: fresh cut flowers and classical background music can establish the milieu. Silverware, fine bone china, and dainty lace napkins create a charming table setting.

The four principal types of tea are:

Black—tea which is fermented, then dried. It contains about half as much caffeine as coffee and comes in various flavours some being: English Breakfast, Earl Grey, Orange Pekoe, and Ceylon. These strong teas may be served plain or with a drop of milk, including unsweetened almond, soya, etc. to smooth them.

Oolong—partially fermented, approximately one quarter as much caffeine as coffee.

Green tea—dried immediately after picking, very little caffeine—said to contain the most beneficial anti-carcinogenic substances of all teas.

Herbal—usually caffeine free, very tasty; certain types are also considered healthful e.g.: Lemon Ginger tea first thing in the morning, especially if you add some fresh squeezed lemon juice, will serve as a wonderful detox.

Preparation of leaf teas: Heat the tea pot before adding boiled water and let it steep for two to five minutes depending on the type of tea. Place your silver tea strainer over each cup before pouring and offer a saucer of thin fresh lemon slices and some type of light milk. Our household is sugar free, but we always have pure honey and organic stevia on hand if someone prefers a sweetener.

What to eat for afternoon tea time? Some people possess a sweet tooth, and others have a salt tooth, craving savoury items, so offer something of each variety. You might begin with a non-sweet like hot cheese sticks and crust-less finger sandwiches such as: cucumber, egg-mayonnaise, roast beef, smoked wild salmon, ham and cheese or tomato with avocado. The sweets normally consist of scones with clotted cream and jam, or various pieces of cakes. In favour of more practical, health-conscious diets, provide sliced fresh fruit as the sweet. Bon appétit!

SPORT AND GAMES

Formal receptions, private luncheons, charity events, opera and film premieres, gallery openings, theatre, ballet—these are the basic artistic and social engagements which top-drawer people are always involved with, however, for those who would indulge their 'sporting' side as well, let's have a look at some other activities. We will begin with games, and then go on to sports.

In years past, billiards was considered to be an upper-class game and many such households had a large snooker table. Later, when the game became common in 'bar' type surroundings, its image took on a different nature, and 'pool' has now been practically reduced to the status of dart boards.

Very few games actually remain in the 'crème de la crème' circles. Chess is one pastime from the old world which has continued to flourish. You will often find a chessboard set up in the library or study of prominent households and also in the private clubs of Pall Mall. Uppers are inclined to admire intelligence, and wisdom like beauty, is one of the few ways that one who is not highborn can enter aristocratic society. Backgammon retains some of its historic cachet, although it takes less skill than chess for there is a bit of luck (dice) involved.

Other standard board games like 'Monopoly' are rarely tried, because want of money seems so vulgar a thing to play at. Playing cards and rolling dice were still socially acceptable a few decades ago, but after the 'casino' boom, they too began to fall from grace. Uppers also feel little need to be competitive, so if one does play cards, it will most likely be a solitary game of Patience played by oneself.

Regarding sports, croquet—once a patrician pastime which was popular in the mid to late 1800s—practically disappeared, until it caught on again some years ago. It remains quite uncommon, like fencing, but both of these activities sustain some character. Horse shoe is out, but horse racing is in (as a social event more so than for speculating) and will likely remain so as long as there is a Royal Ascot, Epsom Derby, Prix de l'Arc de Triomphe, Breeder's Cup and similar events of very high prestige. Riding, polo and other equestrian events are absolutely in; remember that C-people are 'horsey' people. Queen Elizabeth II, at 96 years of age, still attended the Royal Windsor Horse show a few months before her death.

In consideration of other sports, team and group roughing activities smack too much of incivility. Football, volleyball, wrestling, boxing, soccer… are definitely not in the PLU department, and they consider bowling to be for proles like Fred Flintstone. The non-competitive upper-crust tends to prefer pastimes of an *individual* nature: boating, golfing, equitation, shooting, angling, swimming, skiing, but they will occasionally watch a competition like tennis.

Being competitive indicates a mentality of lack and belief that there is not enough to go around. The most successful people realise that the Universe has unlimited abundance and this is why it comes to them more easily. Be a creator, rather than a competitor.

Occupation

CLASS AND CAREER

From peasants to princes, an occupational class system continues to exist. However, today there are so many different callings to choose from. The majority of North Americans, as many others around the world, are self-made. Some begin their youth in the lowest occupational class, and progress with age and wisdom to the higher levels. Showing respect for maturity and knowledge, this system is actually quite fair—an influential and able meritocracy.

Every human is different. Every person has unique talents, dreams and ambitions. We will never all be the same, nor would we want to be. We are the masters of our destiny. Our creator made man unique from other mammals in that we possess advanced intelligence—the capability to re-design our earthly existence.

Every year of life is a process – you can begin at the bottom rung of the ladder and move to the top; or you may choose to stay exactly where you are and still find great happiness—such as Mother Teresa did. There is nothing wrong with being poor, *provided that you still make some contribution to this world*. Also, as Mother Teresa has proven, one can find great satisfaction and joy in any circumstances. More about this topic in the chapter about money.

Now let us return to the occupational class ladder. We are able to alter our financial situation, by changing our career status. Many people start out in their youth with average education and trivial work scenarios. With time and age one reads or studies more, earns extra cash, and can eventually change their career and living conditions. It is not uncommon to see the medical student work as a waiter for extra income throughout his college years, until he becomes a doctor. Never be embarrassed about humble beginnings—everyone has the right to improve their life-style.

How is occupational status determined? The basic concept follows a prevalent pattern: *Employee, self-employed, employer.* Some career options include:

SERVICE WORKERS

Service work might include occupations such as: assistants, waiters, cashiers, bank tellers, domestics, retail or office clerks, beauty salon staff, manual labourers, etc.

PUBLIC INDUSTRY

Public career positions cover: nursing, administration, teachers & counsellors, police & fire, politics & military, sales & marketing, radio & television, professional sports, and employed crafts-people: plumbers, mechanics, builders, electricians, etc.

SELF-EMPLOYED

Attorneys at law, dentists and private doctors, independent craftspeople/tradespeople and self-contracting business occupations from private consultants to estate agents.

SCIENCE & INTELLIGENTSIA

These upper vocations include: architects, engineers, scientists, surgeons, astronauts, religious clerics, fine artists, literary artists, composers, etc.

LEISURE CLASS

The ultimate step on the occupational class ladder is to join the leisure class—those who have arrived and are no longer required to do 'hands-on' work aside from management. They may be agricultural landowners, business owners, art collectors, philanthropists, or have some other aristocratic life-style. They hire the farm hands, domestic staff, accountants, brokers, attorneys and others to handle their affairs for them. They create employment and circulate their money.

Some people move through each step of the occupational ladder and this is very appropriate, considering that we generally have greater health and vitality in our teens-twenties, and tend to put forth more strength than wisdom. One may be a wage-worker for several years to earn extra cash while they study and improve their education.

Some will get their plumbers' papers, real estate licence, or drama certificate—others might achieve a degree in the sciences, or show talent in the arts. I would advise those who are born into a life of leisure, that they still have a purpose. *We are on this earth to communicate and increase knowledge of science, art, and spirit—this is human destiny.*

At some point in time, one should participate in and share at least one of these talents. Science may include anything from medicine to astronomy; the arts encompass written, musical, or visual creations; spirit may be comprised of many different philosophies as well as theology. Infinite Intelligence does not pop down to Earth and design the architecture of a magnificent cathedral; write astounding classical music; sow and tend picturesque gardens; or build incredible material objects.

We are here to serve as *co-creators*, making the world God gave us a more wonderful place to live in. **Look around you and observe the horticulture, architecture, etc. and ask if you are doing the best that you can to beautify and improve life on this planet.**

Now, for those of us who were not born into a life of leisure, let us proceed to analyse. It is interesting to note that the middle occupations often earn more cash than the prestigious upper-middles. Although less book-learning is required—movie stars, models, singers, salespeople and professional athletes have great potential for high income if they are ambitious enough to reach the heights of their professions.

The majority of citizens will remain in a low-wage occupation for only a few years until they have acquired sufficient funds, training, or education for a middle-class career. These vocations are generally where one becomes financially secure. By the age of 30 or 40, having acquired greater knowledge and experience, one will usually place oneself in a position of increased income potential.

These mid-class vocations prepare us for the ultimate life of leisure. Once you begin to flourish, you can always maintain your talents—if an agricultural landowner takes pleasure in gardening, he is regarded differently than the tenant farm worker who does it for money, rather than as a *labour of love* which often determines our quality of life.

MORE IMPORTANT THAN WHAT WE DO, IS HOW WE LIVE. Observe the example of an English butler. It is very possible that his ultimate goal is to become very professional at his vocation, and remain a domestic employee for the whole of his life. Why not—what life could be better? The butler has the opportunity to live in a magnificent house, surrounded by a beautiful ambience, eat the best food and taste the finest wines.

The family retainer works for civilised people who will cherish him until death, just as they would their own grandfather. He practically lives like the aristocracy he serves. Therefore, it matters not what your position is in life, but what your life-style consists of.

I once hired a woman who was past middle age, but would continue to be a housekeeper/cook for many years. Because of her splendid work, she always had the option to serve in fine homes. There was a long list of prospective employers who would constantly urge her to come and work for them. It was not surprising that she found her chosen vocation to be most gratifying and lucrative. I once complemented her on her superior cooking abilities, and admitted that I myself had never enjoyed nor felt peaceful in the kitchen.

She empathised by responding: "I may relish in the art of cookery, but you are capable of running a company which would drive me mad in a day."

Let's not waste time on things we are not suited for... *we all must do what we do best*. I thought much about those words and came to realise that there is great truth in them. What is pleasing to one person, may be completely undesirable or unnerving to another. Personally, I believe that there is no more reward in owning a business, than there is in running a household—*provided that you are fulfilling your desires and using your talents*. We should always specialise in activities that we are good at and which truly delight us, for if we really love what we do, then success and happiness will certainly follow.

SPECIALISATION

One cannot truly perfect themselves at any single activity, unless they devote the majority of their working or leisure time to that particular interest. Who will be the better golfer—the person who golfs every day and does not dabble in other sports, or the one who plays polo, croquet, tennis, etc. and only finds time to golf once in a fortnight? Naturally the person who specialises will become more adept at his favourite sport. The same principle holds true for business.

Remember the old saying: *Jack of all trades, master of none*—this should be avoided. Not only does lack of specialisation often create a poor service/product, but it is detrimental to the economy as a whole.

Have you ever lived in an area where poverty consciousness was rampant? Where people preferred to hoard their money, do everything by themselves, and never hire anyone? For example: women might try to be a housekeeper/cook, a secretary, a teacher/nanny to their children, a seamstress and so on. Men might work a day job, be a mechanic on their motorcars, try to be a gardener, a carpenter, a plumber, an accountant... or put shingles on the roof of their house.

Unfortunately, some of these 'home jobs' are performed inefficiently, and with a great deal of stress. Three years later when the shingles blow off the roof, there will be added expense when the homeowner attempts to re-do his unskilled job. Hire a professional to do the task—circulate your money... one will be amazed how the quality of life improves. If you are in a terribly impecunious position, you can always use the barter system and exchange a service which you are good at, for the service of someone specialising in a different talent.

While residing in a very large city, I frequently received brochures in the post from numerous self-employed professionals who were promoting their services. I hired a helper/cook for part-time cleaning and Saturday evening dinner parties; I had a gardener to do major landscaping; a student to cut the grass; a carpenter to paint the fence; a man who cleaned the eaves troughs; a chimney sweep to dust the chimney; a piano tuner to adjust my piano; grooms, black smiths and trainers to work with my race horses and so on.

We must help to create business for everyone… but now… right this moment… those people who have poverty consciousness will ask 'if you hire so many people, and spend so much money, how can you possibly survive yourself?' All successful people already know the answer: if you are a business person – contracting others to work will actually help you to earn **MORE** money. How? For example, I first began to create projects for other people many years ago when I was self-employed as an estate agent.

Whenever I gave business to my piano tuner, travel agent, accountant, banker, gardener, etc., they naturally sent business to me. Exchange your calling cards, and exchange your service. If you create a job for someone else, they will create business for you. If they don't show this type of loyalty, try to hire someone else who is better concerned about your welfare.

It is not necessary to dabble in someone else's occupation, when you can be more successful as a single link in the economic chain. You will earn more income to live like royalty if you learn to specialise and use your own God-given talents.

AVOCATION AND VOCATION BECOME "ONE"

Do you retire to sleep at night eagerly anticipating the joy which the morrow will bring? Whether your pleasure be gardening, painting, inventing, astronomy, science, philosophy… is it somehow incorporated into your daily life?

If you are one of the minority (though rapidly growing) number of people who work for pleasure, rather than simply for money—bravo! You are already practising one of the main activities of those who live well. For those who have not yet entered this sphere, but would like to… read on.

What portion of your time do you spend working? Take a moment now, add up the hours, and calculate a percentage. If you are awake for 16 hours a day and you spend eight hours on the job, that equates to 50% of your time… incredible, isn't it? (See 'balance' later in this chapter.) Don't allow yourself to remain in a security rut, i.e., the time for cash system. Move into the reward for pleasure mode, and **turn your avocation into your vocation**.

Let your enjoyment become your occupation. Writing is one of my greatest pastimes—otherwise, I certainly would not be doing it. Manifest and create what *you* truly want to do with *your* time. Do you think Tiger Woods simply became a pro golfer to earn money—or might you consider that perhaps he actually enjoys the sport? It is an added blessing, that many people love to watch him golf—thus he also serves a multitude of people… see 'Greater Service Equals Greater Rewards' later in this chapter.

Many of us have hidden dreams and desires which never come to surface, because we are afraid that we cannot *afford* to participate in them. In order to remove 'financial' blocks, and determine what occupation will truly make you happy—do this exercise:

* Pick a quiet spot and peaceful time of day.
* Have a pencil and notepad at hand.
* Relax, and allow your mind to believe that you are now in possession of **ONE BILLION DOLLARS**. Imagine strongly that the money is yours—and you never have to worry about finances again. Don't think about the material objects which you would purchase; but rather, think of the ways in which you would now **spend your time**. Your future occupation is solely to please and inspire—remember, you no longer do anything in the interest of earning money.
* Now write down a list of things which you would **love to do**—beginning tomorrow. Do not write items you wish to have—this is a vocational exercise, write only that which you want **TO DO**. Believe that you can afford any activity.

The following is a sample of the list which I wrote for myself years ago. If I had a billion dollars, I would:

* Become a philanthropist, start a business in the 'sport of kings' and own thoroughbred race horses.
* Socialise more.
* Live in a refined, prestigious location, with a climate conducive to good health.
* Spend more time outdoors—walking, riding, watching polo, golfing, boating, sunbathing, gardening.
* Participate more in the arts—do more writing, spend more time at the symphony, theatre, galleries… and so on.

When your 'love to do' list is complete, you will know *exactly* how you truly wish to occupy your time.

I once met a fellow who told me how much he hated his job, but when I asked him what he would rather be doing, he said he had no idea. I suggested that he clear his mind, and pretend that he possessed a billion dollars. Then I asked him 'what would you do tomorrow?' His response was prompt and enthusiastic—he said 'travel.' He did not produce a complete list of activities, for travel seemed to be utmost on his mind; so, I said fine, that's sufficient.

He was single and free to travel, but he did not really possess the imagined money, and had to work to support himself. After we brainstormed together, he realised that many people such as agents or travel guides and countless others in various areas of the industry, actually 'get paid' to travel. This is how one's avocation (pleasure) becomes their vocation (occupation).

We may not be able to plunge into a new, desired lifestyle the following day, but *we can begin to take immediate steps which will bring us closer*. Returning to the list which I wrote years ago: I could not become a philanthropist, because I did not really possess the imagined money to distribute… so I chose the next best thing for that moment—volunteer work.

In view of the fact that my list also included my love of the arts, I decided to volunteer for the local symphony. This largely fulfilled my desire for socialising, since much of the activity consisted of public fund-raising events.

I later did come to own a thoroughbred company, but it didn't happen overnight. I began by doing a lot of research and initially purchasing only a half share in one racehorse. Also, at that time I was self-employed as a real estate agent and discovered that socialising 'my favourite pastime' could increase business. It's true what they say 'one does meet clients on the golf course and at charity balls.'

Step by step… within a couple of years, I had accomplished several items on my dream list. Four years later, I relocated to a much better climate and achieved more goals which I had added to my list. If you need help to keep focused, create a 'Dream Board.' Take a large piece of plywood or heavy paper and stick on coloured pictures of your future desired surroundings. Look at it every day and imagine how you will *feel* when you are actually in the picture—this will help to get you in the correct frequency for its achievement.

Not all of our desires remain constant—as our interests change, so too might our vocation. My occupation today is different from what it was 20 years ago. It does not matter what career you choose, as long as it is one that you *enjoy*. As the old saying goes, "If you do what you love, you'll never **work** a day in your life."

One of the most inspiring speeches that millions of us have listened to on YouTube, was given by the late, great Steve Jobs as he addressed students at Stanford University: "Love what you do—keep looking until you find it and don't settle. …. your time is limited, so don't be trapped living someone else's life… don't let the noise of others' opinions drown out your own inner voice, and most important, have the courage to follow your own heart and own intuition." What a brilliant man he was, and how great his accomplishments.

If one requires more information on how to determine a suitable pursuit, there are many good sources available. Listen to the recording by Dr Robert Anthony "Doing What You Love, Loving What You Do." Read the book "Creating Money" by Sanaya Roman and Duane Packer, which dedicates a whole section to 'Creating Your Life's Work.'

If you had a billion dollars, what would you be doing tomorrow? If you answered that question, by naming your present occupation—fabulous. If not, begin to take steps *today*, which will set you on course—you can do it!

GREATER SERVICE EQUALS GREATER REWARDS

One of our main purposes in life is to serve others. What some people fail to realise, is that service is also a major factor on the road to living royally. It's important to understand that money is not something which we make, but something which we earn. The better you give to the world, the more wealth the world will give to you. The greater your service, the greater your rewards. Consider your present occupation and income, then ask yourself: 'what contribution am I presently making to mankind?'

There are limitless ideas and ways to be creative and work positively. I will list a few occupational examples which serve:

* You are an actor, and you star in a famous play at the theatre, or on film for the cinema. If a million people watch and enjoy your performance, you have just served one million people!

* You spent many long hours in creative thought, and have just invented a new and entertaining game. It becomes a huge success, and you have served masses of people who purchase it for their family enjoyment.

* You personally design and create a new golf course which brings exercise, enjoyment and camaraderie to the multitudes. As your club serves thousands of people every year, you will be rewarded in thousands.

* You create a high-quality product or sell a commodity which millions of people buy—another success.

* If you are an agricultural landowner and your crops or orchards feed a huge number of people, you will be rewarded in similar numbers.

* If a fabulous vocalist like Andrea Bocelli brings beautiful song to the masses, the singer's success is earned through service.

* If an author produces a fiction or non-fiction book, which entertains or educates a million people, the writer may be rewarded likewise.

* If an artist paints a one-of-a-kind oil on canvass which is of gallery quality and thousands of visitors pay to enjoy viewing it.

* When a scientist develops a new drug which is vital in the treatment or care of thousands, he will be thus rewarded.

* An educator travels from city to city lecturing on something of positive importance. Large groups attend and benefit from his seminars—the instructor will benefit equally.

* A professional athlete who keeps the crowds cheering and paying to watch him or her at sport.

* The architect of an incredible cathedral which will serve multitudes for decades to come.

I could go on writing pages, but I'm quite confident that everyone has taken the meaning. The list of examples all demonstrate good and positive service to mankind. What type of benefits would any of those services bring to the people who render them? Certainly, there would be the reward of loving what they do, as well as the joy from helping or pleasing others. Consider also, the financial wealth. If every person that you served offered to pay you one dollar or pound and you served a million people… how much money would you earn? Simple arithmetic, isn't it?

Do a self-analysis now… add up the number of people which you serve directly in your present vocation. Do you feel that you are being paid according to the numbers which you serve? In the future, would you consider helping more of mankind? Remember: ***The more people that you serve in a positive way, the greater your personal rewards will be.***

Just a final word with respect to service and income. First of all, in order for the system to work best, one should be self-employed or privately contracted. If you work in a large company or for a franchise, and you serve 500 sandwiches per day where the profit is £1 each after expenses, you are not the person who will receive the £500 unless you actually ***own*** the sandwich shop.

Secondly, the occupation which you choose will not necessarily indicate the amount of income which you will receive. Consider 'sales' for instance. There are agents who become very rich, and there are those who earn very little, for their income/commission depends upon their individual service.

Also, success is not solely a numbers game. There is another factor aside from the 'quantity' of people served, which will determine the amount of income one earns. Think again of the sandwich shop, but instead consider a restaurant owned by a famous chef. He might only need to serve a few diners to reap similar rewards because his meals are so incredibly delicious and in such high demand.

Or, picture a carpenter. At first thought—do you believe that most carpenters are rich or poor? While much carpentry is basic, a carpenter can become a specialist of great demand if he chooses. The person who develops a talent for designing intricate carvings in solid mahogany or oak furniture, can realise huge profits. It is hard to find superior quality today, and people who are in search of excellence will pay a high price for it. Always remember that besides quantity, ***quality*** service can be equally important.

TIME MANAGEMENT

The late W. Clement Stone, founder of Success magazine, once had an article entitled **"Do it now!"** For example: Touch your mail only once; if you open it, answer or pay it. **Going back to things wastes time and energy**.

It is quite easy for one to literally 'run oneself ragged' because of poor time management. Remember the old saying: **work smart not hard**. It is all right to work hard at times, but it is equally important to consider how our time can be spent most effectively. Some people work *too* hard—days and nights, with little time for sleep, and even less time for pleasure. The curious thing, is that many of those 12-hour-a-day people, don't seem to be going anywhere fast… why is that?

It is most likely due to poor time management or lack of organisational skills; therefore, let us chart the course, so that we can we reach the destination!

THE AGENDA

The people who you meet which truly live life to the fullest are probably those who:

* Keep a personal journal/diary.
* Use an agenda (calendar/appointment book).

One who has never had a journal, may be a person who has never seen or done anything worth writing about, and that's a pity. But what we will concentrate on presently, is the even more important need for using a daily agenda, which in some respects serves as a diary. Do not simply record items on your phone or computer—go out and buy a proper hard-cover calendar book (if also serving as a permanent journal) or at least a nice leather refillable day-timer if not.

In professional occupations, a daily calendar or appointment book is a must. How would anyone be able to remember a full business schedule, especially these days, when many engagements must be planned weeks in advance? Even if one is a retired professional, life goes on. There are charity events, theatre dates, garden parties, weddings, luncheons, volunteer service… and numerous other activities to plan and partake in.

What kind of person doesn't keep an agenda? Have they never scheduled a game of golf with a friend? A weekend flight to an interesting city? A simple luncheon engagement? If you actually meet someone who does not own a datebook, send them one! The worst time management scenario is when a person sets a date, and later forgets to keep it. Punctuality and reliability are incredibly significant personal characteristics.

Also, never let your own reputation become tarnished. If you break engagements, people will soon lose confidence in your reliability. If you fear that you may not be able to keep a particular appointment, don't make it in the first place, and if you do set up a meeting and something extremely urgent occurs— notify the other person or people as soon as possible.

Every evening before you retire for the night, check your book for the following day. If you have an early meeting… be sure that you will arise at an appropriate hour. You needn't bother to call the other party to remind them of your engagement as it should have been noted in their own register. Hopefully, the people whom you choose to associate or work with will be responsible enough to manage their own time.

An annual agenda is not only vital in recording our schedule, but it is also an important part of goal setting. If possible, keep a calendar which exceeds one year. It will be handy for use in future planning.

BALANCE

Another important factor is learning to balance time constructively. If you feel that you are one of those people who work hard, rather than smart—do the following exercise: Clock a basic, average day in *full* detail… write down every moment e.g.:

7:00 AM. Wake to the sound of radio, relax and stretch for five minutes while listening to the news brief.

7:05 AM. Prayers of gratitude and petitions.

7.10 AM. Slip on sportswear… walk the dog or do exercises.

7:30 AM. Bathe/shower.

7:55 AM. Dress for the day.

8:00 AM. Do personal grooming, hair, shaving, cosmetics.

8:35 AM. Have some fruit, read or watch something inspirational, drink a cup of tea, and go over the agenda for the day.

9:00 AM. Place business calls or answer email.

10:00 AM. Do company business.

12:00 noon. Luncheon with friends or family.

7:00 PM. Read a book; watch a film; play with the children.

Complete your whole day, from the waking moment, until you sleep at night *in detail*. Don't leave it blank between 12:00 and 7 PM as I've done above, but write down minute to minute activities: if you play tennis, attend mass, go grocery shopping, etc. include all.

Now draw a large circle and carve it into appropriate portions. Use a pencil, as you may need to rearrange your sketch. Take your average day—the assignment above which you just completed, and tally up percentages, then fill in the circle, i.e.:

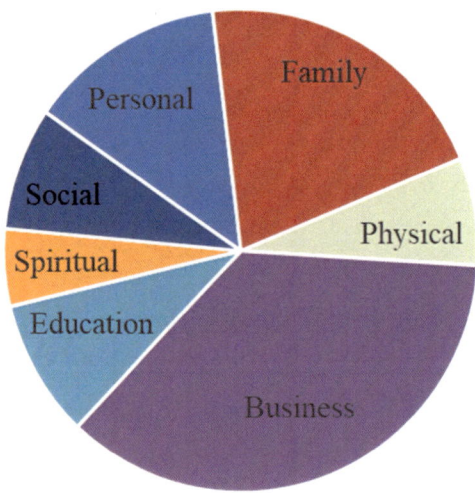

Are you fulfilling all of your needs? The next step in this exercise is similar to the first. Clock a day again, but this time, recreate your ideal 'perfect' day. Does it change? Do you spend more time reading? … entertaining guests? … at sport? What changes or new arrangements could you begin… starting now?

Most of us are not infinitely rich, and must spend time in some form of occupation which also provides extra cash. How can your career become more pleasant and profitable? Years ago, while in business, I found that spending more time at healthy pleasant endeavours, actually increased my clientele, for as I mentioned earlier, *socialising is one key to success.*

What if one were to go for a half hour walk and deliver business circulars on the way... or hand out business cards while window shopping in the mall... or entertain prospective clients by hosting an afternoon garden party... or meet new people while doing charity work? How would the circle change? Preferably the work section would be reduced, while exercise, family, social, spiritual and so forth, would increase. The ultimate goal is to have a ***well-balanced*** life-style.

Let's consider an illustration of how occupation can relate to personal time management. In this example, pretend that you are a person who wants to become a professional violinist: What do you do all day long? Have you found a good source of instruction or a private tutor? Do you practise and study every day? Do you attend concerts for pleasure and inspiration? Did you play the violin in your friend's French restaurant? Have you joined the 'symphony volunteers' in the city where you live? Do you pass along your calling card to people you meet and offer to perform at their soirees? Have you joined a private trio to earn extra cash and increase your experience? Did you take a conductor to lunch? Have you sent your CD to the classical radio station? Do all of your associates ***know*** that this is what you would love to do? Manage your time effectively: work smarter... not harder.

BUSINESS/CALLING CARDS

Once a person has reached adult age, it is a very wise idea to carry some type of calling card. I use the term calling card (also known as a visiting card) on purpose, because it is suitable for everyone—even if they are not in business.

Personal calling cards can be as plain or elaborate as you desire. The design or colours you choose are statements which reflect your personal identity, but I will mention that a classic choice is usually engraved black ink on thick white paper.

Business cards may have a somewhat different look: style of lettering, picture or logo, colours, borders, name of company or organisation and also the way one has their name printed. Some cards add initials relating to academic honours which pertain to the occupation.

Cards can be useful in many different circumstances. First of all, they are a great aid in helping us to remember the names of new acquaintances. Also, they generally provide us with a postal address, email or telephone number in the event that we might like to keep in touch with that person in the future. If you meet someone with whom you do not desire further contact, you should not give them your card.

A major reason for using cards is to assist people in attracting business. When I was first self-employed in my twenties, I remember our real estate broker suggesting that we hand out a ***minimum*** of 10 cards per day.

What a simple and economical way to gain exposure. Even at this current time of writing, 500 basic cards can be purchased for as little as £20. Cards are one of the least expensive and longest lasting forms of advertising. If you enjoy handing out promotional gifts to prospective clients, give a card folder and be sure that one of your cards is in it.

Sometimes people who are unemployed will say 'I wish that I could use a business card, but I have no company.' Why should that make any difference? While the followers *look* for a job—the leaders *create* one. Ask the unemployed student 'what do you study about and specialise in?' If for example, they respond 'computers', then they might have a card printed with their personal name and interest e.g.:

Andrew D. Jones
Computer Consultant
Address/Tel/Email

By handing out their cards they will attract business. They may begin marketing, programming, and instructing on computer use privately, or they might be hired to work for some agency. Everyone has some occupation… tell the public who you are.

If you are a college student, and you want to earn some extra cash during the semester breaks, decide on a service which you are qualified for: window cleaner, gardener, housekeeper, tutor, consultant, pet sitter—anything which you are capable of doing well and handling responsibly. Then have personal business cards made with your name, service provided, and how you prefer to be reached. As mentioned, it is only a £20 investment and at least people will take you seriously. I would be reluctant to hire someone who was not organised enough to present their card.

LENDERS, PATRONS, SPONSORS

I worked and studied through the whole decade of my twenties without taking any major holidays or travels. If you establish yourself when you are young and free from responsibility, one can later relax and enjoy the fruit of their accomplishments. Perhaps I needed to demonstrate my independence by doing things on my own, but looking back now, I wonder if I chose the difficult way. I had been self-employed since my mid-twenties, but couldn't afford to create a business until I was past 30. Do we really have to earn every cent by ourselves, or can one look for outside support?

LENDERS —STARTING A SMALL BUSINESS

Bankers have come to the understanding that the days of lending money solely to large organisations are rapidly fading. They realise that in order to continue their process of giving loans and generating interest, they must also lend money to private entrepreneurs, i.e., people who want to start their own small business. Because of this trend, one now has a fair chance of acquiring a loan. If you are planning to use this method, prepare yourself well. Don't go in to apply with your banker, and simply say 'I've got a marvellous idea here.'

Walk in with a professionally typed out business plan listing all relevant information—projected expenses, profits, location, clientele, everything… give a complete detailed plan of your intended business and how it is going to operate. This preparation, along with references and a good credit rating will give you a very reasonable chance of obtaining a small business loan.

If you don't feel ready to start a new business on your own that is fine, consider acquisitions or mergers. Perhaps you can begin to work with an established business owner and become partners, or take over completely from someone who wishes to retire.

PATRONS/SPONSORS—LITERARY, FINE ARTS, OR SPORTS

The majority of artists and athletes are not born rich, and throughout history, the traditional custom was to find a willing patron. Unless one's work is an overnight success, and they immediately become self-sufficient, it is not uncommon to require financial assistance from a sponsor. Some wealthy individuals and corporations are quite happy to be generous to others and gain a tax deduction for themselves. In order to attract a patron, the beginning artist or athlete requires ambition, obvious talent and a positive attitude.

If one is young and just starting out, they have every right to seek help from someone who is already established. One day, after becoming successful, hopefully they too will sponsor a youth.

SHARE THE WEALTH —CREATE A JOB

Our first responsibility is to create a job for ourselves; our second responsibility once established, is to help create a job for someone else.

If you have been fortunate enough to secure a comfortable position for yourself in the world, try to think about someone else's welfare. If more successful individuals had an attitude of **sharing-the-wealth**, there would never be anyone who lacks. We wouldn't need institutions to take care of people, if people took care of each other.

The majority of citizens spend the first decade of their working life as a wage-earner, employed by someone else until they can accumulate the necessary funds to manage their own business. It is up to the established entrepreneurs to provide jobs for those who are younger and just starting out. If you are already past your thirties, you may likely be self-employed. Perhaps you own a retail store, restaurant, sport club… or maybe you are occupied as a private accountant, notary, dentist, artist, musician, agent, consultant, etc.

If you have become successful, and created your own vocation or business, it is time to give consideration to others. For example: if you are an established business person, consider hiring a part-time assistant to perform accounting, typing, reception. Or, if you want to entertain clients by hosting dinner parties in your house (these expenses are often tax-deductible just as dining out), form a position for a private cook/helper and circulate your wealth.

Once you've reached an age when you have become blessed with success—share it. Hire at least one person, who has just set forth, as you once had to do. When you were a student, someone was probably kind enough to hire you in that first job where you had absolutely no experience. After accumulating some extra cash, continuing our education and becoming self-sufficient… it becomes our turn to hire someone else.

I remember young teenagers delivering newspapers, shovelling snow from driveways, cutting lawns, washing cars, selling homemade lemonade, hauling away refundable bottles, babysitting—anything to feel more independent.

We frequently assisted young people from other countries by giving them live-in positions as Au Pairs. They would do house-keeping and light meal preparations in exchange for free room and board plus a weekly stipend of spending money. Since they had no expenses, it was a good deal for them and a great help to us.

My husband recently purchased a licence for our 14-year-old daughter to sell items at our local antique market in Tuscany—more like a simple boot/garage sale, but she really enjoys earning her own money. Adults have to support the wise and ambitious youth by giving them an opportunity to get started on the royal road of life.

If you are earning £2,000 or more per month, you should have created at least one position for someone who is less fortunate than yourself. How much money will it actually cost you to help someone to achieve that very difficult-to-find 'first' job? For £50 one can hire a part-time domestic for a half day each Saturday. Place an advertisement in your community centre, school, church, local paper or any shop billboard. If you cannot afford to hire a student for a few hours once a week… see a financial planner. For those who would ask 'which student wants to work for £50?' The answer is 'plenty of them.'

Some students clean a different house every evening, and pocket a couple hundred pounds in extra cash per week. Remember when you started out with your first income earning position? Someone, somewhere, was kind enough to hire you; if you're older, now it's your turn to **share the wealth**. This is also a wonderful way to increase prosperity consciousness, which will bring more rewards to you.

Note: Aside from student youth, whenever you hire **adults** for any type of service—whether it be a trainer for your race horse, a domestic for your house, or an assistant for your business—be sure that the individual you hire is a **self-employed contractor**, i.e., one who deducts their own expense receipts, records their own income, and is responsible for their business and income tax. It simplifies matters so that you will not be responsible for workers' compensation, unemployment insurance, or tax statements. This is a very simple and effective procedure which eliminates a lot of paper work, and allows all individuals the freedom to take control and responsibility for themselves.

Hiring Help

Aside from contracting out work to assistants, gardeners and other self-employed individuals, those who can afford, frequently hire household help as well. Some people prefer to use the word 'domestic,' as it became taboo to say servant, but nearly every young individual's first job is either as a private or public servant of some sort. Indeed, most government employees, police, and state school teachers are considered civil 'servants.'

In the countries that I have lived in, property extremes were rare. Tiny 500 square foot cottages and grand 20,000 square foot mansions were not the norm. Most single-family dwellings being built today are basic two-storeys, some with basements, totalling between 2,000 and 3,000 square feet.

The days are long past when each established household had a butler, a cook, a maid, a governess, a gardener, and a chauffeur. So too have the days finally past when people hoarded their money and hired no help at all. Society has finally come to terms and accepted a happy medium.

Properties with very large parks occasionally hire one person as a gardener/handyman/driver. The average household interior by today's standards can easily be maintained by one housekeeper/cook. Some people hire couples to cover both jobs and allow them to live for free in an annex on the property.

The following is an example of a common schedule for one live-in helper.

****

GENERAL HOUSE-WORKER

The house-worker is responsible for all of the details involved in running a household including the shopping, cooking, cleaning, laundry, and general service.

The cook/house-worker wears a uniform—either a simple white or pale coloured dress for cleaning. When she serves you at dinner, or when you have guests, she changes to a slightly dressier, black coloured dress with white collar and apron, or wears a white blouse with black skirt. She should of course, be of neat appearance, and if she has long hair, it should be put up or tied back before serving meals. If male, the standard apparel is white shirt with black trousers and jacket.

The servant addresses the employers as 'Sir' or 'Madam'—or as 'Mr' 'Mrs' 'Miss' 'Lord' 'Lady,' etc. followed by their surname.

When you entertain a dozen or more people you should hire an extra person such as a waiter/waitress to help your housekeeper/cook, unless you intend to do a great deal of the preparations or service by yourself.

The cook/housekeeper eats by herself, either before or after you, as she pleases—she serves herself the same food she prepares for you and has free access to the refrigerator and the freezer. If there are items which you are saving for a special occasion, it is up to you to let her know about them in advance.

Privileges include the equivalent of two days off per week and definite hours to relax every afternoon. Private quarters with telephone/Internet, full lavatory bath, and house-worker's personal decor. Work uniforms are supplied.

Possible schedule:

8 hours a day—4 days a week, plus 2 half days per week = 40 hours a week at £___ per hour. Room and board are deducted, leaving the remaining salary at £___ per month.

Sunday all day; Tuesday mornings and Thursday afternoons off.

Regular hours on working days:

9:00 AM—2:00 PM 5 hours.

2:00 PM—4:00 PM leisure time.

4:00 PM—7:00 PM 3 hours.

7:00 PM… leisure time unless notified and paid overtime.

Duties:

* Kitchen—maintain clean cupboards, refrigerator, and oven; marketing; meal preparation, setting and waiting at table; washing dishes.

* Cleaning house—dust furniture, change linens and set beds, vacuum and wash floors, clean lavatories and fireplaces, polish silver and fixtures, etc.

* Laundry—linen/cotton—everything that is crinkled is pressed. That which is soiled, is washed, pressed, and when in perfect order—replaced where it belongs in the closet. Wool suits are delivered to and picked up from the dry-cleaners.

* Answer door—open the door and conduct expected guests into the drawing room, take coats. Solicitors and unknown arrivals are begged pardon, but may leave their calling card. Answer telephone: Family's surname/town/or company name 'May I tell them who is calling?'

* Entertaining—general service for all special occasions. At garden parties, prepare hors d'oeuvres. At private luncheon parties, offer a glass of sherry or champagne before serving the meal; top up glasses with water or wine.

* Meal preparation—thrice daily, for example: light breakfast and tea at 9.30; serve luncheon at 1:30; serve simple dinner at 6 o'clock. Note: If hosting a formal luncheon, the five morning work hours change to become 10.30 until 3.30- enough time for cooking, serving and wash-up.

* Marketing—Monday, Wednesday and Friday mornings.

Linen—three or four times per week

Cleaning, watering plants, etc.... regularly as needed.

General service as required during working hours.

****

Remember... if you are just starting out and only hiring a part-time student for four hours every Saturday morning, you cannot expect them to accomplish a complete range of tasks. The above was a general 40-hour *full-time* guide, whether live-in or live-out.

Many people are unable to hire a full-time helper, but must be aware that it is quite affordable to hire someone part-time. There is a saying that... 'while the couple from the lower socio-economic order spend £200 per week on cigarettes, the upper-class couple will spend £200 per week on staff.' Which situation is better for one's health and the economy in general? This is just one more example of the difference between poverty consciousness and prosperity consciousness.

SHORT-TERM ACTION—LONG-TERM RESULTS

Suppose that someone begins working as a domestic at the early age of 18 years. Consider that they take great pleasure and satisfaction from their work, and do not want to suffer the trials and tribulations of the business world. This otherwise contented individual has one important question: what about retirement? Will that initial minimum wage income from the early years, contribute at all in helping them become self-sufficient in later life? Absolutely.

Monthly example: 160 hours at £10.00 per hour equals £1600. Less approximately £550 (deducted for room and board) leaves the final balance at £1050 for personal use. Having the employer pay for all living expenses (deducting £550) will mean that the live-in's annual income will be £12,600 which is basically the same as the 2024 personal allowance (£12,570) and means he/she will likely not be required to pay any income tax.

Also, since groceries, toiletries, utilities and room rental fees have already been covered, it should be easy for the live-in domestic to contribute at least £500 per month to their RRSP (Registered Retirement Savings Plan). £500 × 12 months equals an annual total savings of £6,000. If, at a youthful age, one begins to deposit £6,000 annually only for five or six years, the resulting retirement balance could be quite substantial. See the RRSP sample chart in a later chapter.

FAIRNESS FOR MEN AND WOMEN

It matters not if one chooses to run a company, or whether they prefer to be the organiser of activities which enhance their spouse's business. I have found enjoyment in both owning a company and being a homemaker. Fortunately, my whole life has fallen within a marvellous generation where we have always been free to make such choices.

Accumulating extra cash in my early 20s as a civil servant, I earned exactly the *same* income as my male student counterparts. Later, after getting into real estate, I noticed that many female agents were earning far *more* than the men around them. By the time I became a self-employed businesswoman, I was fully convinced that I was getting paid ***consistent with merit—not according to gender.***

I write this for the benefit of women who would use their sex as an excuse for not achieving occupational success. Sadly, in some countries that reasoning might still be legitimate; but in a liberated nation, we can appreciate our good fortune and equal rights. Sincere feminists are hard at work in third world countries striving to achieve emancipation for women who do not yet have it.

EQUAL RIGHTS VERSUS EQUALITY

It has become apparent that a serious confusion exists regarding the difference in definition between *equality* and *equal rights*. Equality means: a state of being equal; not varying; ***uniformity***. On the other hand, 'equal rights' is something very different, perhaps nearly the opposite.

Having equal rights signifies that *EVERY INDIVIDUAL HAS THE SAME FREEDOM TO BE DIFFERENT*. The right to vote, the right to earn capital, the right to be rich (or poor), the right to invest, the right to own property, freedom of speech and opinion.

The right to speak, dress, act, serve, in any manner of your choice—the right of **FREEDOM**. Most people of the enlightened democratic world believe in 'equal rights'—I certainly approve of freedom of choice.

Now let us take a closer look at the definition of 'equality'—uniformity, non-variable, the state of being identical. Have you ever met anyone who wanted to be exactly the same as everyone else? Would you enjoy living in a blue house with a pink roof, if everyone else in your neighbourhood lived in a pink and blue house? Would you be happier if the whole world shared your exact opinions—so that you could never again have an interesting discussion? If everyone was forced to wear blue denim overalls every day, would you feel good about getting dressed in the morning—would there be anything colourful or creative in your style?

It's difficult to imagine that anyone could possibly believe in uniformity. Where would be the spice, motivation, and happiness in life? I can't even think of one person that I would like to be 'equal' with or 'the same as.' I love being free to dress, speak, and enjoy my life the way "I" want to do it.

Fortunately, the world is making some progress—consider the 'Charter of **Rights and Freedoms**' which confirms improved judgement. Returning to the subject of occupation… whatever vocation or avocation one decides to participate in, is totally of their own design. In the civilised world, your rewards will come from merit and nothing else.

FUTURE TRENDS

There undoubtedly exists a right time for every job, and the basic service position can be ideal when we are young. It provides financial security while allowing us plenty of spare time to advance our education, e.g. the daytime dental assistant who studies at night, so that one day they might open their own private practise as an endodontist, orthodontist, dentist, or whatever.

Although the service industry is a fabulous place to start out, there are cons as well as pros. While working as a civil servant, I soon became aware that there are two major negatives of a lower-level position. The first is **DEPENDENCE** on an employer... as the saying goes, "An entrepreneur is a person who would rather work 12 hours a day for himself, than eight hours for someone else." The second is BEING A *WAGE*-WORKER. At the end of the month; one could not go to their boss and say "by the way, I'd like a $15,000 pay cheque instead of the regular $1,500."

We were all paid the same, despite good performance, or lack of it. If one is self-employed, income is based on merit. Consider sales for instance... where in the occasional month, one might actually EARN that 15K in total commissions. Such occupations generally produce higher returns because *they are not on a "fixed" income and they have unlimited potential*.

The most logical aspect of being a self-employed contractor is that *one gets paid for results, rather than by the hour*; it is no longer a situation of 'time for money.' Examples:

* It may take an accomplished author six months to write a best-seller, while the less dedicated writer, spends six years at compiling a similar manuscript. Each book pleases an equal number of readers and earns a similar income. It does not matter how many *hours* went into it—what matters, is the *quality* that comes out of it.

* If one real estate agent works 10 hours per day, and sells one property every two months, while another realtor is busy only four hours per day, but completes a deal every two weeks... who is more efficient?

* When we run a race horse, the contracted trainer receives a commission if the thoroughbred arrives in the "distribution money." Pay for performance is an added incentive for the trainer to prepare the horse well.

* We no longer hire a caterer per hour, but instead, per reception party. What difference does it make if the cook spends two hours making mini quiche, or if they take five minutes with the frozen variety... as long as the canapes turn out *perfect*? The pay per hour routine is finally evolving into a pay per *results* system—we should not need to exchange time for money.

Note: Never ask a mature adult "what is your job?" or "who do you work for?" Such would imply insult equivalent to suggesting that they appear incapable of mastering their own pursuits. You may ask in the royal fashion "How do you spend your day?"

OUT WITH THE NEGATIVE—IN WITH THE POSITIVE

It never ceases to amaze me, when I hear those rare few who actually complain about the loss of horrible jobs… I would counter with the positive.

"The mines are shutting down" … too dangerous for humans.

"Computer technology" … loss of docile clerical positions.

"Factories go mechanical" … robots do the horrific labour.

Why cry over the loss of these terrible jobs? Who wants them? Now that we are post industrial revolution, and have moved into the age of information, we are finally beginning to see such negative practises such as human assembly lines and factory work vanish. The truly humane people say "Good riddance!"

Robots and machines are now the labour behind assembly lines, and rightly so. Human beings are finally free to use their God-given talents. They can create happiness and beauty, art and music, inventions and cures—they can use their knowledge, as well as their hands. People can now concentrate on creating beautiful, intelligent occupations. One's avocation can become their vocation. Old horrible jobs are disappearing, but new fabulous careers are being born! The trend is toward the collapse of large controlling organisations.

Consider all of the service industries which thrive:

* People teaching us how to keep fit and healthy: personal trainers, sports and fitness consultants, massage therapists, tennis/golf/riding/swimming instructors, positive attitude motivational speakers…
* People can set up shop: shoe repair, jewellers, mechanics, music tutors, private tailors, barbers, beauticians, photographers…
* Home offices: accountants, notaries, architects, real estate agents, insurance agents, business consultants, financial planners, computer consultants, web designers…
* Private fine arts: authors, composers, painters, sculptors…
* Public performing arts: opera singers, ballet dancers, live theatre actors, instrumentalists, film stars…
* Recreational proprietors: country clubs, golf courses, spas, resorts…
* Other independents: doctors, dentists, lawyers, researchers…

In "Business Trends 2001—A Window of Opportunity Into the 21st Century", Sarah Purcell and Gary Collins noted: Nearly half the homes in

America will have a home-based business by the year 2001. It also reported that one is 10 times more likely to be successful if you own your own business.

As I write, we have been through a two-year Covid pandemic where many people who were initially reluctant to work from home, soon fell in love with the process and hated going back to central offices after restrictions were removed. How wonderful was the enlightenment: Less commuter-polluters... wasting petrol and time motoring into town, only to work inside the confines of some stuffy office building. In the neighbourhood where I lived, a dentist had set up office in a gorgeous renovated house. I no longer had to drive through the congested centre, or suffer the troubles of pollution and no parking. This dawning of independent occupations and home business creates a healthier and more convenient life-style for all.

My list of examples only skims the surface of new possibilities which exist. We should not cry about losing undesirable jobs of the past—but *celebrate* the freedom of the future! When change does occur, it is often for the better. Consider the example of people who suffer with optical defects. The medical industry now has access to laser beam equipment which can correct astigmatism, myopia (near sightedness) and some far sightedness with a 60 second procedure.

But why does Medicare not provide this cure to the millions who suffer? Because currently, this disability creates much employment in the making, sale, and distribution of glass lenses, spectacle frames, contact lenses, and their numerous solutions. People worry about all of the negative business which will disappear, instead of concentrating on the new positive careers—like laser surgery. Scientists have already been able to grow new teeth in mice—instead of dentists inserting expensive titanium implants and selling us a crown, perhaps one day soon they will be able to fill our gaps with the real thing.

Remember when the 'armed forces' was solely responsible for fighting wars? Maybe in the future we will formally amend the name to 'World Peace and Rescue Service.' The duties have already begun to change, placing concentration on peacekeeping, avalanche control, and emergency rescue operations. Every negative career can be recreated to become a positive vocation. The faster all of society comes to realise this, the sooner all people will be able to partake in pleasurable occupations, and gain more satisfaction from life.

Chapter 5
Tangible Surroundings

Location

I was quite fortunate to have the interesting experience of working in real estate during my early years. I would never forget being taught the three principles of market value: location, condition, and price, but in reality, we really knew that these factors were not of equal importance. In fact, many agents would be heard to say that saleability was strongly based on ***location, location, location.***

Simply having 'an address' can often bring beneficial psychological results. By this we refer to no ordinary address, but one which exudes connotations of success. Why do social climbers want to have Beverly Hills, Billionaires' Row, Trocadéro Paris, Knightsbridge London, or some other prominent location listed beneath their name on their address labels? We have to admit that it sounds far more exciting than living in 'Wretchedville.'

This is not to say that everyone should reside in an already famous place. A truly ambitious person might consider becoming the mayor of an undeveloped town, and transforming it into something wonderful. Turn an abandoned Quonset into a centre for the arts. Have music and drama teachers create an orchestra and theatre groups. Change that acreage of grass into a riding arena, field for polo or other sports. Raise funds for a village library and so on. Every place has the potential for greatness, provided that optimistic people live there.

If one resides in the same city for the whole of their life, chances are that they have a keen understanding of which neighbourhoods are of higher quality. What if one is moving to a different city, province, or country altogether—how can they gather this information? The first method is by referral—speak to C-people who reside in your proposed location. They should be able to share their knowledge. If you don't have any contacts, you may have to investigate on your own.

Call an insurance company, and find out which sub-divisions have the lowest crime rates; ring up an estate agent to learn about property values. Check the professions: dentists, architects, consultants and other independents—which areas do they tend to *reside* in? After you've studied the people of professional business, do research on entertainment. Which zone is nearest the polo club, yacht club, opera, arts, designer fashion stores, private grocers, five-star restaurants, and other amenities of distinction? Don't only search for the positive, but keep a cautious eye open for signs of a low-quality location. Beware the areas with fast junk-food franchises, truck stops, bingo halls and large thrifty department stores.

I have lived in four different countries and the home ownership rates were as follows: Canada 68.5% Great Britain 63% Italy 72% and Norway 80%. In countries with low birth rates, children often inherit a house; but even if buying on one's own with a full mortgage, I feel that ownership is generally the best thing to do since it may bring tax benefits and property values tend to increase over time.

If the beginner, still single and childless, is determined to lease rather than buy, they still should choose the best location. One may only be able to afford a small flat, but limited size in a fabulous area is far better than a spacious home in a danger zone. The UK also currently has a programme called Helpful Housemates, where someone more established, often senior citizens, can take in a lodger for below-market rent in exchange for up to five hours help per week.

If you are presently living in a rough, corrupt area, the very first thing on your agenda should be to *get out*. Move to the absolute best, most prestigious, cultured, civilised neighbourhood in your town or city. Some people prefer to switch cities or counties completely and go as far as is necessary to meet with their new expectations. Birds of a feather fly together—if you establish yourself in a place where you feel confident that people are *living royally*, there should be no regrets.

What if one has to leave behind a very close friend or relation who is also trying to establish higher standards and search for a better life-style? If this kindred spirit still resides in an unrespectable location of your city, the simplest method is to invite them to your new place. Remember—there is no need to undervalue your judgement, nor should one revert backwards. Do the entertaining in your territory. When you go out together to sports clubs or to restaurants, always choose places in the better location. If you've decided to join someone for a film, attend the cinema in the more esteemed area. Prosperity consciousness can only expand and bring rewards, when we truly believe that we deserve the best. Maintain integrity, don't sell yourself short.

Only invite those who share your tastes and ideas. Never force your advanced style on people who are out of character—they may feel uncomfortable, and you will be disappointed with fruitless efforts. People change and grow on their own accord. *In a free country, everyone chooses to live exactly where they are suited to be.*

Don't worry about the planet running out of prestigious neighbourhoods. Remember: *If everyone were to expect the best, the world would eventually provide only excellence*.

If your main residence exists in a climate which has a long winter rainy season, or dreary snow clouds for six months, consider the properties with a resort built in. One does not need to fly to the tropics every winter. By creating an artificial paradise using sun lamps and outdoor props, architects can replicate the 'outdoors' inside. Many buildings I've seen include: an indoor swimming *pool*, an *atrium* with tropical plants, and an *aviary* of colourful song birds. These additions are costly on an individual basis, but are made affordable in condominium complexes. Terrific amenities should be the primary, perhaps only, reason for considering…

COMMUNITY LIVING

Condominiums come in different styles: *apartment*—building with flats and a shared main entrance; *townhouse*—attached terraced row housing with private individual entrances, and *semi-detached* duplex houses which share common grounds.

There is one main reason why a person may opt for community living—*amenities*. Often one family cannot afford to maintain a swimming pool and nine-hole golf course, but 30 families contributing a monthly condo fee can. This will allow the community association to maintain the pool, grounds, etc., which is not only more economical, but removes the tasks from the homeowners.

Demand excellence – shop around for a condo that provides indoor pool, sauna, whirlpool, recreation room, tennis court, etc. If the property manager says that the monthly fee covers yard maintenance only, you would be far better off to invest in your own house and hire a private gardener to do the yard work.

Condominiums should only be purchased if they provide services and luxuries which become more affordable in group ownership.

LAND

Recall the saying "land ... they aren't making any more of it." There certainly is value in this asset, and we've all heard stories about those who've made their fortunes in real estate. Becoming a landowner is one goal, which nearly everyone shares; and if one buys the right size property, in the right location, it will usually be a worthwhile investment.

Canada, which has an enormous land mass, would bemuse foreigners to see a nation with so much space, sometimes crowding homeowners side by side on small zero-clearance lots. This practise was established out of avarice—more units meant more money for 'developers,' as well as income for 'city hall' since they could collect far more in taxes. Developers and city councils often work together to establish high density condominium sites in residential areas, even though citizens protest. In such cases, one can be assured that when an area becomes commonly high density, the upper classes will generally look for *greener pastures*.

Some cities retain certain areas for the affluent in order to keep the town alluring. In the west-side of Vancouver, BC for example, when I lived near Southlands, it had more horses than humans on site—a rare but fabulous environment in the midst of a major city.

One will notice that the aristocratic type generally live where there is an abundance of nature and riding availability. Their ultimate preference is to own an acreage estate either in the countryside or in a specially zoned city sub-division like aforementioned Southlands. If one cannot afford a piece of land suitable for horse and hound, they may settle for a dwelling without acreage, near a riding park like Hyde Park in London, Central Park in New York, or English Gardens in Munich.

Not all major cities offer these privileges, and sometimes one can only find such treasured spots in suburban and rural areas. This creates a different dilemma as high society demands reasonable *proximity to the theatre, racecourse, private clubs, shopping, train station, international airport, and other conveniences*. My homes in Italy and England both benefit from all of the above amenities.

If you own an acreage estate, and can motor to all of the aforementioned facilities in 30 minutes or less, then you have a ***superior*** piece of property. Inner centres will only become less congested, when outer cities begin to provide more of these metropolitan amenities. Many parts of Europe do exceedingly well in this area—no matter where you are, there often seems to be something wonderful nearby. Aside from their geographical benefits like Riviera beaches, one can usually locate a fine restaurant, designer shopping, the arts, and so on. France has 250 race courses—how could anyone possibly live far from the action?

Some locations in North America now develop lots with more than an acre. These semi-rural neighbourhoods not only offer more reasonable taxes, but the benefits of having a large private yard are vast. Not only may one use the space for pleasure—garden parties, tennis, riding, etc., but one can be productive and utilise the land for free-range hens, organic vegetable gardens, berry patches and fruit trees.

Once again, remember when choosing an acreage, to bear in mind the importance of proximity to social amenities; ***space is wonderful***, ***but isolation is not***—an acre of land is most valuable when surrounded by a sophisticated quality of life.

PROPERTY COUNCIL TAX

When choosing your location, be certain to bear in mind the cost of property taxes. In England, money earned through council tax goes towards local services such as the police, fire services, support for the elderly and vulnerable, parks maintenance, refuse disposal and street cleaning. They have a very fair A to H tier system, with the most expensively valued properties in band H. If you own a mansion on St Georges Hill in Weybridge UK, and pay the highest 'tax band H' it will set you back £4,318 per year at the time of writing. This is fair, considering some of the properties there sell in the millions of pounds.

North America has a very different reputation where home owners tend to be exploited for owning expensive properties. Buyer beware—look into this matter very carefully when choosing your location!

HOUSE

For many, the residence can be an all-important source of pride, joy and accomplishment. Not only is it the background of general living and frequent entertaining, but in many situations, it has also become the place from which people operate their business. The fact is, a substantial amount of time is often spent within one's house and grounds, so this should be a place which makes you very happy.

If we were to ask people to describe their ultimate dream estate, we might receive very different conceptions:

* An old brick Victorian character dwelling… stables on a five-acre lot with natural stream running through the English gardens.
* A beautiful bright and modern beach house surrounded by palm trees in a sunny affluent area.
* A huge colonial with private grounds including a swimming pool and nine-hole golf course.
* An elegant European chateau amidst your own vineyards…

We may be long past the gilded age where the Vanderbilts had ballrooms to accommodate 1,200, but even a moderately sized house can display quality. Most grand houses also had a chapel, even if very small like at Puccini's house in Torre del Lago, but they served as a wonderful place to reflect or keep the ashes of deceased loved ones.

Goals and dreams are a wonderful part of life, and I urge everyone to hold the thoughts of whatever they eventually desire to manifest—*the more natural it feels to you and the clearer you can imagine something in your conscious mind as already existing,* the greater the likelihood of obtaining it.

In the meantime, while envisioning and working to establish your wealth, one must often begin with a more frugal standard of housing. When just starting out, perhaps you can only afford to lease a one-bedroom suite in the loft of someone else's mansion. *Be determined to acquire accommodation in a supreme house and location if that is your ultimate desire*. Rather than simply browsing through advertising (magazines, online, etc.), it is a wise idea to post bulletins up at the golf club, yacht club, riding club and parish in your preferred area. Also verbally mention to your older *established* acquaintances that you are looking for a room. Letting a studio in a prestigious house has its advantages. It doesn't cost much to decorate a small space, and the rest of the house will already be tastefully furnished by the owners. If you cannot afford to pay rent—consider becoming a temporary 'au pair' or gardener… to earn your way into a fabulous house.

Proper beginnings are beneficial for future success… one could live rich, until they become rich. You have probably heard the saying: 'fake it—until you make it.' I believe the point is that one must "fake it until they *feel* it." Decorate your room as elegantly as possible—everything you look at should project quality and beauty. This is a 24-hour visual affirmation of not merely what your life will become… but what your life presently *is*. Take an evening off to do a complete inventory on your living quarters. Every item that looks dull, shabby, worthless or in poor taste—remove from the premises. Correct the wall colour, brighten the lighting, improve the blinds, furniture and all personal effects which might transform your room into an attractive, radiant ambience.

Perhaps you are already older, established, and financially secure. You've achieved the funds and means to create *your own* house of distinction.

When designing your dream house, everything should be done to suit your particular taste—it's your masterpiece. It does not matter if your house is going to be of classic design: a character structure with antique furniture, hardwood floors, Persian carpets, crystal chandeliers, and oil paintings… or done in futuristic design: of modern decor with marble flooring, track lighting, abstract art, contemporary furnishings and so on. Regardless of what style you choose—certain things will always exude good taste. For example: if one desires a piano in the drawing room, they may choose a solid walnut upright pre-World War I antique, or a modern white baby grand… there is a perfect piano for every house.

No matter what style we favour—certain designs are considered essential, especially pertaining to structure. Let's look inside a basic two-storey with basement house:

MAIN FLOOR (ground level)

Most people adore sunshine, for it tends to induce a healthy, happy atmosphere. Whether the architecture of a house is modern or character, the main floor should incorporate high ceilings and tall windows to provide an abundance of natural light. This effect is especially welcome in the ***drawing room*** where people gather to socialise.

The next area of the main floor, equal in importance to the drawing room, is the ***formal dining*** area. This room is significant and vital for tasteful entertaining. Cosy breakfast nooks in the kitchen may be charming for your children, but a dining suite which seats six to a dozen guests, is a necessity for the adult cirque. Lighting is less important here as candles can be used anytime.

The main floor of a house should also provide a ***library***; plus, a ***study*** and/or ***sitting room*** for leisurely moments. Such areas require bright natural lighting for daytime, and should be equipped with good reading lamps and a wood-burning fireplace for evening enjoyment.

The ***kitchen*** will be located just off the dining area, and the ground floor of the house will also provide at least one ***lavatory*** with sink and toilet.

BASEMENT

Basement houses are still the preference, if only for their ***wine cellars*** and extra storage. Full size basements with bright windows near the top, can be used adequately as living space. Since the area could generally be left large with few walls, in the past it was common to find a 'games' room. Card tables, shuffleboard, or billiards could be fitted for those who took delight in such pastimes. More frequently these days, high basements are turned into a ***suite***, providing accommodation for a live-in domestic.

Unlike a century ago, when the servants were expected to stay in the uppermost storey, possibly a stuffy attic—in present times, attractive quarters are often provided downstairs for the help. The suite will contain a kitchenette, full lavatory, bedchamber, and sitting room. If your domestic also serves as a nanny, a nursery/playroom will be available downstairs to make child-care more convenient.

FIRST FLOOR (second level up)

One flight above the main floor, the upstairs of the house is designed for bedchambers and office space. Any ***guest room/s*** should be of reasonable size and furnished with twin beds, occasional chairs, and a desk. The desk should provide a looking-glass, pens, stationery, and an intercom telephone to reach other rooms in the house.

Ideally all bedrooms would have their own private ensuite. This has long been one feature which truly distinguishes a house of quality. Every lavatory should be complete with sink, toilet, bathtub, overhead shower and possibly a bidet if desired. When designing your house, opt for the more expensive full bathing tubs with 'built-in' shower surround, as people do not appreciate dashing out of their comfortable bath and into some tiny shower stall for the final rinse. The maid will also thank you for easier clean-up.

The ***master bedroom*** should take precedence over all other bedchambers, for it may become partially responsible for one's marital bliss or distress. There should be two separate dressing rooms so couples need ***NEVER*** watch each other do personal grooming, and they should also have separate sinks. Sharing a room for intimacy is far more gratifying than crowding someone's space while they wash, dress or groom. Finally, if sharing a bed with your consort, be sure to buy a super king size for adequate space and comfort.

FIREPLACE

Every great house has at least one fireplace, and the natural wood-burning variety is often the preference. In the older character homes, before central heating, one would often find seven or eight fireplaces—one in the drawing room, dining room, study, and every bedchamber.

Of course, today, dwellings are equipped with modern central heating, but there remains a certain atmosphere which only a fireplace can create. What could be more enchanting than the mesmeric flames which flicker as one stokes wood in the hearth? To avoid excess smoke and fumes, consider buying compressed logs which are more environmentally friendly than forest wood. Having said this, there are also some very realistic gas fireplaces which provide excellent sources of heat.

What a very fine ambience is created, when we sip cognac with friends, hound at our feet, or simply curled up with a book in front of a warm fire.

FLOORING

The preferred quality floorings are oak hardwood, marble or ceramic tile, and movable Persian rugs. These types of floor coverings tend to be expensive, but are attractive, provide higher resale value, are longer lasting and even more healthful. The floors can be vacuumed or swept and sponge mopped with disinfectant cleaner as required. Whereas, wall-to-wall carpeting may produce health hazards… although formaldehyde, a known carcinogen is no longer supposedly used in the glue, apparently other toxic chemicals still are.

Dust mites, the same microscopic organisms which can be found in curtains, old mattresses/bedding, etc., are often found in carpets. Fortunately, most houses now opt for blinds; also, white linen/cotton bed-sheets and pillow covers are usually laundered in hot water and cleaning fluid to reduce dust mites. Small rugs can be beaten, spray washed and/or dry-cleaned, but glued wall-to-wall carpeting is rarely washed so thoroughly or frequently. Regular dirt and dust mites are quite harmless to most people, but can be a serious problem for sensitive people with allergies.

HINT: The upper-crust ***do not*** remove their shoes when entering a house—this practise is unsanitary and unnecessary in houses with quality flooring; ***but*** there should ***always*** be a coir rug in the foyer or just outside the front door on which to wipe the dampness or dust from the soles of your shoes—most people will know what the coir mat is for. There is ***never*** a sign that reads 'remove your footwear' or 'wipe your feet'.

FRESH CUT FLOWERS

I have rarely seen a truly elegant home without vases of fresh cut flowers. Colourful, fragrant blossoms can add a touch of extravagance and beauty to almost any room of a house. The main entrance, drawing room and sitting room are favourite spots. Bouquets may also be displayed on dining room tables, but should be unscented (so one's olfactory sense may be used to savour the delicious aromas of the food and wine) and low, so people dining will have unobstructed vision across the table.

The truly discriminating will prefer to display flowers which are in season. Naturally, this is characteristic because the blooms are always fresh cut from one's own property. Gardening has long been the pleasure and pride of the affluent. From spring freesia and tulips, to summer lilacs, hydrangea or bougainvillea and autumn roses, a colourful outdoor park will be seen throughout the year. Fortunate are those who can afford the privilege of living in locations which boast pleasant climates throughout the whole calendar.

If you do not yet possess your own flower gardens or if you live in a colder climate, be sure to keep some indoor plants such as tropical, orchids, etc. They should be live-potted; no plastic, silk or dry arrangements, as those with refined taste generally abhor anything artificial. Live succulents like Sansevieria also provide health benefits in that they purify air by absorbing toxins through the leaves and producing oxygen. This easy to care for plant would also be ideal in bedrooms as it cleans the air we breathe. For rooms with less light and more moisture, such as a bathroom, try a Peace Lilly.

THE YARD

It is likely that the established will have a fair-sized property with room for not only flowers… but a berry patch, organic kitchen garden, and possibly fruit-bearing trees. Even regular size lots (e.g. 50 by 150 feet) in the midst of a city can be arranged very well with the initial assistance of a professional gardener's designs. A surrounding border of shrubbery may provide privacy to parcels of land which are in close proximity to neighbours. The general idea is to keep everything as green and natural as possible.

Wooden fences which require painting are not easy to maintain, but stone masonry walls, perhaps displaying ivy or bougainvillea are very practical and can look quite lovely. Cedar fencing may be used for paddocks and cedar decks are for boat piers. Cement patios are best suited for social areas of your garden and pool surrounds. Interlocking paving stones may be used for garden trails or motor drives.

RECOGNISE QUALITY AND BEAUTY

The main theme to follow regarding the property's **exterior** is ***fresh and invigorating***. A natural garden with green grass, trees, flowers—beautiful colours.

The house should be built from quality materials like brick or stone and provide plenty of tall windows for natural light. Avoid dull, stucco grey, concrete appearances. Garages should be located away from the house or inconspicuously underground.

Indoor items: having aesthetic objects in the home is of greater value when they are ***useful*** as defined by our senses:

- A bouquet of garden flowers adds visual and fragrant appeal to a room; artificial ones cannot compete.
- A bowl of fruit displayed on a table, should be fresh and ready to eat; non-edible, plastic fruit displays are in poor taste.
- The polished silver tea set may be a marvellous sight, but it becomes far more spectacular when used to serve your daily tea.
- What good is a study/library without a selection of great books? Or the piano, if no one is allowed to play it?
- The fine bone china, crystal, and silverware should not be gathering dust, but should be used by the adults of the household for their enjoyment at every meal.

One could go on and on with this list, but I believe that everyone has taken the main point, which is: high-quality is always in fashion and ***to be used***.

The search continues... ***excellence***... distant or attainable? Is it really as difficult as people like to believe, or can excellence be experienced by everyone? One of the principles of this book is to acknowledge that everyone deserves the best; and of equal importance, that it is within reach for all, no matter how humble one's beginnings.

Much can be attributed to our own expectations—see 'poverty or prosperity' consciousness... but enough of that. You've studied how the sub-conscious mind works, you've done affirmations and exercises to get rid of inferiority thinking, you realise your true value. You know that you have style and deserve the best that life has to offer. Now what? While improving one's education, establishing a more enjoyable and lucrative vocation, time passes by. Must one wait years to see results, or can they realise some changes immediately?

When I first lived on my own, I had very little money to spend, and the furnishings in my flat showed as much. The sitting room contained cheap, poorly made glass and brass coffee tables which wobbled menacingly. My taste wasn't even modern, it was traditional. I went to a furniture store and considered buying a pair of French provincial tables. The cost was $1,000 for basic pine topped with cherry-wood veneer, and sprinkled with black dots—referred to as 'antiquing' by the sales clerk.

The design was tolerable, the price was high... the quality wasn't even genuine. A few monthly payments could have bought the new furniture, but I decided not to rush. The following week I went to an estate sale and purchased two magnificent solid mahogany French provincial tables for my sitting room at one quarter of the price-$250 for two pieces of perfection, rather than an inferior, over-priced product from the department store.

Always choose quality, shop around... check the local paper or website for sales, visit antique shops, or consult private carpenters. I later found a French provincial sofa and chair, in sturdy condition, for the same price. A $70 steam cleaning revealed the most extraordinary original material. Next came a solid walnut antique piano... and so on. Decide with your mind what quality you desire... then determine what price you can pay. After that you will be conscious of opportunities when they arise.

I have often heard it said that opportunity knocks, but we don't always open the door. Make yourself aware, and you will notice good fortune when it appears. It never fails to amaze, but it's true—two households on the same income, can experience totally opposite life-styles. **WE DON'T NEED TO BE RICH TO LIVE WELL.** Changing our physical surroundings can be the quickest and easiest of all improvements as we choose to live like royalty.

Material Possessions

Before proceeding with this subject, one must first understand that the world is abundant and there is enough to go around for everyone. Joe Vitale mentioned in "The Secret" ordering from the catalogue of life—and why shouldn't we? First of all, if we need more, more will be created.

Secondly, we all have different desires. A young girl might be hoping above all else, desiring more than anything, a new pair of figure skates as a Christmas present. That does not mean her wish will be wanted by everyone—the last time I went ice skating, I broke my arm, and therefore skates are the least of my desires – we do not all long for the same things.

PRESENTS WITH FINESSE

One of the most splendid privileges which comes with the acquirement of style, are the presents. When people understand that one has evolved to refined, discriminating taste, they will rarely be disconcerted by the arrival of unwanted objects. If anyone should receive an ill-chosen item, they are certainly under no obligation to keep it. Ashtrays, polyester clothing, bric-a-brac souvenirs or T-shirts with words printed on them, can be donated to the nearest charity shop.

What type of gift should one give to those who have an appreciation for excellence? Any choice item which is appropriate for a fine standard of living. Consider that we desire to promote more quality and fewer inferior objects in this world. Presents can vary from highly expensive to inexpensive and still exude style.

Some of the items on our 'preferred gift list' are quite expensive, and others are not, so everyone will be able to choose articles which suit their budget. It does not matter whether something is costly or of a lower price—***good taste*** is what's important.

PREFERRED GIFT LIST

* Opera glasses or small racing binoculars.
* Leather bound classic books by writers like Jane Austen, Shakespeare, etc.
* Interesting hard cover modern books, especially if signed by the author.
* Silk satin clothes hangers.
* Loofah natural sea sponges, scented Epsom salts or other treats for the bath.
* An aesthetic care package: manicures, back massage, etc.
* A box of compressed logs for the fireplace.
* Good quality pen like Waterman, or Mont Blanc.
* A fine watch—Cartier, Rolex, Piaget, etc.
* High-quality stationery, such as correspondence cards with envelopes from Smythson or Debrett's.
* Genuine diamond, pearl, precious gem, or gold earrings.
* Private box seats to the race track or opera.

* Complimentary limousine service if recipient does not already have a private car with driver.
* Specialty food items like wild smoked salmon, caviar, saffron, truffles.
* Fine champagne, vintage port, cognac or a choice bottle of wine for the cellar.
* Silverware or table items like fine bone china or crystal—try to find out which brand/pattern they use: Royal Doulton, Steuben, Baccarat, etc.
* Bouquets of roses, an orchid or other live potted plant.
* Tins of *loose-leaf* Ceylon or other fine teas—perhaps from Fortnum & Mason.
* Luxury cruise tickets—choose a destination they adore.
* Perfume or cosmetic items, if you know their preference.
* High quality hair brushes e.g. solid teakwood with boar bristles.
* Sable hair cosmetic brushes for women.
* Classic films like Pride and Prejudice, A Tale of Two Cities, Jane Eyre etc. from BBC on DVD.
* 100% white cotton bath towels, 100% silk sheets, 100% Irish linen or 'Porthault' bedding.
* A string quartet gift certificate to provide classical music at a private soirée.
* White silk handkerchiefs for men's coat pocket.
* Cotton and lace handkerchiefs for women.
* Gold, silver, or mother of pearl cuff-links for men—traditional style, two identical sides joined by a chain shank.
* Cotton summer gloves, leather gloves with silk or cashmere linings for winter.
* Silk ties for men, silk scarves for women—think Hermes.
* Cashmere scarves or polo-neck jerseys for cool seasons.
* Socks of natural fabric 100% wool, cashmere or cotton.
* Cotton or silk briefs (only for your consort or children please)
* Hand-beaded clutch or leather envelope style bag for women.
* Ladies' silver compact for translucent powder; leather mirrored lipstick case.
* Men's silver money clip or a leather billfold.
* A high-quality house fragrance diffuser like Rituals.

- A pair of fine candlesticks or candelabra with candles; or one scented candle.
- Tickets to opera, ballet, or live theatre.
- Leather agenda book, leather passport holder, key holder or luggage tags—think Aspinal of London.
- Mother-of-pearl spoons for boiled eggs or caviar.
- Classical tapestry cushion for sitting room chairs.
- Leather jewellery case for travel.

The above list is very general—if you know the recipient on a more personal level, you can purchase something of a more individualistic nature. For example, if your friend's hobby is creating art, they will always appreciate more supplies—just be sure that if you are buying paints, a new brush, etc. you will buy the best quality available.

People naturally prefer to receive top quality when they spend their extra cash, so consider where the best items might be made – examples include: Persian carpets, Swiss watches, Russian caviar, Belgian chocolate, Canadian maple syrup, German pianos, Italian shoes, French perfume, Irish linen, Chinese silk, Indian cashmere, English fine bone china, Spanish sherry and so forth. Most countries supply some luxury or specialty products which enter into stately residences around the globe. What connotations fill one's mind when they read the list above? A first thought may be extravagance, but on more careful study… its true meaning is *excellence.* We should try to acquire objects which are noted for their high grade. It is a great necessity that more of society learn to accept only the best quality, for if one does not support the finest, then they are, in effect, promoting faultiness.

If for example, you want to purchase a picture—would you hire a young artist to produce an original oil on canvass, or would you go to a thrifty department store and buy a tacky print. It takes less time, cheaper materials, and little skill to manufacture the print, but what does one gain? An inferior product plus the disgrace of having supported big business rather than an individual craftsman. Furthermore, the artist might become famous one day!

This is not to suggest that one should never purchase anything which is produced in larger quantities. As long as the quality is upheld, then the product has value. A woman may choose to own a Chanel handbag, because the design is exceptional. If I want practical, well-wearing, very attractive leather shoes, I do not always have them hand-made in Italy, but frequently purchase Salvatore Ferragamo, Roberto Capucci, Amalfi, or Gucci. We may buy a Waterman pen, not only for its style, but because of the lifetime guarantee, which is another sign of quality. One might select a Cartier, Patek Philippe or Rolex watch because they maintain their value. Moreover, we all know of the precision which goes into a Bentley or Rolls, but it does not matter what 'name' you choose to buy, as long as you believe that it is of *superior* quality.

IF PEOPLE SEARCH FOR EXCELLENCE, THE WORLD WILL BEGIN TO PRODUCE MORE OF IT.

It should not be misinterpreted that all good things must come at great cost. Prices of products often vary due to supply and demand. If everyone purchased only original art, the world would afford a great many more artists. Costs of materials also fluctuate a good deal, like gold and silver. Currently, superior cotton is very inexpensive – *prices needn't be exorbitant, only quality is of priority*.

STATUS SYMBOLS

Do not get too wrapped up with flashing 'status' symbols of designer initials. During the affluent eighties era of power dressing, this proclaimed to the world "I have arrived." But swindlers quickly caught on, and soon a lot of *imitation* products 'were arriving' on the fraudulent black market.

There are so many material items which one can buy, and we certainly wouldn't want to bore ourselves by listing them all, so we'll choose only one to use as a basic example. It seems as though the most common and much-loved object in North America, is the motor car. If one's household does not own at least one of these, they would appear to be rather unusual indeed. I bought my first car as a teenager before I had a driver's licence, so that I would have something to practise with.

Upper class, middle, or lower socioeconomic… if you live in a country of vast expanse, like Canada, you're likely to own a motor car. If one has decided to buy a car, let it be the best that they can afford for two reasons, practicality and prosperity consciousness.

Study example: Imagine a purchaser who saves over £500 per month and currently has £1000 extra cash. They have a steady business cash-flow, a good credit rating, and he/she always pays their bills on time. Which car should this person buy?

A. An old, heavy consumption vehicle which is likely to need repairs in the near future—for exactly £1000 cash—to be bought as is.
B. A much newer, clean, attractive, electric/hybrid or other economy type of car for a cost of £1000 down and a monthly payment of £500.

Not only is the purchaser choosing between poverty or prosperity image, but consider the logic. The extra petrol and high repair costs of A could create more expenses every month than payments of the newer, economically sound, more attractive car. We don't need to buy the most expensive car on the market, but a clean, efficient one is the obvious choice. There is such a thing as 'affordable quality' in all forms tangible… the wise and determined, will always find a way to locate it.

Part III
Underlying Basics for Greater Joy

An artist can produce the most extraordinary painting with his brush, but remove the three primary colours from his palette and notice how difficult it becomes for the creation of his masterpiece. Although personal development and life-style will greatly determine whether or not one lives an abundant life… there are three basics, which once established, can make the other goals arrive with greater ease. Freedom is the backbone of all success—the ability to grow and develop into everything wonderful which we are capable of. Emotional well-being, physical health, and financial stability, will give one this freedom. Work hard to achieve these three fundamentals, and then enjoy more rapid progress in attaining your additional ambitions.

Chapter 6
Health and Well-Being

Introduction

One can experience little success or happiness, unless we first possess reasonably good health. We've all been touched by illness at some point in our lives. It may have been something common such as a cold, influenza, an infection; or in some cases, a more serious matter. Surely everyone can understand what an impairment any degree of affliction can be. Therefore, one of the prime foundations which enable us to experience a wonderful life is to first establish, and maintain, a sound bill of health.

HISTORY AND FUTURE TRENDS

When we study the history, present, and possible future of various events, we see how quickly things can change. Over the years… health, well-being, and even sickness have altered greatly. Illnesses which were often fatal in the past such as tuberculosis, scarlet fever, or smallpox… are of relatively little concern for the developed world today. The discovery of penicillin in 1928 by Sir Alexander Fleming relieved many common ailments. However, as we find cures and remedies for old diseases, we are often faced with new problems such as the recent Covid pandemic.

Another serious disease is AIDS, which has been a top concern since the 1980s. The Economist magazine of 13 August 2022 said, "So far, it has ended the lives of some 40 million people…" It is our hope that research will develop a cure for this illness; but for the moment our only consolation is treatment/control and the advantage of knowing how to 'prevent' it.

A future trend regarding health… is the long overdue, concentration on **PREVENTIVE MEDICINE**. How can we eliminate emotional anxiety? How can we avoid sexually transmitted viruses? In what way can proper nutrition and exercise lessen our leading killer—heart disease? How might regular check-ups lower the risk of cancers resulting in death? As a society in general, we have become more cautious—our motorcars are equipped with air bags, and people actually *use* their seatbelts.

Preventive medicine will become a major business in the future. People will learn to relax again with mindfulness—perhaps at a massage salon, soothing health spa, at the beach, in a yoga class, or maybe on the golf course. There will be a high demand for most enterprises related to well-being. We will also see a need for qualified nutritionists, personal trainers and other people who promote a healthy life-style. **No human should die by cause other than peacefully in their sleep of old age.**

Emotional Well-Being

Not only has disease and illness changed over the centuries, but so have our methods of dealing with physical or emotional malfunction. How different were the women of a century ago—who, when faced with stress or shock, could glide into an elegant relieving faint? They would then be gracefully swept up, revived with a little smelling salt, and offered some laudanum. Today, when people are unable to govern their emotions, rather than fainting, women and men alike, frequently have a 'panic attack.'

It is no longer common to simply drop over when gripped by intense fear, so we allow our bodies to respond with an erratic heartbeat, throbbing headache, wet palms, shortness of breath and other unpleasant symptoms. The late Dr Wayne Dyer once created an excellent recording called "Choose to Live and Love"; on it he said: "There's no anxiety in our world, our world is a perfect place. There's no stress in our world—there's only people thinking anxiously—there are only people thinking stressfully, in any given way."

I tend to agree with psychologists who believe that people do in fact 'choose' their emotional reactions. One can literally decide to keep their wits, faint, or experience temporary derangement (the cry for help)—whichever method appears to be the least painful at the time. Nervous or physical ailments have touched everyone, even if mildly or rarely. If you have ever suffered from the common cold, then your body has experienced breakdown.

This low immunity may be caused by poor nutritional habits, but is just as frequently preceded by emotional tension—perhaps one has worked too hard, or functioned under stressful circumstances. A person becomes wrapped up in the pressures and deadlines of life in the fast lane and the next thing they know, they are feeling run down and lying in bed with a fever. This can happen to people who don't allow themselves time to slow down. I recall working very long hours, and going without any holiday when I was 27 years of age. Subsequently, I contracted chicken-pox, and became indisposed for a few days. My body was saying 'enough... if you don't slow down, I'll make you take time off.'

Something that should be noted here... which some may not realise, is that ***too much idleness can be just as detrimental as the strain of overwork.*** Many people who struggle with depression, do so because of a *lack* of positive physical and emotional energy. ***We must keep a healthy BALANCE of activity and rest***.

It is important to have control over your own emotions, and learn that relaxation can be a part of our daily occupational routine. Remember that ***stress is self-induced***. Don't react like our animalistic ancestors with the fight or flight instinct; instead, take a breath and respond calmly. Remember that you can disagree without being disagreeable and being kind is better than being right. If you always do what you know to be right, nothing should bother you. For those who already follow the practises which are suggested in this book, it is likely that stress has already become a stranger—excellent!

Just use good judgement and always do the best you can; also, try to associate with positive up-lifting individuals. If one ever feels extremely down, they must analyse the absolute worst that could happen; quite often, things are not really as bad as they seem, and the majority of our 'worries' never actually manifest. Say to yourself: ***tomorrow will bring a new day—it can be a very different day***... never give up. Then take affirmative steps to improve the situation, and don't be afraid to ask your loved ones or professionals for emotional support.

We are told that marital problems, financial troubles, loss of a loved one, changing careers, re-locating, and numerous other situations will often cause stress or emotional collapse; but we need to look at the bigger picture. I believe that depression occurs whenever necessary—it is like a rap on the head, whenever the human student fails to look beyond what they see on the radar screen. ***It surfaces when a person becomes too overwhelmed by earthly matters***.

Depression hits to wake people from an illusion. To remind them that they may be God's greatest creation, but not His sole creation. There are ***billions*** of people on earth, and ***billions*** of solar systems in the universe. Look at the whole picture, surrender your worries, put your faith and trust in eternity and as the saying urges, "Let go and let God." Then as we go on about our daily lives, simply doing the best we can, one will be at peace with oneself and the universe.

HARMONY AT HOME

I was raised in a family where 'hugs' were in constant supply, and 'hearty belly laughs' resounded through the rooms every day. ***Loving physical touch and genuine natural laughter are two requisites of emotional well-being.*** Therefore, if you choose a spouse who loves to exchange gentle amorous strokes, and also possesses a fine sense of humour, you will be doubly blessed. Some people become so involved in public decorum and outside protocol, that they forget how to behave around intimate associates. ***True, one should be a lady/gentleman in private, as well as in public, but this does not exclude laughter and passion.*** Create a happy, harmonious ambience at home and share pleasant emotion with your loved ones.

To avoid repetition, I will not go into further details pertaining to emotional health under this section. Much has been covered under the chapter on 'Inner Improvement' where the power of mind and attitude are discussed. Indeed, the entire contents of this book are designed to help people choose a more pleasant way of life—and when carried out, emotional well-being tends to follow automatically.

Physical Health

EATING PATTERNS

One of the most important factors which may determine our state of health concerns eating habits. What we eat or drink is extremely vital; but first, let us analyse our eating patterns. How often and how much do you eat? The following is a list of common eating times:

Times	Menu examples
8:00 AM breakfast	* Fresh fruit, toast, cereal, eggs etc.
11:00 AM brunch	* Salad, soup, sandwiches, etc.
2:00 PM luncheon	* Potatoes/rice, meat/seafood, vegetables
4:00 PM tea	* Sandwiches, scones

6:00 PM dinner	* See luncheon
8:00 PM Supper	* See luncheon

Throughout the day: snacks of berries, fruit, raw vegetables, cheese, yoghurt, olives, nuts, seeds, dark chocolate, etc.

As you can see, there are many occasions when one might choose to eat throughout the day. Just imagine what would happen to our bodies if we actually indulged at every possible opportunity. The negative results would soon show up in overweight or a poor state of health.

During the regular daytime eating period, the majority of people generally crave food approximately every four hours. If a parent, you might remember the feeding schedule of infants, once past six months and no longer being fed on demand, they are generally moved towards the 2/6/10 schedule and eat at: 6am, 10 am, 2 pm, 6 pm, 10 pm and the dreaded 2 am slot! Adults however, can easily manage with 3 meals a day.

Since people have become aware of the great health benefits regarding daily intermittent fasting; i.e., eating within an 8-hour window and fasting the other 16 hours, many of us have cut back on eating too often and too much.

My current mealtime schedule is something like this:

10 AM	Fresh berries/avocado/fruit; occasionally a slice of ham or wild salmon; eggs; etc
2 PM	Meat or seafood and vegetables
5–6 PM	Meat or seafood and vegetables

If I ever have a healthful snack as those listed earlier, I take it *immediately* before or after a meal, because I no longer agree with the concept of 'grazing' all throughout the day. My meals are approximately every four hours (like hunger) and I avoid foods containing preservatives. Upon rising in the morning, I sometimes have a cup of tea or coffee, because I feel it does not affect my fast.

Some people prefer to start their food day later, but can still remain in the eight-hour window—for example, 12 noon (brunch/lunch) 4 PM (teatime) 8 PM (supper). I like to eat a light and early dinner—Benjamin Franklin said, "Eat few suppers and you'll need few medicines." This is especially true for the many of us who have hiatal hernias and are not supposed to retire to bed for at least four hours after eating.

One might ask then; how can a person ever entertain? We can make some changes; now, I only host garden parties, luncheons and daytime receptions. In current times, many people work from home and are able to create their own hours; plus, many of us have children who are in school all day; ergo, the only private family time we have with them is in the evenings.

When I first began my new programme, I met with some resistance as I started to decline all late dinner invitations and only attend morning or afternoon receptions, champagne teas, luncheons and other traditional daytime gatherings like weddings, Christenings and so forth. Fortunately, there were also many people 'in my court' who appreciated that most of the finer engagements: Royal Ascot, Royal Henley, Epsom Derby, the 4th of June at Eton, polo and other glorious events, at least when we are in England, all tend to occur between noon and 5 o'clock. I also noticed that many of our invitations from the Diplomatic Corps were now earlier as many embassies had moved their receptions closer to midday/early afternoon. Since making the changes, I feel much better and lost 10 pounds which I should not have been carrying—you can do this too if you wish!

You might notice on my list of luncheon and dinner items above, that I did not include certain carbohydrates like pasta, bread or rice. I do *occasionally* eat *organic brown* pasta or *wild* rice and I consider *sweet* potato tubers to be on my list of vegetables. If you want to be super healthy, my best secret tip is that you **empty your refrigerator, cupboards and pantry of all "white" items**—and that most definitely includes refined sugar!

Another excellent recommendation which you might have heard is*: **Eat what God has made, not what is made by man.*** Now, this does not mean that humans shouldn't help out—we are co-creators for all greater goodness. In my *organic* Tuscan garden, which benefits from its own watering well, I have sown a kitchen vegetable patch plus 10 different types of fresh herbs for cooking. When it comes to fruits and berries, I have planted and now enjoy a variety of citrus and other items from Turkish figs to physalis.

The saying at the top of the last paragraph means that we should avoid man-made ***processed and packaged*** food items—think of boxed cereals, biscuits and other products which often contain preservatives and have sat ageing on a grocery shelf. Try to eat fresh seasonal foods as they come from the earth, the sea or free-range pastures. The ducks and geese on my childhood farm loved freshly grown lettuce; the chickens ate mainly grass and insects as did their ancestors, and there were no antibiotics ever given either. Today, many people with the garden space, once again keep free range hens and have a supply of healthful egg as an extra bonus.

DRINKS

I recommend that people limit coffee to the morning hours due to the high caffeine content in most brews. We then drink teas and plenty of sparkling or filtered water throughout the day. Pure vegetable juice like V8 or home-made green juice is nice occasionally, but avoid drinking *fruit* juices because they can cause a spike in your blood sugar — it is better to 'eat' your fruit fresh. If you would like to study menu examples, beverages, and additional diet information, see Appendix #4 at the back of the book.

BODY WEIGHT

One's weight is often indicative of their state of health. Those who are either too thin or too heavy, may be suffering from a physical or emotional disorder and should visit a doctor to determine if this is the case. Thyroid or glandular problems, anorexia or bulimia… all require special care and treatment.

Healthy individuals who exhibit increasing weight may include growing children—who ***should not diet***, even if they appear to be somewhat heavy. Their nourishment can consist of three proper meals every day, and if a child or young adult still feels hungry, they should have access to as much fresh fruit and raw vegetables as they desire. Packaged snacks containing preservatives and fast-food items needn't be a part of any youth *or* adult's food intake. Proper nutrition is vital to achieving optimum health and a first-rate life-style.

People have generally finished growing and reached their ideal weight by the age of mid to late twenties. Normally, a sign of proper health… is a steady, stable weight—from the duration of this maturity throughout one's life. Aside from child-bearing females, one's weight, once established, need never fluctuate. Note also, that from the age of 20 to 60 our metabolism should not change.

Your appropriate weight can be determined by your height and bone structure (fine, medium, large) frame. There are BMI (Body Mass Index) charts where one can find out if they are currently in the recommended zone. A good way for people to control their weight is to keep a scale handy, and make a point of weighing in regularly. Once an adult has established their desirable weight, they will be able to notice immediately if they have gained a couple of pounds.

I weighed 120 pounds when I got married and gained a pound a year—now, just after my 20th anniversary, I have finally returned to my wedding weight. Do not procrastinate—make a point of eliminating excess weight before it gets out of control. It is much easier to lose two pounds, than 10. If you only weigh yourself once a month and you've already gained a stone, it may be more of a struggle to reduce. Thus, *if your weight has a tendency to fluctuate—do a daily check on it*. Even those who do not own a scale should be able to notice when their clothing becomes too tight.

Try to avoid dressing in baggy oversized sweaters or sweats with elasticised waists—this type of apparel permits a lack of discipline and psychologically makes people feel bigger than they are (remember: what we think, we often become). I wear tailored, well-fitted jackets, skirts, dresses and trousers—if I gained 14 pounds, I would be required to replace my entire wardrobe. One's apparel at the age of 30 can still fit perfectly when they reach the age of 60 and beyond.

I realise that no one can be expected to maintain a perfect diet especially if they are often entertained as guests. Also, when hosting luncheons, I frequently ask the cook to prepare those marvellous rich dishes like orange duck, veal fricassee, chicken a la king and my special puddings like Grand Marnier chocolate mousse, Marsala tiramisu or perhaps cream cheese cake with Cointreau strawberries. Not to mention the aperitifs we consume like champagne and the wines which follow—alcohol is full of useless calories. Our bodies may be able to tolerate such feasts on occasion, but let us not become a decadent and indulge in extravagantly heavy meals on a daily basis.

There are several points involved in maintaining a healthy weight and physical condition. Although some people do follow a reasonable diet, they still find themselves gaining excess pounds. We must remember, that it is not solely **WHAT** we eat, but also how **FREQUENTLY** throughout the day—try to stay within the 8-hour window.

Now let us move on to an equally important topic…

EXERCISE

There exists a vast selection of books, DVDs and YouTube tutorials pertaining to exercise; therefore, one will require little input from me on this subject. The only suggestion which I would offer will be directed at those people, who like myself, find routine exercise to be somewhat tedious. Although Isometrics, Callisthenics, Aerobics, Yoga, and such are extremely beneficial... for those of us who tend to get bored easily, it can be difficult to discipline ourselves, on the much required, daily basis. If, like me, you suffer a lack of enthusiasm for organised work-outs, try something recreational instead.

In this way, one will gain emotional pleasure, plus physical agility, burn off calories and so forth. I wear my pedometer on most days when I am at home and generate many steps just from gardening and walking the dog... the real secret is simply to **MOVE YOUR BODY**. Even when in bed, stretch your body full out every morning and night—with hands high overhead and toes pointed as far as you can. Maybe you can dance around the room to some fabulous music—Jazzercise is also making a comeback.

Consider taking up something entertaining or sporty—swimming, rowing, cycling, skiing, skating, tennis, riding and fencing are some excellent calorie burners. I may not have exhibited much talent during my sports lessons or ball-room dance classes, but I certainly gained a great deal of emotional enjoyment and physical exercise. Engage yourself in something invigorating today!

The Great Outdoors

Have you ever permitted business and life in the fast lane to take a toll on your nerves? Has your physical body ever lost vitality, for lack of sunshine, fresh air and exercise?

Weather and health permitting—why not consider following, what I call the 'the outdoor treatment', that is: make an effort to **spend one to two hours outside on a daily basis**. There are numerous ways to incorporate the open air into your lifestyle:

* We have to eat, so try a picnic in the park, or lunch at an alfresco bistro.
* Take up a sport like riding, golf, sailing, skiing, swimming, tennis, etc.
* If one can't participate, become an outdoor spectator—attend the races or a polo match, watch outdoor golf or tennis tournaments.
* Walk a dog, or take a run through the park.

* Be a horticulturist—spend more time gardening.
* Attend an outdoor mass or theatre.
* Enjoy a concert or fashion show beneath the stars.
* Try your occupation or hobbies in the open air—painting, writing, photography and numerous other avocations work well.
* Host a garden party or reception outside.
* Instead of motoring, ride a bicycle whenever possible.
* Visit with friends on the patio or terrace rather than in the sitting room.

Many people believe that the ancient Athenians lived so well, because they spent very few of the daylight hours inside. If you make a habit of spending **one or two hours** in the fresh and free outdoors *every day*—you may be surprised at how quickly physical and emotional well-being improve. Nature, like love, can stimulate an incredible emotional high, which costs absolutely nothing and is available to everyone.

Vitamins

People and medical advisors seem to possess varied and numerous opinions regarding vitamin supplements. Some people say don't go without them; and others advise that they are totally unnecessary if we are consuming the right foods and beverages. Whether or not you do decide to take extra vitamins will depend on your own personal requirements, and should be determined together by you and your doctor.

A well-balanced diet that includes an abundance of protein, fresh fruit and vegetables, should provide an adequate amount of nutrients, but many people still choose supplements; for example, those who do not eat enough oily fish, might take Omega 3. If a woman requires more iron or calcium, her GP should advise her.

I take one multi vitamin/mineral tablet, plus a zinc, an Omega 3 soft gel, and a time-release vitamin C as an antioxidant. Even though I spend plenty of time outdoors, I also use vitamin D3 which strengthens the immune system to fight off colds, influenza and disease. If you are not sure what your personal requirements are, consult your doctor. If you do decide to take a supplement, my recommendation is that you choose a natural one, which has no artificial colours or flavours and no preservatives, sugar, or starch.

MEDICAL PROCEDURES

Medicare is a fabulous system and aside from judicial/policing/fire departments, it is one of the few programmes which the majority of people are happy to support through taxes. Most illness can be safely treated in countries with Medicare or a National Health Service as well as in private practices.

Regular check-ups are very important for they frequently detect ailments which could otherwise become too advanced. As the saying goes: ***an ounce of prevention, is worth a pound of cure***. Getting annual blood tests, a full body ultrasound, and maintaining optimum health, is far less costly for the medical system than allowing illness to progress to a state where hospitalisation or expensive treatments are required.

Having said this, note that there are also people who go to the opposite extreme. Many of us have met a 'hypochondriac' who not only rings the doctor once a week, but also worries continually… telling everyone how sick they are. These people have no idea how detrimental this is. Whatever they ***speak*** about, the mind will eventually ***believe***, and the body will literally ***feel***.

I am diagnosed with severe myopia, scoliosis, hiatal hernia, polyps, IBS, paroxysmal atrial tachycardia and a heart murmur; but if you see me or ask, I am in good health. I have learned to ***avoid activities which cause me pain*** so that I do not have to think about the ailments. If motoring distances by car creates agony for my crippled spine or aggravates my IBS, I can choose to travel by luxury ship, plane or train where I can walkabout, lie down, etc.

Also beware of medical practitioners who like to do too much. I maintain my tonsils and wisdom teeth despite having suffered infections, and calls for their removal during my youth. These body parts may appear relatively useless, but is that reason enough to dispose of them? Unless one has a dangerous condition such as malignant cancer, a ruptured appendix, etc., think twice about having surgery.

Some people learn very little about the operations which they agree to—this includes cosmetic face lifts, breast alterations, thigh reductions, and so on. Try non-surgical procedures like exercise and better nutrition first. We now have access to educational material, where one can view the particular procedure which you are contemplating on video—the reality of what the body must endure during surgery might make you re-consider.

SLEEP

Sleep... what a wonderful relaxation! Considering that we spend approximately 1/3 of every 24-hour day in this way, I hope that you enjoy its blissful tranquillity as much as I do. The refreshing moments when our subconscious has the opportunity to re-join the ethereal world... if only in our dream-state.

Slumber is dominated by our last waking concepts, so do not go to sleep feeling discouraged or dissatisfied, nor in the consciousness of failure. Just imagine everything you really want and allow yourself to smile and trigger positive emotions, for as Neville Goddard said, "Sensation precedes manifestation."

Then, there is another marvellous benefit referred to as **beauty sleep**. Why is it that one may notice many wrinkles at 10 PM, but very few at 10 AM?

Not only the texture, but even the complexion of our skin becomes rejuvenated—good bye 'red blotches', hello 'peaches and cream.' Dark circles beneath one's eyes are known to become lighter and nearly vanish, when people drink enough water, and take enough *rest*. Sleep is such an incredibly important part of emotional and physical health that I could not omit the mention of it.

Studies have indicated that eight hours seem to be the average amount of required sleep, although some people prefer slightly less or more; just a few decades ago, the average was nine hours. It has also been recommended that we try to form a habit of going to bed and getting up at a similar hour every day. If possible, choose a general schedule like 6 or 7 AM until 10 PM to spend your active hours. I agree with the philosophy that *it is preferable to rise early, and not to sit up late*. If we sleep in line with our individual body clock (circadian rhythm), possibly the best sleep we can have, are the two hours before midnight.

There will always be 'owls' and 'larks'—those who are nocturnal, and those who rise with the sun. It should be noted, however, that whether one is currently a night person, or a day person, they can change positions if they desire. Many youths tend to go through wild years during their student or college days and very few are able to escape the temptation of late nights. On school breaks or weekends, a whole group may celebrate until dawn, and consequently must sleep in late on the following day. I remember blending into the party-scene of youth, and actually believing that I was a 'night' person. This is a popular misconception, for most young adults will eventually grow out of the adolescent tendencies.

A person can certainly condition oneself to become an 'owl' if they decide to work graveyard shifts for example, but this is not an inherited characteristic. All humans are born 'larks' and only behave nocturnally by choice or necessity. After the student years, when I reverted back to the early bird life of rising with the sun, my physical health and overall spirit, became far superior to what it was during the nocturnal period. The human body and brain thrive in the glory of natural sunlight, which is impossible to acquire during the dark hours.

Mankind has different needs for the various periods of life. Infants require a great deal of sleep because they are growing and learning at such incredible speed. Some adults require less sleep during the night, but compensate by taking more frequent day-time naps. Speaking of naps… if one lives the traditional day life not exceeding 16 hours, they may not require this practise. However, when one rises normally at 7:00 AM, but must attend a late-night function which will carry on well past midnight, it is best to take at least a 20-minute refresher nap during the afternoon.

Another important point about sleeping habits, is to never jump out of bed to the resounding sounds of an alarm clock. I use my inner 'biological' clock only, and wake naturally at a similar time every morning, probably because I retire at a similar time every night. Only if one is not well-rested, might they require something more reliable; in that case, set your radio alarm to something pleasant like classical music.

Providing that one has not weakened their mental sensitivity (by sleeping with radio or television on), they will be able to wake easily to the mellifluous symphonic sounds. One needn't rouse with a start, but should awaken peacefully, and indulge in a long luxurious stretch, before actually leaving the bed. Prior to rising, while still in the alpha rhythm, perhaps while listening to some baroque music, many people also like to meditate, pray, recite positive affirmations or give gratitude. After rising and with your morning cup of tea, you might simply watch 10 minutes of beautiful affluent pictures accompanied by verbal positive 'I AM' affirmations, readily available on YouTube. Try out some of these ideas, and see how much better your day begins.

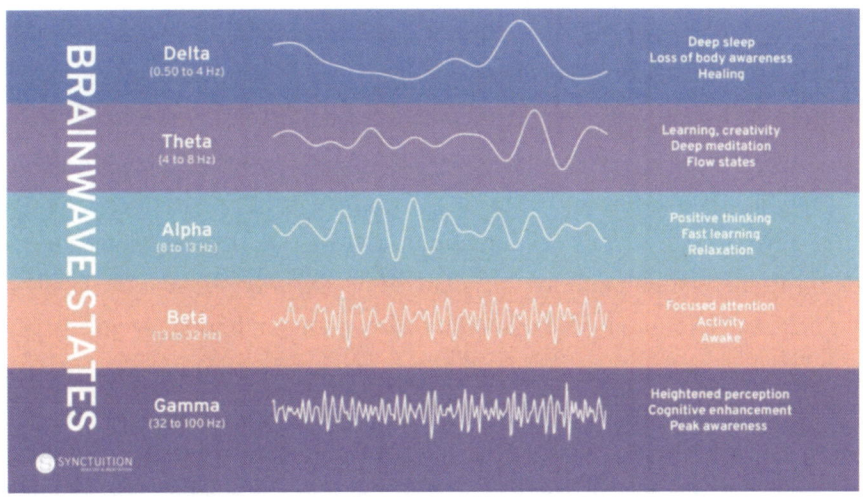

INTIMATE HEALTH

With more and more people choosing to marry in their late thirties, after they have become established, one can hardly expect such adults to remain celibate until their nuptials. Therefore, our youth might as well be educated at an early age.

The responsibility of sexual education initially lies with all parents or guardians, as they are expected to educate the young adolescents. One should not depend on schools, churches, or other institutions to enlighten their children. Young people must be made aware of how to **prevent an unwelcome pregnancy or transmittable illness before it occurs**. If the youth is very chaste and chooses celibacy, that's splendid, but many students involved in long term steady relationships are very likely to indulge their biological urges.

Better safe than sorry… the caring guardian will educate their charge. Unlike some illiberal countries which suffer tragic restrictions, our unconfined society permits the use of numerous forms of protection. Everything from pills (either birth control or day after), to condoms are readily available. Aside from rape, we have no excuse other than lack of intelligent education since AIDS, STDs and unwanted pregnancies are all **preventable**. Life is precious—play it safe!

Avoiding Self-Destructive Compulsions

"We first make our habits, and then our habits make us"—John Dryden.

What is a self-destructive compulsion? It is an uncontrolled impulse to perform some action which tends to be harmful or destructive to oneself. Major fixations like smoking, drugs and over drinking can be serious health hazards.

Compulsions such as smoking may begin for emotional reasons, but will usually develop into a physical addiction. Most young people initially take up smoking to alleviate a common problem—*low self-image.* As a teenager, one may think that smoking is an indication of freedom, adulthood, or power; but if they possessed a healthy self-esteem, this delinquent prop would never be necessary and addiction could be avoided.

Other dependencies can be even more serious than cigarettes. Years ago, Nancy Reagan did the world a wonderful service with her "Just Say No" campaign on the war against drugs—youth today really need to be inspired to take control and not succumb to peer pressures which reduce their health and social status. Remember, you become limitless when you set limits.

Smoking for a prolonged period of time, like drugs or heavy alcohol, will often develop into physical dependence, where not only the mind, but also the body requires the stimulant. If you presently have concerns about any of these three topics, please see Appendix #5.

Over eating has already been discussed under 'Diet and Health,' so in this section we will concentrate on compulsions of a lesser nature, but which are none-the-less, detrimental to wholesome living. Before analysing various compulsions, we should first consider what leads people to initially indulge in them.

Habits like daily TV viewing or gambling are 'emotional' addictions, i.e., something one does to alleviate mental boredom and general dissatisfaction with life. Many children today have also become obsessed with computer games and playing on their smart phones.

These youth and adults consider such 'actions' to be entertainment, although spending the day in front of a visual screen or slot machine, can hardly be called activity. Mental addictions can often be overcome by simply 'getting a life.'

TV OR NOT TO BE?

"So please, oh please, we beg, we pray, go throw your TV set away, and in its place, you can install a lovely bookshelf on the wall." Roald Dahl.

One may wonder why I am devoting writing space to discuss the habit of television viewing. The answer is **because TV has become one of the greatest alibis for failure.** It is vital that people acknowledge its detrimental effects, and take heed.

What is a TV? A harmless screen with some electronic entrails. Was it designed to be destructive? Unlikely… it could have been more beneficial; unfortunately, commercials and propaganda have reduced its potential as a vehicle for enlightenment.

Television, which was once considered the "baby sitter" of poor children, has now also evolved and become the 'keeper' of lower-middle class adults. It consumes the time of those who have neither business nor pleasurable activities to keep occupied with. TV is the ruler over the land of 'boredom' and its subjects often become poorer for lack of aspiration and intent.

If you are a success-oriented individual, chances are that you've attended some educational/motivational seminars. What's the first thing that the instructor or speaker often suggests? *"If you want to get rich – sell the TV."* Not only does time wasted in front of a television, prevent one from earning money, but it destroys their valuable social life as well. **TV's negative connotations warp weak minds into believing that a low standard of living is normal**—hence the synonyms: **boob**-tube, and **idiot**-box, for this is what the majority of programming seems designed to cater to.

Like many students who took that excellent motivational advice, I too got rid of TV decades ago. Today; however, one needn't be quite so extreme. With the advent and rapidly expanding use of computers and DVD players, commercial television is becoming less desirable and somewhat passé on its own demise. Unlike television, a disc player gives people *the freedom to choose commercial free programming*—from classic film entertainment, to educational documentaries.

Some films and many instructive tutorials can be watched for free on YouTube. Also, cash otherwise squandered on 'pay' TV or licences can be put towards more enterprising use like the purchase of quality discs which can be handed down from generation to generation. If there is a wonderful historical drama made for TV, it will usually soon be available on DVD for private ownership.

If one is not ready to eliminate TV, at least do not situate it in the drawing room—this area is for real life socialising, just as the dining room is only for dining. One should never keep a set in the bedroom, unless they are medically immobilised—bedchambers are for two things and they both begin with 'S.'

Television fanatics might consider placing the set in their home gym, so they can ride an exercise bike or work out on a cross-trainer while watching instead of just frittering their time away. Still, music usually encourages one to exercise better and if you do not use television at all, well done you!

Something which offers free viewing choices like a computer or DVD player may be placed in the study or den. Some people turn a family room into a home cinema area which is comfortable and fine; but please, never spend more than an hour or two viewing each day.

Unless you are extremely old, indisposed, or living with penguins in freezing Antarctica, what could possibly tempt you to spend your time viewing television? Don't watch life – live it. It is much better if you are active in business, studies, exercise, sports, dancing, family, church, attending performing arts, travel, socialising with a wide circle-of-influence, or any other aspect of real life. You are 'living' and you don't have the desire to participate in pretend life.

Those people who *do* watch TV may be thinking—well television is reality. National Geographic, Documentaries, Olympic Games and major sports events aside, is it? Perhaps 98% of programming is unnatural, rehearsed or acting. I visited a home where a youth was watching a violent programme. I asked the adolescent if he was enjoying the show and he replied 'yes, it's so real, you see people get shot every day.'

I then asked the young chap how many people he had seen get 'shot' in actual life. He was stumped, and replied 'well nobody ever.' What a co-incidence, all of the adults in the room including myself, had never witnessed any shootings, stabbings or violent crimes either. We were in Canada at the time, and aside from the country's war veterans, the majority millions have fortunately never been subject to that sort of barbarism. Reality is where *you* choose to live, and the ambience that *you* have created in your own life.

While in Canada, I once saw an excerpt in the Vancouver Courier which read: 'Hundreds of residents of the Indian city of Bombay have taken a direct approach to the problems of excessive violence and sex on the boob tube. They simply threw their TV sets out the window and into the street. Now, the news story informed us, none of the 1,200 residents of two fashionable apartment buildings owns a set.'

It is important to remember that *what you think about, you may bring about*. Every truly cruel or extremely violent act which I have ever seen, I have viewed either on film or TV news. The most horrendous scenes which are stored in the average person's mind, were first imagined through delusive programming. For more information about the mental effects of such programming, read about the 'sub-conscious' in the earlier chapter I wrote on Mind.

What about the news—isn't that an important TV service? When we consider that the majority of news is negative and feeds pessimistic thoughts to the sub-conscious mind, we will quickly realise how important it is to *keep it brief*. First of all, if you are a social person, and something major occurs, like war or peace, chances are you'll hear about it. One cannot afford to waste an hour watching negative programming, when we could hear the news from a few minutes of direct radio information.

RADIO THEN?

Radio might be as detrimental as television if one is not discerning with respect to lyrics since audio messages can be as strong as visual ones. In September 1996 you may have heard about the murder of the rap singer whose destructive words became a self-prediction (auto suggestive affirmation) to his own violent end. It is important to also avoid stations with opinionated phone-ins, which is just as bad as "chatting" on social media.

Wherever you currently reside, it is likely that you will be able to join those of discriminating taste and tune in to a sophisticated station. A good choice will cater to the enlightened intelligentsia. It may offer interesting reviews, play mellifluous classical music which is free from depressive lyrics, and there will be few or no commercials.

IN CONCLUSION

Being aware of a compulsive addictive disorder, we seek a solution. As well as doing the obvious steps—getting rid of television, cigarettes, or what have you—there is one final process. One must constantly envision the person that they want to be. Never use any ***negative*** material or verbal terminology. Don't think or say "I'm addicted to TV; I binge drink; I can't quit smoking/taking drugs; or I'm overweight." Make a habit of concentrating on what you desire to become—see yourself as a physically and emotionally healthy individual. Affirm that you are prosperous, successful, in control of your life and happy. This is the secret… learn it… practise it. Study the information on positive mental attitude, auto-suggestion, and affirmations found in the chapter on 'Mind.' Also remember that the easiest way to shield oneself from self-destructive compulsions, is to raise a protective barrier known as 'good emotional, spiritual and physical health.'

Chapter 7
Financial Freedom

Introduction

It is quite possible that you take some interest in money, or you may not be reading this sort of material. There may even be a few of you who have skimmed through the table of contents and opened the book to this chapter first. Very few people have an aversion to extra cash, and it should not be considered objectionable, unless it has been **stolen, accumulated illegally**; or, if you **use** your money for **unacceptable purposes**. Money is not to be used for prostitution, human trafficking, drug trafficking, etc. If you buy illegal drugs, then you are supporting the evil drug cartels who sell them and you are partly responsible for the horrible crimes they commit.

Money itself, is *not* the 'root of all evil,' such a notion merely depends upon what the cash is used for. Education, health centres, architecture, the arts—some of the world's greatest wonders exist because there was money to provide them. If one has negative feelings towards currency—release them; learn to concentrate only on the positive benefits which it can provide. Money is attracted to those who feel good about it and are prepared to use it for the good of all.

If one believes that money is bad, chances are that they will rarely see much of it. Fortune, like most circumstances, will attach itself to those who are open to receive. Many people have been brainwashed into believing that money is evil. How can paper or coins possibly be evil? They are simply items which are designated some value, and can be used to create good conditions or destructive ones.

Others have seen wealthy people who are miserable, and blame their unhappiness on money. Despair usually comes only to the *idle* rich—those who make no effort to find a purpose and contribute to fields of learning – science, the arts, spirit or any other form of expansion and worldly development. The idle can become bored due to a lack of creative ideas and are often prone to indulge in self-destructive compulsions, simply for want of passing time. Such idleness need never occur, and wealth need not bring misery.

Can one do better with money or without it? Free services such as churches, libraries, and health clinics are supported by generosity. How could these valuable services come into being without the charitable support of those who not only have money, but share it?

Some people actually feel guilty about having a surplus of money. Is it sinful to be rich? Not according to the Bible; however, it does state that with greater riches, comes greater obligation. ***The more riches you possess, the more benevolence you are required to show towards others***. I Timothy 6:17 reads: "Charge the rich of this world not to be proud, or to trust in the uncertainty of riches, but in God, who provides all things in abundance for our enjoyment. Let them do good and be rich in good works, giving readily, sharing with others, and thus providing for themselves a good foundation against the time to come, in order that they may lay hold on the true life."

Ecclesiasticus 31:8 reads, "Blessed is the rich man that is found without blemish: and that hath not gone after gold, nor put his trust in money nor in treasurers." Ecclesiasticus 13:30 reads, "riches are good to him that hath no sin in his conscience: and poverty is very wicked in the mouth of the ungodly."

There-in lies the truth; money is good when used for good and charitable works—this should not be so difficult. People who have trouble with this concept, might try using this affirmation: 'I like money, and use it for good things only. I release it with joy, and it flows to me in abundance.' Saying or writing this affirmation can help to re-programme the subconscious of those who find themselves either in a poor or selfish position. Remember that **THE MORE YOU GIVE, THE MORE YOU SHALL RECEIVE**. Never hoard money, learn to circulate it toward good things, and more will be given unto you… see upcoming section on charity.

What if you are just beginning this enlightened process, and you want to be generous, but you find yourself in an impecunious position. You have absolutely no money to give… what can you do? When walking down the street, *imagine* that you are giving large amounts of money to the people who pass by. Notice how you will begin to smile while doing this exercise. Even simply thinking generous thoughts will help to improve your situation by raising you to a higher vibrational level suitable to receive abundance.

I also asked someone 'what can I do?' many years ago, when I was just starting out and had no extra cash. He answered with a Persian saying, which when translated means '*IF YOU MOVE, GOD WILL PAY YOU.*' People who are without occupation and stay indoors watching TV or playing with their smart phones all day, will find little reward. Go out and move. People find money while walking down the street—they find opportunities as they read the bulletins, or while out communicating with others. Get the momentum going so that when an opportunity shows up, you can take it.

When I was given this advice so long ago, I decided to 'move.' I went out and began doing volunteer work. At the time, I was just beginning self-employment and had few prospects to keep busy with. The charity work brought me many wonderful friends and clients! Do something positive with your time and the money will follow.

One may be wishing that I will provide some 'get rich quick' advice—I won't. I will; however, share some ideas which may help people to accumulate money with greater ease. If one has patience and persistence, they may nearly be guaranteed success.

If you already have a financial planner, or successful mentor, I commend you—you're on the right track. If you have spent time reading about the rich to discover their methods for success, once again, I must say that you have extreme potential. *STUDY THE RICH, AND DO AS THEY DO*. If you mimic those who are lacking, you may have some difficult financial times ahead. *Pigeons fly with pigeons, and eagles fly with eagles.*

Every chapter in this book should help people to lead richer more pleasant life-styles. Blessings come in many different ways—good health, loyal relationships, and doing what you love to *do*. Rich is not solely money in the bank—it is a life-style. Some people have great financial wealth, but live poor unhappy lives. Others still, do not have vast fortunes, but live with joy equal to the greatest life of royalty. 'Wealth' is really just another W based on the five—who, what, when, where, why. Who you associate with, where you live, what you do, and so on. *One's quality of life revolves more around behaviour, than around money.* Jim Rohn said: "You can have more than you've got, because you can become more than you are."

Still, I too admit that poverty holds no attractions for me. Hopefully the following sections will help to guide people away from poverty consciousness, and towards the life which all of God's people deserve.

Don't fall for the myth that "It takes money, to make money." It does not matter whether a person has pots of money or whether they don't have a bean. Lack of money is not the problem—lack of money is the result of the problem! For example, instead of simply working for a boss, find a way to make yourself extremely valuable to the company, so that your employer will take you on as a partner or at least as a shareholder.

Another thing to do when starting out is to find ways to create equity and accumulate assets which increase in value. Rather than throwing money away on rent, one would take out a mortgage on the type of property which normally increases in value. Even if house prices do drop, a poor investment is no worse than a useless spend. Do not be afraid of the word 'debt'—it is good when you use it to buy items which make you more money. Owning a house can generate money in other ways aside from appreciation. The UK government has a Rent a Room scheme where hosts with an extra furnished room, can let it out and earn up to £7,500 a year tax-free.

The two suggestions above are ways that people can begin to generate money without starting out rich.

Success System for Financial Freedom

I believe that the very best way to achieve financial freedom, is to learn how to follow an appropriate system of budgeting one's income. Take the 100% or your net earnings and try to divide it as close as possible to the following success chart:

| REINVESTMENT—50% |
| FOOD/NECESSITIES—20% |
| UTILITIES—10% |
| SAVINGS/CHARITY—10% |
| ENTERTAINMENT—10% |

Reinvestment is by far the most important aspect of financial success. The smart and wealthy generally put 50% of their income towards their own private business, house purchase, and other commodities expected to increase in value. Some people with good income and permanent job positions, often make the grave mistake of renting. It is fine to put money toward ownership—as a car payment, house mortgage, and so on, but it is never wise to throw one's earnings into the wind. You will notice that the success chart does not allow any income to be put towards rental fees aside from utilities, and even there, people are wizening up and becoming more self-sufficient by installing solar panels, etc.

Another word about investments… which person do you think will accumulate more money: The one who spends 90% of their time considering ways to save, or the person who spends 90% of their energy developing new ways to earn more money? Remember the wise saying: ***It is easier to earn a large income, than to learn how to live on a small one.*** Join the smart and wealthy—earn more money. Invest 50% of your income into business, shares, or property. If you make good choices, this will generally show the greatest rate of return and quite possibly offer you the luxury which most of us desire which is passive income: *'making money while we sleep.'*

Back to the success chart. Food and necessities are self-explanatory. If one's net income is £2,000 per month, they would have £400 to put towards groceries and toiletries. This percentage should be sufficient for a healthy life-style, providing that one does not waste money on self-destructive compulsions, like drugs or cigarettes.

Charity is fundamental; consequently, I have dedicated another section to it below. Tithing is important for prosperity consciousness and for the good of mankind in general. With respect to saving—see the section on RRSPs and ways to retire as a millionaire. The book "Richest Man in Babylon" by George Samuel Clason is one of the greatest reads to encourage saving; it says, "A part of what you earn is yours to keep. It should be not less than a tenth no matter how little you earn." Some people also say that you should tithe 10%—I have joined the two together as people must determine what they can manage.

It is good to begin saving early in life. My parents wisely had me open my first savings account when I was only six years of age. I will never forget, because I had to be taught how to 'write' my signature—I was still printing at that time. Certain members of my family are thrifty; but alas, I was a black sheep—the 'spendthrift.' My father used to say to me, "save for a rainy day" and I would reply "it *is* raining!"

This brings us to the final chart percentage—entertainment, the one category which often imbalances my budget, for I tend to spend more than the allotted 10%. I have a motto also— 'spend on a rainy day.' I will share an anecdote as an example.

When I was younger, and had just become self-employed, my income was most irregular—sometimes three or four thousand dollars per month, and at other times—zero! Once, after having a particularly good summer, I decided to purchase season tickets for the symphony and theatre; plus membership to a private leisure centre which had a swimming pool, tennis courts, etc. That autumn I bought my first new car, and although I paid mostly cash, I still had to finance for three months.

Unfortunately, my business became very sparse during that winter, and I was just able to make the car payments and buy necessities like groceries and toiletries. What a blessing it was to have those season tickets to carry me through until spring! Although my funds were temporarily depleted, I still had the opportunity to live rich throughout the tough times, because I had made provisions during the prosperous days. Social activity is very important—see the chapter on entertainment. Always budget effectively for this—be sure to stay active, even during bleak financial times.

WORRY REPELS MONEY

Have you ever heard someone say: "I have to worry about money because I don't have enough to get by!" Or the opposite "I never worry about money because I always seem to have plenty." Chances are that you've heard both statements, although the first (poverty consciousness) does tend to be more common than the second (prosperity consciousness). Are these statements accurate, or actually some twisted paradox of reality like the old question 'Which came first, the chicken or the egg?' Perhaps you should *assume* you have money before it arrives. *If one constantly worries about money, they might never attract any.* The more a person worries about a lack of money, the *harder* it will be for them to earn any; whereas, the person who *never* worries about money, should find that it flows to them in abundance.

Notice how one often will not receive something, until they no longer NEED it. Change your thinking first, and the tangible will follow. If you currently suffer from poverty mentality, begin working with a prosperity affirmation as soon as possible.

TRUE WEALTH IS INDEPENDENCE

Many people have a misconception about what 'wealth' is. True wealth is the means to survive, should the 'system' collapse. Think of the historically based television series "The Waltons" about a typical North American agricultural family making their way during the Great Depression.

Appearances can be deceiving—picture two examples: One is a smart dressing government appointee who rents a fabulous apartment and a Jaguar motorcar. The second is a small landowner with an acreage large enough for some fruit trees, a vegetable garden and hay fields. He has a water well, some cattle, laying hens and a stream with trout running through his land.

One appears to be a rich executive, and the other appears to be a simple farmer. But if governments should fail, inflation rise and dollars become valueless—which person is *independently* stable? This is one of the distinctions between the old aristocrats and the nouveaux riche—the former never part with the country estate. Many of us today live a rich lifestyle and have an affluent business, but in order to have true freedom, we must also become wealthy. Webster's Collegiate Dictionary clarifies the synonyms:

Rich—implies having more than enough to gratify normal needs or desires.

Affluent—suggests prosperity by increasing wealth.

Wealthy—stresses the *possession of property* and valuable things.

INDEPENDENCE YES... AVARICE NO

In the book "Psycho-Cybernetics" by Maxwell Maltz, we read: "… that unhappiness is the sole cause of all psychosomatic ills and that happiness is the only cure. The very word 'disease' means a state of unhappiness—*dis-ease*." What truly brings happiness—must one become a multi-millionaire, or is it all a state of mind?

If you believe that you will never be content unless you become super-rich, then most psychologists would tell you right up front that you will never be happy. If on the other hand, you can take pleasure in simply 'having enough', then you are very likely joyful already. The happiest people whom I know, generally live very simple lives. They have fine food and drink; a happy healthy family with a great circle of friends; they work for themselves by doing whatever it is they love without worrying about pleasing a 'superior'; they own or are gradually financing their own property.

If an individual believes that they cannot experience joy without possessing a yacht, a jet, a huge company, tonnes of jewels, and so forth, then such a person has a misunderstanding of the word 'success.' Success is achieving a favourable outcome. I think several royal ladies, including our late Queen, would have happily settled as chatelaines running a fine house – gentlewomen farmers with a garden to tend, horse and hound, an interesting private vocation and a fine circle of friends.

In Dr Wayne Dyer's recording entitled "Choose to Live and Love" he talks about the psychology of ARRIVING rather than the psychology of STRIVING. He speaks of the disease called 'MORE' and says "If you don't know how to appreciate what you have *totally*, then you don't need anything else."

Be independent, happy, and productive… but do not succumb to avarice.

RRSP/Investments

IN RETIREMENT

The majority of people have wondered at times how they might spend their senior, leisure years. Most of us want to have enough income for the basic comforts of life, and perhaps more importantly, enough to retain our independence. How many people are prepared to lose their freedom or to become forced to live in an old-age group home? Very few, I would imagine.

A purpose of this book is to help people accept the best and live royally, so consider the English royal family for a moment: did the late Queen Mother, Prince Philip or Queen Elizabeth II reside in a public care home? Of course not— it would be out of the question. In upper circles this simply is not done. One usually lives on their own estate as long as they can afford to keep up the private help—maid, nurse, or whatever care is needed.

Children usually help out and sometimes live-in, but what if a senior has no heirs? Should the government claim responsibility? Nice thought, but many health care systems do not provide free out-of-hospital carers. Also, some pension plans will likely have disappeared completely by the time Generation X or the Millennials reach a senior age. Therefore, we all must plan carefully in our youth. If one is wise, and begins RRSP contributions in their late teens or early twenties, contributing for several years, they should have no difficulty in achieving independence in later life.

RRSP

One of the simplest and best proven ways to acquire financial independence is by contributing to an RRSP (Registered Retirement Savings Plan). The reason why RRSPs are often chosen over other interest-bearing options such as GICs (guaranteed income certificates), is because tax on the interest of the RRSP is not payable until funds are actually removed. Therefore, one can make deposits and let early contributions grow for years, without having to pay tax. Until that glorious day when income tax exists no more, RRSPs will have to do. If one does desire to remove funds without paying tax, the best way is to do so when they have little or no other income e.g.: retirement, returning to school, taking maternity leave, starting a private business, etc.

In my lifetime, interest rates have varied from as low as 1% to as high as 21%—so for demonstration purposes only, we will use a middle figure of 12%. How fast could one double their money? Use the rule of 72, i.e., divide 72 by the rate of return. If we divide 72 by 12, our money would double approximately every 6 years—not too bad.

EARLY BEGINNINGS=LARGE REWARDS

If we were to deposit a meagre $200 per month... how many years would one be required to contribute, in order to be a millionaire by the age of 65? ... 50 years? 40 years? 30 years? 20? How many of you said 5? 5 years multiplied by $2,400 per year, equals a total contribution of only $12,000. Could $12,000 actually turn into a million? Try a million and a half!! What's the secret? The strategy is to *BEGIN EARLY*.

If one person deposits $2,000 per annum for only six years, and another person deposits $2,000 per annum for 35 years—which one will accumulate more money? It depends who began contributing at an earlier age. Even five or six years earlier will make an enormous difference. See the chart below. Would you contribute $12,000 if you knew that it could make you a millionaire? Who wouldn't? *Encourage young people in your family to begin their RRSP by the age of 20.* Help them out if you can and also deposit some of the money they receive for Christmas, birthdays, Confirmation or other presents throughout their youth.

YEAR	AGE	DEPOSIT	PLUS 12% INTEREST		AGE	DEPOSIT	PLUS 12% INT
2024	21	$2000	2,240.00	Person #1 begins young	Person #2 only begins six years later		
2025	22	2000	4,748.80	and makes deposits for	and must therefore contribute more		
2026	23	2000	7,558.66	only six years	than 30 years to accumulate		
2027	24	2000	10,705.69		a similar amount!		
2028	25	2000	14,230.38				
2029	26	2000	18,178.02				
2030				20,359.38	27	$2000	2,240.00
2031				22,802.51	28	2000	4,748.80
2032				25,538.81	29	2000	7,558.66
2033				28,603.46	30	2000	10,705.69
2034				32,035.88	31	2000	14,230.38
2035				35,880.18	32	2000	18,178.02
2036				40,185.80	33	2000	22,599.38
2037				45,008.10	34	2000	27,551.31
2038				50,409.07	35	2000	33,097.47
2039				56,458.16	36	2000	39,309.16
2040				63,233.14	37	2000	46,266.26
2041				70,821.12	38	2000	54,058.21
2042				79,319.65	39	2000	62,785.20
2043				88,838.01	40	2000	72,559.42
2044				99,498.57	41	2000	83,506.55
2045				111,438.39	42	2000	95,767.34
2046				124,810.99	43	2000	109,499.41
2047				139,788.30	44	2000	124,879.33
2048				156,562.89	45	2000	142,104.84
2049				175,350.42	46	2000	161,397.42
2050				196,392.48	47	2000	183,005.11
2051				219,959.57	48	2000	207,205.72
2052				246,354.71	49	2000	234,310.40
2053				275,917.27	50	2000	264,667.64
2054				309,027.34	51	2000	298,667.75
2055				346,110.62	52	2000	336,747.88
2056				387,643.89	53	2000	379,397.62
2057				434,161.15	54	2000	427,165.33
2058				486,260.48	55	2000	480,665.16
2059				544,611.73	56	2000	540,584.97
2060				609,965.13	57	2000	607,695.16
2061				683,160.94	58	2000	682,858.57
2062				765,140.25	59	2000	767,041.59
2063				856,957.08	60	2000	861,326.58
2064				959,791.92	61	2000	966,925.76
2065				1,074,496.69	62	2000	1,085,196.80
2066				1,203,962.90	63	2000	1,217,660.40
2067				1,348,438.40	64	2000	1,366,019.60
2068				1,510,251.00	65	2000	1,532,181.90
TOTAL EARNED BY EACH AT AGE 65				1,510,251.00			1,532,181.90
TOTAL EACH PERSON DEPOSITED				12,000.00			76,000.00

It almost makes one wish that interest rates begin to pay out 12% again!!

EVERYONE CAN BE A MILLIONAIRE

Even though interest rates are not paying out as high as they once did, things could certainly change again, especially with inflation currently on the rise. More and more people today are beginning to realise how easy it is to become a millionaire. Why wouldn't they, with all of the financial information which abounds to promote this pleasing prospect? We have already discussed that the sooner one begins investing, the more rewards they will reap. Someone who bought their first cheap house 30 years ago may well be sitting on a million-dollar property today. Bear in mind; however, that *even starting to save and invest late, is better than not at all*.

When a young adult is just starting out on the road to riches, you may hear them say "Save money? ... I hardly earn enough to live on." Many of us have been in that position, but don't forget that: *To sacrifice early, provides huge dividends later on*. Go back and read the previous page RRSP sample one more time—would you rather save for six years, or 35? Think long and hard about that one.

Consider a young wage-earner who works for eight hours a day at one full-time job, or has several part-time positions which total the average of eight hours a day. Multiply that by five days to get a 40-hour work week. If the person earns minimum-wage, what will be their total monthly income? Not much—so let us investigate a very low-income example below:

Remember the example of a live-in domestic who might work 40 hours a week at 10 dollars per hour, producing a monthly income of $1,600. The householder subtracts $550 to cover the helper's room and board. The income remaining is $1,050. Fortunately, there are no additional costs incurred for rent, food, toiletries, utilities or transportation. The $1,050 is disposable income, and even if the domestic spends over half of that on personal items like entertainment, he/she could easily deposit the remaining $500 in an RRSP.

Not every minimum-wage earner has the benefit of boarding where they work. Some will need to find a different economical form of shared accommodation, or live with family for the first few years. The important thing to do, is contribute a decent amount each month to their savings.

If the individual in the case study remained in their low-salary position permanently, but began saving at an early age, he/she is almost guaranteed to accumulate a fine nest egg. The dishwasher in the restaurant where you dine may well be a millionaire one day if they invest wisely in property, savings, shares, etc. at an early age.

OUR FINANCIAL SITUATION IS A PERSONAL CHOICE.

If a person who is broke, asks you for advice on becoming rich… try to help them. But remember, that not everyone will take the appropriate action, or follow wise advice. If someone truly accepts being poor, we cannot force them to change. In liberal countries, people have the right and freedom to be rich or poor—believe it or not, some people actually choose the latter.

Credit Rating

In most financial systems, it is hard to think of anything which surpasses the priority of one's personal credit rating. If you are not sure where you presently stand on this vital issue, contact your local Credit Bureau. Credit scores typically range on a number scale and are placed into one of five categories: poor, fair, good, very good and excellent.

As an example, consider the North American system which uses a number scale from 0-9. Zero may represent new or unused accounts; unfortunately, this does not give prospective lenders any information on whether or not one is reliable. R1 is the best rating, and indicates that some person or institution has not only given one credit, but it also indicates that the receiver was responsible, and made all payments on time. R2 may indicate a payment which was received 1 to 30 days late. A three rating would represent a payment which was received up to 60 days late, etc. R9, of course, is indicative of a problem, delinquent credit rating.

The bureau should kindly answer your inquiries, and explain dates and reports which have been filed for or against your record by various agencies. Most countries have a similar system, and after you have become aware of your current status, you can proceed to improve upon it.

Good credit ratings are established by borrowing money in the form of a loan, or by using credit cards ***and making all repayments on time or early***. As your credit rating and personal collateral increase, so too, can one increase the amount of their ***line of credit***. We know that large developers like Donald Trump did not build projects with cash taken directly from their pockets. If you want to go far, you need to establish strong financial backing. Begin early—apply for a credit card as soon as you have secured your first job and begun to earn a pay cheque.

If a person possesses a responsible attitude and always pays their bills on time, a good credit card can only benefit. Dependable people can enjoy free credit for one month, while their cash earns interest in a bank account, and many cards offer wonderful benefits like 'cash back.' After establishing a good rating, one can usually narrow their plastic down to two or three ***gold/platinum*** cards—maybe a Visa, an Amex and a MasterCard.

Every few months, they can telephone the agency of the card which they use, and ask for an increase in the amount of the credit limit. Extend this limit as high as you feel is necessary. I once went into a piano shop and bought an inexpensive used piano. I asked the gentleman if I could pay with my credit card, and he said certainly. Then he proceeded to tell me of one other client, who bought a new grand for $45,000 and put the whole amount on their gold card. Imagine if that person were using a card with benefits, such as aero points—they would be well on their way to a free flight.

Some credit cards also offer free air travel life insurance, car rental insurance, medical travel insurance, purchase insurance, and various other benefits. If someone was over 30 years of age and still did not possess a gold/platinum card, they might seriously reassess their education regarding finance. By that time, most people have spent a decade in different lines of work or business, and should have established a good rating; but remember, it's never too late.

Probably the best part about creating a reliable reputation will be the fact that commendable financial institutions will then offer one a ***personal line of credit*** at a much lower interest rate. Establishing a strong personal line of credit is very important for those who have high expectations of going far economically.

When I speak of using plastic cards—please be aware, that I refer only to the purpose of creating and maintaining a good ***credit rating***. I would ***never*** use personal ***debit*** cards to make purchases because they offer no benefits! Cards are for using OPM—other people's money… never your own. You want to establish a CREDIT rating… not a debit rating. For convenience's sake, I might use direct-debit to pay utilities, although if I could score points by paying them with my credit card, I would.

EASY MONEY?

Easy money, alias 'get rich quick' schemes, are attempted often, but succeed rarely. This sad technique is generally practised by those we consider to be gamblers. Gambling basically refers to luck without strategy, for example: playing slot machines or buying lottery tickets. True, somebody usually wins, but millions of other people do not. If you do tend to be intrigued by chance, why not consider becoming a speculator, rather than a gambler. Speculating is related to gambling; however, it allows one the privilege of adding ***knowledge*** to luck.

People speculate on horse races, or playing the stock market. Speculating can offer more security than gambling if one studies their subject properly. If there are only eight horses running in a race, and you invest in the best horse to 'show', your odds of being in the money are good. If you invest in mid-price range stocks which have a stable steady growth, you should do all right.

By playing it safe, one may not make 'big' money, but they can make quick money. Speculators lose their investments, when they become careless or avaricious. If one is susceptible to greed, and invests too frequently on 'long shots', they may end up wasting money just as most gamblers do.

Remember also that stocks, race-horses, and such are generally owned by private investors like yourself. Speculating supports personal free enterprise, but gambling supports big business. Big casinos, bingo halls, and other large systems where only one party has control and ownership should, in good conscience, be avoided.

Another get rich trap, can be risky over-hyped business ventures. Don't be taken in by smooth talking con-artists, who are eager to spend your money, but reluctant to invest any of their own. Business can be excellent, providing that you have done your research, and left no rock unturned. Approach all business ventures with caution.

CREATIVE SPENDING

Many people experience great difficulty and assume a position of distress, because they are obliged to make certain purchases for their daily activities. Have you ever heard someone complain about the price of fuel? This is one commodity which many people utilise on a daily basis. The question is… how can one make the necessary expense more acceptable, and less aggravating? Be a wise business person; learn how to receive the most value from your purchases.

Since solar panels have become more popular and widely used, there are homes which run completely on electricity without even requiring a gas-line to be connected. Also, instead of driving a large, extremely fuel consuming automobile, consider purchasing an electric, hybrid or at least a low consumption petrol motorcar. *Be a wise consumer—this may determine whether you smile or sob following your purchase decisions.*

INSURANCE

Insurance is a somewhat controversial subject. Some people swear by its importance, and others swear that it is merely self-serving. One thing that we all know: *Insurance companies are in business to make money, not to lose money.* Try to remember that. Another odd thing about insurance is that 'when we are poor, we often can't afford it—and after we become rich, we rarely need it.'

I believe that some types of insurance are quite necessary: medical—when travelling or in countries without free Medicare/NHS; motorcar—accident liability; property—loss of possessions or house fire—and other forms which are incurred by accidental acts of nature. Becoming ill cannot always be prevented, likewise, if lightening should strike your house and set it ablaze, compensation would be nice.

Unfortunately, many other types of insurance are the product of the 'blame' mind set. People refusing to take responsibility for their own misfortunes and trying desperately to make someone else pay, often by form of a lawsuit. We don't want to assume the shameful and degrading reputation of being known as a 'sue-you' society.

We can see where this attitude has led, as we go to pay our car insurance premiums. When it begins to cost $2000 per year for vehicle and personal liability, it gets to the point where insurance is no longer as feasible as it once was. Indeed, often the car repair costs less than the insurance. If one were to omit the purchase of insurance, and be fortunate not to have any accidents for approximately 10 years, they could save an amount of money equivalent to buy a brand-new car. Personal injury claims may also become a practise of the past, as insurance companies can no longer afford the continual abuse of questionable 'make me rich quick' lawsuits such as fraudulent whiplash injuries.

Back to insurance... what about life insurance? This seems to be a wonderful programme, if you are selling it and making the commission, but should one actually buy it? If you have a spouse or dependants who rely completely upon your support and you are not yet able to leave a substantial bestowment, you may wish to purchase life insurance. Life insurance can be a blessing for the survivors of a deceased person who was not yet financially established.

On the other hand, people who manage their money wisely, and deposit into saving programmes or make good investments, can arrange to leave everything to their beneficiaries, and may not need to purchase life insurance. NOTE: The very ill or aged, who are aware that they have a short time remaining—usually transfer major accounts, investments, and property titles *before* they become deceased. My neighbour used to call this 'giving with a warm hand instead of a cold one.' This protects the inheritors from disputes and high legal costs afterward.

BEGGARS ARE NOT BORN

How many babies have you seen lying outside in the street begging? None... because people are not born to be beggars. The Bible instructs us to give alms to the poor, and we certainly must abide by this, for there are often times when people find themselves in a *temporarily* impecunious position. But what of those who choose to make a 'career' out of begging?

II Thessalonians 3:8 "Neither did we eat any man's bread at his cost, but we worked night and day in labour and toil, so that we might not burden any of you." Unfortunately, what some beggars do not realise, is that they often work much harder for their money, than the average person. What appears to be acquired for free, can actually take hours of degrading work. Washing dishes in a warm restaurant, or shining shoes in a hotel lobby, would likely provide far better rewards emotionally and monetarily.

If a baby were left in a basket on the sidewalk, certainly someone would adopt and care for it. Begging is not the lot of infants, but the choice of adults in need of education. Instead of merely tossing a few coins to those who approach you, whenever possible, offer them some form of part-time work.

TWO ROADS TO FINANCIAL FAILURE

ENVY: The negative emotion of envy is so unworthy, that it actually made the list given to Moses. Remember the 10th Commandment— "Thou shalt not covet thy neighbour's goods." Not only does this command forbid all desire to take or keep unjustly what belongs to others, but it also forbids *envy* at their success. One is obliged to return what they've borrowed, and one must not envy their associates for possessing it.

A priest once shared a story during his homily: An impecunious man was living in a democratic capitalist country, and one day he dropped to his knees, and looking up to the Lord, he prayed with sincere gratitude "Heavenly Father, thank you so much for giving my neighbour a fine house and good milk cow— please provide me with blessings also." In another corner of the world, a similarly impoverished man was living in a state of communism. This fellow looked up to the sky and said, "God, I have nothing… my neighbour has a new house and a fat cow—let his house burn and the cow die!"

How did Winston Churchill sum it up? 'Capitalism is the unequal sharing of blessings—socialism is the equal sharing of miseries.'

An attitude of envy only serves to create misery for all—happier the man who can rejoice in his neighbour's blessings. More rewards will surely come to the first man who was able to be grateful, rather than envious.

GREED: The second path to failure is through avarice. With envy we observed the faults of the man who had *less*, but greed can be the curse of those who always want *more*. In modern times, the cow may be considered your private business, and the milk might be your knowledge and profits. If you are the wise person who has earned a good cow—what harm will come if you share some of the milk?

If your church takes up a special collection to help those where a natural disaster has occurred or for the poor immigrant family who has just joined your parish… are you prepared to give? Everyone has something to offer. Some can afford a lot of money; others are practically cash broke, but will donate a blanket, kitchen ware, or simply their time to the new family. There is no excuse for lack of charity—as the Bible says in the book of Tobias 4:9 "If thou have much, give abundantly: if thou have little, take care even so to bestow willingly a little."

It is naturally wise to budget your income, but recall that the success system allows 10% for savings and charity. Circulating money is vital to accomplishment—what you send out often returns more easily. Hoarding money has an opposite effect. It brings loneliness and loss of respect from others. Who wants to associate with the rich person who is cheap and unwilling to share? Who wants to constantly treat the moocher, who has plenty of their own money, but never reciprocates?

We also notice that those who scrimp and save and struggle with poverty consciousness have such a difficult time accumulating money… while luxuries seem to flow endlessly to those who are generous.

CHARITY

Some people may think that allocating a percentage of their income to charity is too difficult, but notice how these are generally the same people who are struggling with poverty consciousness and lack. Why is this? It is because hoarding puts a stop to the system of circulation—as money moves away, so too it can flow back. Those who circulate their money freely should always find that it returns more easily. The Bible explains it best of all, see Luke 6:38 "Give, and it shall be given to you, good measure, pressed down, shaken together, running over, shall pour into your lap. For with what measure you measure, it shall be measured to you."

I doubt that being generous with money or time, has ever harmed anyone. We are told to abide by faith, hope and charity; but the greatest of these is charity—for charity is *love*. When being charitable, do not do so in expectation of reward; be a giver, not a trader. Share with those who are not able to repay you, like religious nuns and priests. Give solely for love and the satisfaction of giving.

What should we give? Give to others, that which you believe is worthy of sharing, that which you would enjoy having yourself. Whatever you need the most, spend time giving it. What if one is broke? A philanthropist is a person who donates time, money, material possessions, experience, skills or talent to help create a better world. Therefore, everyone can contribute something to the welfare and success of others. Find a channel of service to humanity. Charity does not need to be a monetary action. Do volunteer work: share your time and also give emotional support to those who need encouragement. You will achieve your full potential more readily, when you help others to reach theirs.

If you want to be philanthropic, and you *do* have money to share with worthy causes, be very selective. Remember that your money should only be used to promote the POSITIVE aspects of life. For example: If you want to bless people with free education you could donate to libraries, or find a way to help individuals. One might provide free advice as I offer on our website livingroyally.uk and don't be afraid to over-deliver.

If you wish to promote peace and charity… give to churches which support humanity. If you desire more natural beauty… support the environment and wild-life organisations. If you want to expand cultural beauty… donate to the live arts—galleries, opera, theatre… or become a sponsor for a new writer or an artist.

Tobias 4:7 "Give alms out of thy substance, and turn not away thy face from any poor person: for so it shall come to pass that the face of the Lord shall not be turned from thee."

BE GENEROUS—SAVE TAX

In some countries saving our receipts from church and other charitable donations can be used at the end of each year as a tax deduction. This is a wonderful system which encourages generosity. When I lived in Canada, the deduction rate was a mere 17% up to $250, and 29% on the balance of donations.

If you are partially or totally self-employed, one can take greater advantage by *converting donations into gifts* For example: A real estate agent enjoys supporting the symphony, and would like to make a $100 annual contribution. By making a $100 donation they can claim 17%, i.e., only $17. If, instead, they purchase concert tickets, or one symphony charity ball fund-raiser ticket for $100, they could give this present to any associate/prospective client. Not only will they be able to claim the whole *gift* amount of the $100 as an expense, but at the same time they will be making their clients very happy, and effectively promoting the orchestra. *Change donations into gifts*—this way all three parties, the giver, the recipient and the organisation will benefit.

BE GRATEFUL

It may be a nice gesture that people give thanks on Thanksgiving or other special holidays, but it is of more importance that we learn to be grateful *every* day. This is one of the most important steps in creating 'affluence' consciousness.

After one has achieved or accomplished something, they shouldn't simply take it for granted; but rather, appreciate it. If all of your life, you wanted a piano, and now you've finally bought one—enjoy it! Play it, polish it, be glad, and thank God for your blessings. Try saying an affirmative prayer, such as: "The world abounds with blessings from an infinite supply—God provides all of our needs—thank you Heavenly Father for thy blessings now." Learn to always have an attitude of gratitude for this will elevate your vibrational frequency and bring better to you.

INCOME TAX

I would like to begin this topic with a quote from Alex Doulis' book entitled "Take Your Money and Run." He writes "In order to escape from the system you have to maximise your earnings. If you assess your current situation, you will find that your highest cost of living is taxes. Eliminate the luxury of taxes and you double your income." In Canada, just over a century ago, a *'temporary'* tax was initiated to pay for the first world war. Alas, the war ended, but the *workers' income* tax remains.

SUFFER FEW FOOLS—ENDURE FEW TAXES

We are a very unique culture —*capitalists with a social conscience*. We sing the praises of free enterprise and Medicare in the same breath and this is a wonderful thing.

Governments were originally established long ago strictly to provide a *judiciary court, police system, and military*. Most of us are prepared to reach gently outside of those boundaries and support the very important *medical care* services as well; but we cautiously reject government ownership in land or business.

Our social morality insists that we contribute enough tax to provide free medical services for one and all. This includes welfare assistance for orphaned children, destitute seniors, and all others who are *physically, mentally or emotionally unable to care for themselves*. Legally, in Canada, no one can be turned away from a hospital or elderly care home… even if they are penniless. One can rightfully be very proud of this humane system and most of us agree that the four uses of taxes mentioned are quite acceptable.

How many people are aware that one simple material (spending) tax *would provide revenue for both medical care and judicial, policing and military*? A reasonable tax on merchandise (non-food) items is fair for all—the more luxuries purchased; the more tax contributed. Like karma, the more one takes from this world, the more one must return. *Spending taxes, sometimes referred to as IVA, GST, VAT, etc. should be sufficient.*

If people were not forced to pay income tax on their labours, they would have much more money to *spend* on home improvements, or items like a new motorcar, jewellery, accessories and such. This would *greatly improve the economy* and the government would generate *more income* from 'spending tax' than from 'working/income tax.' Which tax sounds fairer and can be better regulated? We already have council tax on our home property to pay for the neighbourhood fire department, rubbish collection and street repairs.

So, what went wrong… why are some people burdened with worker's income and other outrageous taxes? As the decades did pass, some countries became relatively 'absorbed' by government. Alex Doulis explains "You see, governments, like all institutions, have as their first objective their own self-preservation." Horrible, but true—political bodies often took control of utilities, schools, business, postal, transportation and even property rights.

Mandatory unemployment insurance and workers compensation should be private and optional like fire, car, life, and all other forms of insurance.

When governments confiscate too many freedoms, they also inherit a burden… this is known as *'deficit.'* The worst scenario is the *'valueless'* dollar which can occur if spending is not curtailed and deficits reduced. People do not appreciate overbearing; hence the popular saying *the government which governs least, governs best*.

What solutions? Libertarians are too civilised to display violent revolt, but too independent to tolerate socialist control. With quiet determination, more and more individuals become self-employed, self-sufficient, and escape the perils of mandatory programmes and taxes.

Rather than fight 'the system' many entrepreneurs simply prefer to abandon it. ***Most would agree to pay a single merchandise spending tax to cover the greatly important medical care and judiciary/policing, but employment/income*** tax is quite another matter. North Americans of pioneering spirit in general, do not appreciate being punished for working hard. Therefore, as would be expected, many take their business elsewhere—at the time of writing, there are nine states in the U.S. which do not charge income tax.

Fortunately, not all countries have been swallowed by 'state-control.' If you are becoming established and successful, ask your financial advisor which countries will 'cater to your intelligence' rather than 'penalise it.' Not all nations expect payment from those who engage themselves in occupation. Many countries are relatively tax friendly—consider: Andorra, Antigua, Austria, Bahamas, Bahrain, Barbados, Belize, British Virgin Islands, Caicos, Cayman Islands, Channel Islands, Gibraltar, Grenada, Guatemala, Isle of Man, Ireland, Liechtenstein, Luxembourg, Monaco, Netherlands, Switzerland, and San Marino on the Italian peninsula. Hopefully, one day our tax systems will be revamped so that hard-working people will stop wanting to leave otherwise fine countries.

I spent part of my time living in a province which even had a property purchase tax—imagine that people were actually ***punished*** for becoming homeowners! This shameful practise also goes on in many European countries and is sometimes referred as 'stamp duty.' This should only be used as a ***spending tax*** when one purchases multiple properties—it should never be charged for a person's ***principal inhabited*** residence. Nor should there be an inheritance tax on a property if the inheritor makes it his or her main house to occupy and maintain.

Some parts of North America also have exorbitant property council taxes. It is not only the 'young working people' who are being hurt by this, but many senior citizen homeowners who are considered 'PROPERTY RICH—CASH POOR.' They have two options—sell their hard-earned life-time homes, or re-finance them in order to pay the exorbitant property taxes. England has a much fairer system of council tax.

One of the wisest ways to avoid the punishment of '***working tax***' is to do as much as you can by ***trade*** also known as the ***barter system***. If you're a photographer and your house need re-shingling, while your friend is a roofer who needs a photographer at his wedding—do a trade! Exchange no money… pay no tax… help thy neighbour. Having said this, one cannot expect to make a living using the barter system; this is why most people prefer a spending tax as opposed to a worker's income tax.

Keep a business card file—the wise person has a contact in every field. If one is just starting out in life, and still has few contacts, or is not yet capable of offering a service in return—they may have no option but to pay; ergo, when you do hire, use **self-employed contractors. You should not be held responsible for workers' compensation, income tax records, or other bureaucratic red tape.** Consider the example of a real estate office: Most real estate agents today choose to be self-employed because they will retain a higher percentage of the total commission, and they will also have the liberty to work as they please. The self-employed sales people are responsible for keeping their own records—tax registration, income, expenses, and so forth. The company or franchise often serves merely as an umbrella—to offer a name, manager, or sales tools.

Canada, like many countries, has a wonderful guideline, known as the '*Competition Act*', which permits freedom of pricing in private business. This act encourages competitive fair terms and *prohibits price-fixing*. For example—your realtor, dentist, music instructor, or any other private professional cannot insist 'this is the standard fee in our occupation'—*every rate must be negotiable, and everyone has the right to search for the best value.*

What does the future hold? Will hard-working residents find any reasons to remain in over-taxed countries or will they follow Alex Doulis' advice by 'taking their money and running?'

In the meantime, if you are prepared to brave it out, read plenty of financial books and ask a wise accountant for good counsel. Some people who have small businesses find that incorporating or creating a Limited Company can save tax dollars.

The true secret to 'the good life' is *freedom*—disconnect from all or any controlling bodies. The upper classes have known for centuries that *independence* and 'royal living' are synonymous[2].

---

[2] Regarding public and private enterprise—one might consider taking advantage whenever governments let loose of their controls. The moment that Royal Mail decided to go private, my husband and I immediately bought shares. It is important to help such traditional services flourish, especially in these days of 'Big Brother' monitoring every move one makes. We all know (or should know) that mobiles, email, etc. are not private forms of communication while postal mail is.

TALK IS CHEAP

There is a common understanding in high society, that those who have money, never discuss it. C-people consider it very tacky to haggle over prices or discuss the cost of items. On the reverse side of the spectrum, we notice that people of lower social class or culture are typically preoccupied with money—perhaps because it is such a novelty to them.

If someone is impertinent enough to ask you about money, there is no need to rebuke them. You may answer in a very kind manner by pleasantly saying 'I'm terribly sorry, but that is a private matter.' When someone enquires 'may I ask a personal question?' You might respond: 'I don't promise to answer.'

It is amazing that some people will look at one's new motorcar and ask how much it's worth. The information could be discreetly obtained by online research or a single call or email to an automobile sales office. If one has a desire to know what someone else's Gucci shoes cost, they can find out for themselves at any Gucci shop or website.

No one should ask the cost of an item, unless that item has been offered 'for sale.' Those who are curious about someone's net worth, should be able to make accurate deductions without asking them. What colour is their credit card? What company or assets do they own? If they have clear freehold title to a house in a much sought after, expensive location, we can assume that they are worth some money. Asking personal questions about the obvious, **will not** make a person appear very clever.

Oscar Wilde's definition of a cynic—someone who "knows the price of everything, and the value of nothing." It's not what we have, but how we live. The person who tells others that they spent a fortune on magnificent china, but fears the pleasure of eating from it, mystifies me. There is little value in talk—much more in action.

ONWARD AND UPWARD

Once in my younger years, after I had already experienced personal and financial success, I made the decision to change occupations and soon found myself in a rather sparse position. There is a favourable aspect to this account. Although my funds were depleted, I 'the person' remained the same. Of course, I still owned a motorcar, and some very fine accessories which I had accumulated in the previous years. I also possessed high quality business apparel—one doesn't really lose the shirt off their back. Bills could be paid by credit for some time, since I established a good rating while the grass was greener.

I had knowledge and experience in business—and taste, once cultivated, does not readily dissipate. I rationed the meagre earnings of my new state, and apportioned a small budget for live arts, the occasional ball, and other cultural delights of which I had previously partaken. I dressed and behaved in the same manner as when I possessed plenty of 'extra cash.' I did not give up my circle of sincere associates—loyal friends are for life.

Because everything appeared as usual, new acquaintances and old alike, automatically assumed that I was financially secure, even though I was temporarily monetarily disadvantaged. So, one may ask—what is the principal message of this anecdote? Having little money does not have to insinuate poor or reduced social distinction. This is a very positive axiom… to understand that a great deal of success is 'internal.' *How you feel about yourself, is generally how others perceive you to be*. Once you have arrived, nothing should ever detract your accomplishments.

There is more good news. Because I assumed a continued state of prosperity, the money very quickly began to return. *Abundance moves in the direction where it is expected to travel*. Perhaps this is the reason why people who have earned riches once, and lost or spent them, often find it easier to acquire their second fortune.

If one is currently going through an unprosperous phase, they should first learn how to direct their scant budget towards a quality lifestyle. Second, but just as important—they must have powerful mind control, and continue to manifest an affluent way of thinking. This book has listed dozens of ways to live rich even if you are not… it is not solely the 'money', but rather the 'attitude' which makes one triumphant.

As I mentioned on a previous occasion, if we have a desire to progress in a certain area, we would be wisest to follow the examples of those who have already attained similar objectives. I love to study people, historical or current, and one interesting personality I read about was Wallis Windsor. If you are familiar with her biography, you may recall that her mother became widowed early—and although surrounded by others of affluent life-styles, theirs was a constant financial struggle to merely keep afloat.

Wallis may have possessed good taste early on, but money was another matter—and consequently she battled with this disadvantage well into her thirties. Despite no skill for earning cash, Wallis still had powerful attributes to her merit. In Anne Edwards' "Wallis: The Novel", the author uses the phrase "must have, will get" which was very likely characteristic of Wallis's nature. Somehow, she always managed to travel extensively, which is one of the greatest forms of education and opportunity. Her 'royal' road was partially paved due to communication skills, since she also possessed the marvellous talent for socialising.

Most important of all... despite her limited financial position, she **always retained determination to live prosperously**. Read that last sentence again, and remember that these are the qualities which make up the foundation of most success stories. If you are not yet practising them, why not give it a try?

Goal Setting

If *we achieve what we think about all day long*, then let us start thinking about our goals. It does not matter if you have money, you first need to ***build your vision and set your purpose – follow this by faith and gratitude.*** Release any limiting beliefs – use affirmations until you are convinced you can accomplish your goal; and the people, events and circumstances will start to move towards you. Consider your goal and then ask yourself "who do I need to become—what do I need to do?" Begin to think, dress, speak and act the part now. Many people make a goal card to carry and read throughout the day. You might write "I am so grateful and happy now to be super healthy and wealthy!" Finally, surrender and enjoy the journey. When inspired to action, do it and keep following the trail of momentum.

Use the following worksheets regarding your own personal ambitions. If you can think of additional objectives which you would like to plan for, use a regular sheet of paper, and simply follow the worksheet example, substituting the name of your goal at the top of the page.

Planning is a vital part of making our dreams become a reality—do this exercise when you have some peaceful time all to yourself and can concentrate seriously on what you truly desire to create in your life. I will now illustrate with an example to show how this goal setting sheet is to be used. Let's use TRAVEL for the illustration:

The following is a goal setting example which I wrote in my youth decades ago.

PAST: Only North America—Canada and U.S.

PRESENT: Travelling throughout Italy.

FUTURE: Immediate future—wish to travel through more of Europe—England, France, Austria, Germany, Spain, Hungary, Belgium, etc.

More distant future: Would like to see the other four main continents: South America, Africa, Asia, and Oceania.

WHAT ACTION REQUIRED TO ACHIEVE THE DESIRED RESULTS?

- Renew passport and international driver's licence.
- May live in Italy, because it is located abroad, and would make European travel more accessible.
- Remain involved in occupations which can travel with me—namely private business and writing.
- Study basics of various foreign languages.
- Research each location on my immediate travel list.
- Make arrangements with friends and travelling companions.

Always be specific; clearly name your precise goals—where you want to go... what you want to do. Equally important to writing/setting goals is the follow up. Be sure to actually do the activities, which you have written under 'required action.' Let's say you want to publish a book. After selecting your topic, you should immediately choose your date for the launch; then commit to your project ... do research; set aside time for writing each day, and so on.

WHAT CHANGES WOULD YOU LIKE TO MAKE?

Chapter one of this book began with one's name—you might want to alter yours or simply some aspect of yourself—you can begin here.

****

YOU
PAST:
PRESENT:
FUTURE:
WHAT ACTION REQUIRED TO ACHIEVE DESIRED RESULT?

****

LOCATION
PAST:
PRESENT:
FUTURE:
WHAT ACTION REQUIRED TO ACHIEVE DESIRED RESULT?

****

DWELLING
PAST:
PRESENT:
FUTURE:
WHAT ACTION REQUIRED TO ACHIEVE THE DESIRED RESULT?

****

OCCUPATION
PAST:
PRESENT:
FUTURE:
WHAT ACTION REQUIRED TO ACHIEVE THE DESIRED RESULT?

****

EDUCATION
PAST:
PRESENT:
FUTURE:
WHAT ACTION REQUIRED TO ACHIEVE THE DESIRED RESULT?

****

SPIRITUAL
PAST:
PRESENT:
FUTURE:
WHAT ACTION REQUIRED TO ACHIEVE THE DESIRED RESULT?

****

ACTIVITIES
PAST:
PRESENT:
FUTURE:
WHAT ACTION REQUIRED TO ACHIEVE THE DESIRED RESULT?

****

CLUBS/MEMBERSHIPS
PAST:
PRESENT:
FUTURE:
WHAT ACTION REQUIRED TO ACHIEVE THE DESIRED RESULT?

****

TRAVEL
PAST:
PRESENT:
FUTURE:
WHAT ACTION REQUIRED TO ACHIEVE THE DESIRED RESULT?

****

LANGUAGE AND SPEECH
PAST:
PRESENT:
FUTURE:
WHAT ACTION REQUIRED TO ACHIEVE THE DESIRED RESULT?

****

MIND/THOUGHT PATTERNS
PAST:
PRESENT:
FUTURE:
WHAT ACTION REQUIRED TO ACHIEVE THE DESIRED RESULT?

****

FINANCIAL
PAST:
PRESENT:
FUTURE:
WHAT ACTION REQUIRED TO ACHIEVE THE DESIRED RESULT?

****

PHYSICAL
PAST:
PRESENT:
FUTURE:
WHAT ACTION REQUIRED TO ACHIEVE THE DESIRED RESULT?

****

EXERCISE
PAST:
PRESENT:
FUTURE:
WHAT ACTION REQUIRED TO ACHIEVE THE DESIRED RESULT?

****

PERSONAL HABITS
PAST:
PRESENT:
FUTURE:
WHAT ACTION REQUIRED TO ACHIEVE THE DESIRED RESULT?

****

ASSETS
PAST:
PRESENT:
FUTURE:
WHAT ACTION REQUIRED TO ACHIEVE THE DESIRED RESULT?

****

CLOTHING
PAST:
PRESENT:
FUTURE:
WHAT ACTION REQUIRED TO ACHIEVE THE DESIRED RESULT?

****

ASSOCIATES
PAST:
PRESENT:
FUTURE:
WHAT ACTION REQUIRED TO ACHIEVE THE DESIRED RESULT?

****

Besides writing out your list of priorities and the actions to be taken; you should also inspire yourself by creating a Vision Board. I mentioned this briefly before, when I also called it a "Dream Board." It is a picture board with cut and pasted (preferably colour) pictures of the items, places or situations which you desire the most. You can include positive sayings on the board, like "Today is a beautiful day!" beside a photo of a sunny beach; or "I am full of vigour and energy" beside a picture of yourself riding a bicycle or working out. My young daughter's board says "Go Girl!" and other youthful phrases to keep her inspired and motivated. Look at pictures or brochures which excite you: luxury trains or cruises, jewellery, a house, a new car, etc. See yourself in the picture and imagine how it feels. Some people have been known to go one step further and actually get a picture taken of them sitting in the new car which they desire—this can really help one to imagine their wish fulfilled more intensely. Have fun with it!

Creating Abundance

An important factor when setting goals, is learning to find the perfect balance between the incredible and the attainable. A common reason for not achieving what one desires is the fact that some people simply do not aim high enough. Consider that on a scale of one to 10, our ultimate desires being 10, we may reach five or six. For instance, if you affirm that you are going to earn $100,000 next year, in actuality, you might earn 55 or 60 thousand dollars. Why not aim for $150,000 (if attainable in what you currently do) and actually earn $90,000?

On the other hand, some people are almost unrealistic when setting 'near future' goals. If they say that they are going to earn $90,000 next month… it is quite unlikely unless they are already established in an occupation which provides that sort of income. Begin with steps which you know you could accomplish—this will empower you to believe in yourself as you achieve them.

On the previous pages, we have given examples of various goal setting projects of which you can choose one or several, or create your own. As mentioned earlier, it is a programme to be completed when one can truly devote some quality time. As for this moment, I will provide a short, inspiring exercise which you can do in about 20 minutes. Take a pen and sheet of paper right now, and create a list of all the marvellous ambitions which come to your mind.

Don't think about whether or not they are attainable at this point and do not concern yourself with the 'how'—simply jot down all of your deepest desires and know that the treasure exists. Aim as high as you wish… design whatever would appear in the perfect lifestyle for YOU. Some notations on your list may be continuous actions such as a fascinating occupation. Other items may simply be things which you would indulge in less frequently like champagne, or travel. The following is a sample wish list:

HAVE/DO/BE/SHARE

Polo, riding, country club, golf, boating, horse racing, travel.
Film premieres, gallery openings, museum previews.
Opera, ballet, symphony, fine restaurants.
Old guard music, art, antiques.
Garden parties, private luncheons, pool parties.
Gourmet food, caviar, champagne.
Classic tailored suits, salons, grooming.
Sunshine, smiles, flowers, perfume.
Prestigious location, fabulous climate.
A country estate with horse and hound.
Character house, traditional decor, fireplace.
Loyal efficient staff that is happy and very satisfied.
Culture profession, fascinating occupation, success and extra cash.

Security, assets, investments.

Philanthropy, church, charitable organisations, volunteer committees.

Etiquette, grace, taste, manners, civility, politeness, elegance.

Tranquillity, peace, harmony.

Clear mellifluous speech, good vocabulary and pronunciation.

Love, timeless romance, attractive charisma.

Executive, professional, successful, intellectual, prosperous, generous, kind, faithful, honest, loyal—consort, friends, associates and self.

Membership to private clubs like White's, Boodles, Brooks's, The Athenaeum.

After you have completed this enjoyable exercise of letting your true desires come to light, we will move on to the next step. Read over *your* list. How many of the events, activities, or conditions will you be able to HAVE, DO, BE, or SHARE in the very near future? Much will depend on your current status, age and so forth. The established person who is 40 years of age may be much closer to owning the fine house in the country than the individual who is just starting out at the age of 20.

The first person may consider this item to be one of her 'near' future goals, whereas the second individual may decide to place it into his five-to-10-year plan. Other objectives will be immediately possible—grooming, or behaviour for instance—circle what you can begin to improve immediately and feel your deserved sense of accomplishment. Indeed, almost all of our goals are attainable—it's simply a matter of time, planning, discipline and ***actions***.

We must be wary of inactivity in order not to miss opportunities—switch from bored and stagnant to active, alive, creative. Amazing things do not happen in our comfort zone—human beings crave expansion. We are here to grow with a sense of meaning, not to be inactive—comfort is nice, but growth feels so much better!

Type up a copy of YOUR dream list, and read it aloud with emphasis, desire and confidence every morning as a verbal affirmation. Fabulous results often being with words. Remember:

Words create thoughts.
Thoughts inspire actions.
Actions produce results,

When determining your goals, it is important to bear in mind that we should not simply focus on luxury or self, but consider how our ambitions can bring pleasure, occupation, or success to others as well. Also remember to appreciate the basics. The book "Angel Power" by Janice T. Connell reads: "People do strive for comfort. We experience God smiling upon us when we appreciate the soft wool of the sheep, the sweet taste of the orange, the warm water that fills our baths, the company of loving friends." If such blessings are already present in your life—be grateful!

Look at your past actions and you will understand exactly how you came to be where you are. Humans were given the benefit of many wonders, including those of major consequence: *'thought'* and *'freedom of choice.'* These two factors will determine your state of being and eventual happiness… and with that notion I will close this topic with another quote from Connell's book: "Do not focus on the problems of the day. If you focus on the problems, you actualise them. God wants you to accept divine peace, live divine peace, and spread divine peace."

People, who choose a positive behaviour and ambience, tend to live very pleasant lives. In contrast, those who choose or simply even permit negativity to influence their words, thoughts, associations or surroundings, frequently live a life less fortunate. Will making yourself poor make someone else rich? Will making yourself sick make someone else healthy? Create goodness and build a better economy in your own house as a starting point for choosing abundance over scarcity. Then, sow generously to reap generously; go the extra mile in your vocation, always giving great value and a sense of increase to others.

Living Rich

Perhaps the most important step in attaining financial freedom, is mastering the art of 'living rich.' We can earn money, save it, share it, and re-invest it to make it grow… but in order to quicken the pace towards an affluent life-style, the key is to **live royally**. External succeeds internal. A person who thinks rich, feels blessed, and behaves in a noble fashion, will find that the external rewards automatically follow. This is the reason why it was necessary to present so many various aspects in this book. The way a person speaks, dresses, behaves… who they associate with, what activities they participate in, and so forth, will largely determine their odds at happiness and success.

The quality clothing, beautiful ambience, fine manners, pleasing vocation, civilised associates, prestigious location—these initial steps will help one to actually **FEEL RICH**. When the feeling exists, belief will follow—and with belief comes reality, for *whatever man believes, he can achieve*.

With time and practise, the confidence and social graces, which seem to come so naturally to the highborn, will become an automatic presence. Once attitudes and behaviours have been improved so that we expect quality in everything from items to relationships, we will become like a magnet which attracts only the positive and repels the negative. One will 'miraculously' always seem to find oneself in the right place, at the right time.

Wonderful people, opportunities and good fortune will follow, but the wise know that these are not really 'miracles' in action. The bountiful events and progressive life situations are largely the results of our own belief system combined with behaviours and good habits. One who is born a prince, may choose to live a miserable, unwholesome life; just as, one born a pauper, may choose to **LIVE ROYALLY**.

WHAT IS SUCCESS?

To laugh often and much;
To win the respect of intelligent people
and the affection of children;
To earn the appreciation of honest critics and
endure the betrayal of false friends;
To appreciate beauty;
To find the best in others;
To leave the world a bit better, whether by
a healthy child, a garden
patch or a redeemed social condition;
To know even one life has breathed
easier because you have lived;
This is to have succeeded.
—*Ralph Waldo Emerson*

CONCLUSION

TRUE HAPPINESS COMES FROM WITHIN

When I was young, I often wondered why God dropped me off on such a primitive planet. A world with war, crime, and punishment sanctioned by governments. But maybe the earth is not so foul after all… perhaps it is simply the way people choose to think or behave, for it truly is a remarkably beautiful planet.

Happiness is our true nature—think of how happy young children are before adults suppress their joy by saying things like "calm down, grow up, be quiet." Let people live and laugh; even more than this, join others in expressing the happiness which is inherently inside of us.

If we release the striving and struggle, then we could indeed realise paradise on earth. Observe the beauty and perfection of God's natural creations—the trees and streams, birds and furry friends, heavenly clouds, the sun and stars. Wallace D. Wattles in "The Science of Getting Rich," wrote: "Everything you see on earth is made from one original substance, out of which all things proceed." We are here as co-creators for the expansion of this greater goodness.

I have written about external measures which can be taken to bring more pleasure, peace and harmony to one's life-style. Fine and good, but remember that true happiness must come from within. Without love for our Creator and our fellow man, we might find few royal rewards either in this life or the next. Be a libertarian with a holy conscience—enjoy your freedom and care for yourself, but also care for those who surround you. Do not worship mammon, control, or power; for if you do, then you have taken everything out of context. This book was written for the God of love, that we may all live with peace, joy, freedom and charity towards each other. So be it!

Appendices

Education—Appendix #1

TYPES OF EDUCATION

There are three commonly known types of education:
TUTORS – Privately hired in-home tutelage
INDEPENDENT – Privately supported schools
GOVERNMENT – State owned schools

Before one determines how their youth is to be educated, they should not only consider the future aspirations, but also, what is best suited to the child's personality and demeanour. Each system possesses pros and cons of varying degrees, which guardians should discuss with their charge before making any serious commitments.

GOVERNMENT SCHOOLS

PROS

* Little or no upfront expense
* Peer companionship and interaction
* Equal opportunities for various income levels

CONS

* Grade system—students initially placed by age rather than intellect
* Mandatory pre-arranged programmes
* Limited choice of subjects
* Numerous students per teacher—less individual guidance

- * Peer influence from lower middle classes
- * Higher rate of disorderly conduct and delinquency
- * High drop-out rates
- * Poor dress habits if uniforms are not worn
- * People pay through higher taxes

INDEPENDENT SCHOOLS

PROS

- * Peer companionship and interaction
- * Prestigious ambience and reputation
- * Sense of security and stability
- * Strong bonding—V.I.P. contacts
- * Highly qualified instructors
- * Often stronger ethics and less misconduct
- * Fewer pupils per teacher-more individual guidance
- * Classic neat apparel

CONS

- * Expensive
- * Schools are limited to certain locations
- * Boarding may be required
- * Student must meet certain requirements for acceptance

PRIVATE TUTORS

PROS

- * Beneficial for self-disciplined independent students
- * Highly individualised, one-on-one, tutor-pupil personal study
- * Grades can be completed earlier at much younger age
- * Unlimited subjects: sports, languages, music, business, etc.
- * Pupil may receive instruction indoors, outdoors, anywhere, anytime

* Student will never fail or be expelled
* More available time allows child to participate in other activities
* Ideal for families which travel frequently or have global responsibilities
* No transportation or boarding costs
* Creates employment for private instructors—no drain on tax system

CONS

* Expensive
* Isolated—unless child becomes involved in arts, sports, church, clubs, or other group organisations

The three types of education are also characterised by other dissimilarities, which do not necessarily fall into a pro or con category. For instance, one should consider what type of sports the youth is interested in. Government schools tend to offer team sports like baseball, football, etc., while independent schools often include traditional events like rowing, polo, fencing, beagling and so on.

The entrepreneurial eighties saw the young urban professionals (Yuppies) scrambling to get their children on the prestigious *independent* school rosters. This trend has continued somewhat, as each generation demands a greater degree of excellence.

Private tutelage, once considered the glorious upper-class privilege of the past, has just begun its comeback. Like everything else, educational trends move in cycles of change. The three types of schooling will likely always exist, but some will be more predominant at certain times, under different conditions.

Families with very self-disciplined, independent offspring will find that private tutelage offers a quicker and more efficient way of learning. Many students now become involved in the family business, independent vocations, or arts at an earlier age. Times may soon resemble our historical past, when geniuses like Mozart had the freedom to create wonders while still in their youth. The important thing is not degrees and diplomas, but actual results and achievement. The disadvantage to home schooling is the lack of group communication. Fortunately, alternatives are springing up at a rapid pace. More and more intellectual, church, music, theatre, and sports clubs cater to youth. It really doesn't matter what type of education one should choose, as long as they always keep learning.

Mind/Spirit—Appendix #2

Mankind has understood for thousands of years that a relationship exists between the ethereal world and our own, and that this bond is called *spirit*. Upon physical death, we know that the human *body* will return to dust or ashes. The only method of preservation (excluding cloning and cryonics) is through the creation of an heir. Unless genetic cells are reproduced in this manner, that unique physical/mental pedigree will discontinue. Our physical pedigree is continually evolving, and the only way to terminate a particular blood-line, is by deciding not to procreate. We have evidence that physical reincarnation, including the brain's computer chips, is passed on from one generation to the next, but 'spirit' is an entirely separate matter.

Scientific research and recent genetic studies confirm that we not only inherit features like our father's long nose and dark eyes, but our mind bank (genetic brain) also inherits some ancestral memories which occurred *prior* to our conception. ***Our physical cells contain the genetic memories and attributes of our ancestors.*** Not merely bodily health and physical resemblance, but strengths, weaknesses, and attitudes as well. Think of your instincts—perhaps an inherent fear of spiders because most contain venom, which you instinctively knew as an infant even before anyone ever told you; and the 'fight or flee' response which humans still carry, stemming from the behaviours of our ancient ancestors.

In this scenario, re-incarnation is not viewed as the re-birth of a soul, but is considered to be a partial re-birth of body. Therefore, it is not unusual when brain cells seem to recall the 'past lives' of their ancestors, for that is where these cells originated. The concept was explained well in the book 'Embraced by the Light' by Betty J. Eadie— "I learned that all thoughts and experiences in our lives are recorded in our subconscious minds. They are also recorded in our cells, so that, not only is each cell imprinted with a genetic coding, it is also imprinted with every experience we have ever had.

"Further, I understood that these memories are passed down through the genetic coding to our children. These memories then account for many of the passed-on traits in families, such as addictive tendencies, fears, strengths, and so on. I also learned that we do not have repeated lives on this earth; when we seem to "remember a past life, we are actually recalling memories contained in the cells." Is this what the Bible refers to in Deuteronomy 5:9… visiting the iniquity of the fathers upon their children unto the third and fourth generation?"

Those who disagree with this view might have the theory backwards—if they believe that they are 'an old soul in a new body.' In actual fact, your body cells are ancient—they have been reproducing themselves since the dawn of man. As for spirit, apparently this world has never held this number of bodies previously in all of history; consequently, in consideration of logic, a large proportion of souls would have to be here for the first time.

For those over-attached to physical life and wanting to believe that spirit/soul returns, consider "The Silver Cord" by Martha Josephine Barham and James Thomas Greene, which reads, "One does not accumulate karmic debts or payments over lifetimes. Karma is nothing more than consequences within a lifetime."

Regarding the physical, can cells which contain information be transplanted from one brain to another? Possibly, according to the example from the book 'The Human Brain—Mind and Matter' by James A. Corrick, where we read: "Pietsch's final test was to place the brain of a tadpole into one of the young salamanders. Later examinations showed that the brain segment from the tadpole fused with the nervous system of the young salamander. Tadpoles are vegetarians, unlike young salamanders which are meat eaters.

"The salamanders with tadpole brains no longer would eat other animals. They had now, from the fragment of tadpole brain, become vegetarians." Two paragraphs later, the book goes on to say: "In the future, if you aren't satisfied with your own memories, you will go to a memory bank and have a new set grafted into your mind."

So, it is established that the brain affects the body, but what then influences the brain? Our soul, spirit, energy, life-force—the **uncontainable** part which, unlike the body, never dies. Although temporarily residing in mortal flesh, ***our eternal spirit has the ability through sub-conscious energy to communicate with our Creator***.

Never doubt the power of the sub-conscious mind, which can achieve whatever the conscious chooses to believe. When one has reached a level in life where their mind and spirit are ready for a spiritually transformative experience, it will occur. It is important to remember; however, that the experience will manifest in whatever method, shape, or form that the person's sub-conscious is open to. If one is practising the occult, they may meet an avatar or entity. If one is involved in religious study, they may be greeted by an angel. If one is intrigued by the possibility of UFO encounters, they might attract an 'alien' vision.

Through infinite intelligence the sub-conscious mind has the power to re-create anything which the conscious mind has first imagined, i.e., programmed into it. The experiences which these people have with such contacts are definitely real to them. They may experience pain and turmoil, or they may experience joy and healing—this depends on their expectations, meditation, or form of prayer. God has given mankind the power of thought and free-will, which literally opens us up to the universe, and all negative or positive forces which exist therein. We cannot condemn, disbelieve, or judge people who have chosen to have negative experiences; but at the same time, we must realise that we also have the right to our own preference. The right to create *our* reality. What exists for one person, does not necessarily exist for the next person as people are different. Freedom to create is one of the greatest privileges which God has given to mankind. "As he thinketh in his heart, so is he."

Spiritual experiences come when a person is open to them, not necessarily on demand. This is why it can be unwise to 'hire' a psychic to do a reading. As Dr Yvonne Kason explains in her book "A farther Shore"— "Following the initial experience, psychic episodes often recur only irregularly and unpredictably, and even highly psychically open experiencers find they can't always make the abilities appear consistently."

A final word—even though our brain is influenced genetically by nature, remember that nurture can play an equally important part in determining the path your life will follow. This is why I have written so much about thoughts and environmental factors, because behaviours and surroundings can usually be chosen.

All experiences of the mind are determined by each individual's belief system. If one is plagued by self-doubt; succumbs to control; has fear, or dependencies—they will have negative experiences, because they are living on a lower level of consciousness, and vibrate at a lesser frequency. If one has prosperity consciousness—complete freedom, plenty of faith, thinks abundantly and with much love—more positive things are likely to happen.

Speech—Appendix #3

STATUS ENUNCIATION

In upper-class English, a few words are pronounced *differently* than they appear.

Ex.: derby sounds like 'darby.' They never sound the 'L' in golf. Nor do they sound the 'H' in forehead. Private when changed to 'privacy' exchanges it's hard I for a soft i. Likewise hygiene (hi jeen) becomes hygienic (hi jen ik). Uppers tend to pronounce girl as (gairl) rather than gurl.

U-people prefer to stress syllables in certain ways: ex.: **duch** ess, **count** ess, prin **cess**.

'EI' words have always been rather confusing—'leisure' rhymes with pleasure, having a soft E as in Ed. While 'neither' is pronounced (nie ther), first syllable sounds like sky. Similar to neither, German names with I & E are also pronounced in reverse of their appearance, ex.: '**Einstein**' is (ine shtine), but 'Friedman' is (freed man).

This reminds us to be cautious with other languages. It is very déclassé (deh klahs seh)/ (day kläs ay) if one cannot pronounce 'noblesse oblige' (no bles o bleezh). You will not be sentenced to the guillotine (gee yo teen), but it is embarrassing. More information under 'foreign words.'

Many words are pronounced *exactly* the way they appear:

already (al ready) sound the 'L' not... a'ready
all right—same idea
amateur (am a **tur**) tur not 'choor'
aunt (**ah**nt) not ant (distinguishes humans from insects)
coupon (**koo** pon) not q-pon
education (ed **u** ca tion) yoo not 'joo'
garage (gar **azh**) there is no 'D'—garidge or garadge are incorrect
fortune (for **tune**) not 'chin'
issue (is **syu**) not 'is shoe'
opportunity (op or **tu** nity) too not 'chew'
schedule (**shed** yule) not 'sked jel'
Tuesday (**too's** day) not 'chews day'
vegetable (veg e ta ble) pronounce all four syllables

Proper pronunciation of famous names will demonstrate one's level of cultural/historical knowledge:

Beethoven (bay toe ven)

Chopin (show pan)

Freud (froit)

Gandhi (gan dee)

Goethe (gu te)

Jung (yoong)

Tchaikovsky (chi kof skee)

Having the money to buy haute couture will usually be associated with the correct pronunciation of designer names:

Armani (ahr mahn nee)

Cacherel (kash ar rehl)

Chanel (shah nehl)

de la Renta (day lah rehn ta)

Dior, Christian (krees tyehn dy ohr)

Gigli (jee l'yee)

Givenchy (zhee vahn shee)

Grès (grey)

Hermes (ehr mays)

Ricci, Nina (nee nah ree chee)

St. Laurent, Yves (eev san loh rahn)

Versace (vchr saw chay)

Place names are usually pronounced properly by people who travel often, or associate with global travellers:

Argentina (ar jen tee na)

Buenos Aires (bway nos I ras)

Gloucester (glos ter)

Hertfordshire (har for sh'r)

Norwich (norridge)

Rio de Janeiro (reo day zha na ro)

More word and name samples were written in the Canadian edition of 'Learning to Write' by Reed Smith.

(1) PLACE NAMES

Abitibi (ab-i-tib'-i)
Argentina (ar'jen-te' na)
Azores (a-zorz')
Banff (bamf)
Bombay (bom-ba')
Buenos Aires (bwa'nos i'ras)

Calgary (kal'-ga-ri)
Cataraqui (kat'-a-ra-kwi; kat'-a-ra'kwi)
Chicoutimi (shi'-koo'-ti-mi)

Esquimalt (es-kwe'-mawlt)

Genoa (jen'o-a)
Gloucester (glos'ter)

Himalaya (hi-ma'la-ya; less correctly him'ala'-ya)
Houston (hus'tun)

Iowa (i'o-wa; not wa)

Kapuskasing (kap'-us-ka'-sing)

Leicester (les'ter)
L'Orignal (lor-nel')
Los Angeles (los ang'gel-es or los an'jel-es or ez)
Louisiana (loo-e'zi-an'a)
Louisville (loo'is- or loo'i-vil)

Madawaska (mad-a-wos'-ka)

Newfoundland (accent either first or last syllable, not the second syllable; but Newfound'land dog)

Okanagan (o-ka-nah'-gan)
Omaha (o'ma-ho)

Penetanguishene (pen-e-tan'-gwi-shen')
Pompeii (pom-pa'ye;-pe'i)
Port Said (port sa-ed')

Quebec (kwi-bek')
Quinte (kwin'-ti)
Quito (ke'to)

Rainier (ran-yay)
Restigouche (res'-ti-goosh)
Rio de Janeiro (re'o da zha-na'ro)

Rio Grande (re'o gran'da)
Rouen (roo'an)
Rouyn (roo'-on)

Saguenay (sag'-e-na)
Saskatchewan (sas-kach'e-won)
Sault Ste. Marie (soo sant-ma-re)

The Pas (the pah)
Timagami (te-ma'ga-mi)
Tours (toor)
Tucson (too-son')

Manitoulin (ma-ni-too'-lin)
Miami (mi-am'i)
Mojave (ma-ha'va)

Nanaimo (na-ni'-mo)
Nassau (nas'o)
New Orleans (or'le-anz)

Uruguay (u'roo-gwa; oo roo-gwi')

Utah (u'to; u'ta)

Worcester (woos'ter)

Yosemite (yo-sem'i-te)

(2) FAMOUS PEOPLE

Beerbohm (ber'bom)
Beethoven (ba'to-ven)
Boccaccio (bok kat'cho)
Boswell (boz'wel)
Brahms (bramz)
Bronte (bron'ti)
Buchan (buk'an)

Chopin (sho'pan')
Clough ((kluf)
Corot (ko'ro')

Dante (dan'te; Italian pron., dan'tay)

de la Mare (de la mar')
Debussy (debu'se')
Don Juan (don' ju'an; Sp., don hwan')
Don Quixote (don kwik'sot; Sp., don keho'ta)
Dvorak (dvor'zhak)

Freud (froit)
Froude (frood)

Gandhi (gan'de)
Gauguin (go gan')
Goethe (gu'te)
Gogh, van (van kok')

Hohenzollern (ho'en-tsol'ern)

Lowell (lo'el)
Masaryk (ma'sa-rek)
Maugham (mom)
Maurois (mo'rwa')
Mayo (ma'o)
Medici, de (da med'e-chi)
Morse (mors)

Nietzsche (ne'che)
Nobel (no-bel')

Paderewski (pa'de-ref'ske or res'ke)
Pasteur (pas tur')
Pepys (peps; peps; pep'is)
Petrarch (pe'trark)
Plato (pla'to)
Proust (proost)

Rebelais (ra'ble')
Ravel (ra vel')
Robespierre de (de ro'bes'pyar')

Sienkiewicz (shen-kya'vich)
Strachey (strachi)
Synge (sing)

Tchaikovsky (chi-kof'ski)

Vermeer (fer mar')

Jung (yoong)

Kublai Khan (koo'bli kan')

La Verendrye (la va'ran'dre')
Leacock (le'kok)
Leeuwenhoek, (van la'ven-hook)

Vespucci (ves-poot'che)
Vinci, da (da vin'che)

Wagner (vag ner)
Wycliffe (wik'lif)

Xerxes (zurk'sez)

Zweig (tsvik; tsvig)

(3) CLASSICAL NAMES

Achilles (a-kil'ez)
Aeolus (e'o-lus)
Ceres (se'rez)
Circe (sur'se)

Erebus (er'e-bus)
Hades (ha'dez)
Hebe (hebe)
Lethe (le'the)

Niobe (ni'o-be')
Penelope (pe-nel'o-pe)
Pleiades (ple'ya-dez or pli'a-dez)

Psyche (si'ke)
Satyr (sat'er or sa'ter; distinguish from *satire*, sat'ir)

Ulysses (u-lis'sez)
Zeus (zus' or zoos')

ADDITIONAL WORDS OFTEN MISPRONOUNCED

I
1. alias (a'li-as)
2. ally (ally')
3. amateur (am'a-tur')
4. Appalachian (la')
5. apparatus (ra')
6. athlete (ath'let)
7. auxiliary (og-zil'ya-ri)
8. aye, ay (ever, a)
9. aye, ay (yes, I)
10. bade (bad)

II
11. bicycle (b*i* sik'l, but motor syk'l)
12. bouquet (boo-ka'; bo-ka')
13. chastisement (chas'tiz-ment)
14. column (kol'um, not yum)
15. coupon (koo,' not ku)
16. creek (kreek, not krik)
17. culinary (ku'li-ner'i)
18. data (da' or da')
19. desert (waste of sand, dez'ert)

III
20. dessert (sweets, dezert')
21. diphtheria (dif-, not dip-)
22. docile (dos'il; do'sil; dos'il)
23. dour (door)
24. draught (draft)
25. droll (drol)
26. encore (ang'kor)n.
27. envoy (en'voi)
28. err (ur)
29. facile (fas'il)

IV
30. forehead (for'ed)
31. fragrant (fra'grant)
32. genuine (jen'u-in)
33. gratis (gra')
34. hearth (harth)
35. height (not heighth)
36. hcinous (ha'nus)
37. humble (sound the h)
38. imbecile (im'be-sil; im'be-sil)
39. joust (joost or just)

V
40. lenient (le,' not len')
41. literature (lit'er-a-tur, not -choor, -cher, or -toor)
42. longitude (lon'ji-tud)
43. long-lived (livd, livd)
44. mineralogy (ral,'not rol')

VI
50. partner (not pardner)
51. penalise (pe'nal-iz)
52. perfume (verb, per fum')
53. perfume (noun, pur'fum)
54. precedent (noun, pres'e-dent)

45. motorcycle (motor sike *l*, but bicycle, sik l)
46. nape (nap)
47. neither (ne'ther or ni'ther)
48. often (do not sound the t)
49. parliament (paa luh ment)

55. precedent (adj., pre-sed'ent)
56. quoit (kwoit or koit)
57. respite (res'pit)American (res pite) British
58. route (root)
59. salient (sa'li-ent)

VII

60. senil (se'nil; se'nil)
61. short lived (livd)
62. sleek (rhyme with leak)
63. soften (do not sound the t)
64. status (sta')
65. subtle (sut'l)
66. unprecedented (unpres'e-den'ted)
67. usually (sound the a)
68. version (vur'shun)
69. wont (accustomed, wunt)
70. zoology (zo-ol'o-ji, not zoo-ol'o-ji)

SPEECH AND CLASS

Unseemly though it may appear, people have always associated the class status of others by the way they speak. The most common way of noticing this behaviour is through actual life associations. Most people will find that as they progress in life—travel more, become more established in occupation and social class order, their speaking habits change naturally.

If a middle-class individual has never conversed with either the elite, or with people who speak a lower dialect, they may never notice the different speech patterns... except through written information or broadcasting. For obvious reasons, we will concentrate on speech improvement rather than inferior usage.

As previously mentioned, proficient speech can often be heard on classic film. Another method of instruction is through the use of written material like Jilly Cooper's 'Class' or 'Noblesse Oblige' by Nancy Mitford. It was in the book 'Noblesse Oblige' that Professor Alan Ross coined the expressions: *U* (upper-class) and ***Non-U*** (not upper-class) with respect to speech and other behaviour.

If one hasn't yet had the opportunity to review such books, here is a sample list of what was considered to be upper-class and non-upper-class speech:

****

It is interesting to note that some words are kept *formal* by U-people. For instance:

U SPEECH versus	NON-U
present	gift
notecase	wallet
bank note	bill
expensive	costly
vegetables	greens
relation	relative
one	I/you
children	kids
son	boy/lad
daughter	girl/lass
aunt	antie
wife/husband and children	family
dinner guests	company
servant	help
schoolmaster/schoolmistress	teacher
goodbye	ta ta/bye bye
polo-neck jersey	pullover/turtleneck
dressing gown	bathrobe
stockings	hose
counterpane	bedspread
drawing room	living room
sitting room	family room
study	den
lavatory	bathroom
lavatory paper	toilet paper
writing paper	note paper
looking glass	mirror
influenza	flu
motor	drive
petrol	gas
bicycle	cycle

spectacles   glasses
sun-specs   sunglasses
tiresome   boring
telephone   phone
telegram   wire

In other cases, U-people tend to consider modern words inflated and prefer to stick with the *basics*. For example:

U SPEECH	versus NON-U
what?	pardon?
yes	that's right
suppose	presume
remember	recollect/recall
cloth	tea-towel
napkin	serviette
nappies	diapers
gift-wrap	wrapping paper
formal clothes	formals
black tie	tuxedo
dress	gown
jacket and skirt	two-piece suit
coat	overcoat
jacket	blazer
shirt	blouse
gum boots	wellies
bag	handbag
main course	entrée
helping	portion
meat	roast
grouse	poultry
pudding	sweet
jam	preserve
drinks	cocktails/beverages
glasses	crystal
car	vehicle
the car and driver	limo and chauffeur
buy	purchase
rich	wealthy
of good family	well-connected
deb	debutante

flowers	corsage
scent	perfume
sweat	perspire
mad	mental
pregnant	expecting/family way
crippled	handicapped/disabled
sick	ill
die	pass on/away
to hurt	to pain
very	quite
stamp	postage stamp
England	Britain
The States	America
Scotch	Scottish
false teeth	dentures
big house	mansion
beautiful house	elegant home
boxroom	utility room
chimney-piece	mantel-piece
curtains	drapery
sofa	couch/settee
civilised	cultivated/cultured
smart	classy
cheeky	impertinent
dirty	soiled
the washing up	do the dishes
wash hair	shampoo
dark hair	brunette
red hair	auburn
fair hair	blonde
woman	lady
male/female companion	escort

Do these differences in speech ever create a communication problem? Indeed, they do. Consider for example: U *spectacles*—which non-U refer to as *glasses*. In U speech *glasses* represent what the non-U refer to as *crystal*. The U word for angry is *cross*, while non-U say *mad*... but *mad* in U speech means the same as non-U *mental*. U *company* refers to one's business, although *company* in non-U is equivalent to *guests* in upper speech. And don't even mention the word *handicapped* to a U person unless you are referring to the race track or their golf game.

Although the above samples may seem confusing to some, in actuality the code is quite elementary. 'Formal' and 'basic' both embrace one similar precept—*traditional*. When in doubt of what to say, simply stick with correct, original language.

Finally for certain situations they simply have their preference:

	U versus	**NON-U**
eating around noon	luncheon	dinner
male over 21 years	man	boy
pre-marital commitment	engaged	going steady
exam preparation	working for	studying for
in cards	knave	jack
U-people are horse people	riding	horseback riding
	horse is lame	mount is limping
	goes up	rears
	on heat	in season

Note: to say 'horseback' is redundant—in upper language, riding always refers to horses. We motor in cars; on two wheels we cycle or go biking.

None of the above words or phrases are incorrect. The sample lists were merely provided for the interest of those who have not had the opportunity to associate with people from various life-styles.

SLANG

Slang is definitely non-U. If one has any foul word in their vocabulary, they need to isolate the culprit, look up an appropriate synonym in a thesaurus, and permanently replace all non-traditional language.

An alternate word exists for every piece of language—e.g.:

VULGAR/SLANG	ORIGINAL/ACCEPTABLE
brown-nose	ingratiate
bull-shit	nonsense, rubbish
give heck	reprove, rebuke
oh brother!	indeed!
pig-headed donkey	obstinate
shit! damned!	shoot!
crappy	unpleasant

... and so on

There is no excuse for swearing, slang, and other vulgarities—such talk only serves to make one look bad, and risk losing respect from others. If one should ever hear this type of language, they might take a clue that they are not in the greatest of places, or with the most civilised people. If you are truly living a good, successful life, your ears will never be subject to such drivel.

FOREIGN WORDS

Foreign names are a focus of attention even more sensitive than foreign words. People love to hear the sound of their own name, but only if it is pronounced correctly. Take the German name 'Hans' (properly pronounced 'Huntz'), or 'Frans' (Fruntz). If one could not master the German enunciation and were forced to convert them to English, the names would *not* become Haans or Fraans, they would be 'John' and 'Frank.' Beethoven's first syllable does not sound like the vegetable used to prepare borsch. Show respect for other cultures—always articulate correctly.

How do foreign words affect your class status? In lands of opportunity, it is not uncommon to notice the occasional 'parvenu' (someone who got rich before they became cultured). Have you ever seen someone driving an expensive imported motorcar and not know how to say the name of it? Common examples are Jaguar (correctly pronounced 'jag yu wahr') not 'jag war' or Porsche (por shuh) rather than the incorrect one syllable 'porsh.' Money can buy many things, but prestige has to be acquired.

We certainly would not expect everyone to go out and learn seven languages, but it is very simple and easy to learn the words which are universally recognised. I highly recommend that you memorise 'foreign words and phrases' from the book 'Outclassing the Competition' by Jan Darling. Those few pages will provide extraordinary advantages in your travels and royal life-style.

Health & Diet—Appendix #4

Try to eat properly whenever you can—if you have been given a restricted diet from your doctor, follow it. If you don't need a special diet, but would like a list of ideas—this is the regime which I follow:

FRUIT AND VEGETABLES DAILY

Fresh berries and fruit: include melons, avocados, tomatoes, etc. Raw natural fruit is preferable—a 2nd choice would be tinned without syrups; avoid dried, jams or jellies which are all high in sugars.

Vegetables:

* Steamed, baked or lightly sautéed vegetable recipes.
* Fresh, raw, cleaned vegetables: asparagus, sliced cucumbers, courgettes, red or yellow sweet peppers, broccoli, cauliflower, celery and carrot sticks, etc. May be eaten with homemade tzatziki, or sour cream fresh herb dip (I can provide excellent recipes for both).
* Tossed salads: may flavour with some extra virgin olive oil, a wedge of lemon, salt and pepper. If you want to add protein, you may top with: feta cheese, cooked shrimp, chicken breast, boiled egg, etc.

STARCH CARBOHYDRATES

* Avoid white bread/rice/potatoes, crackers, cereals with added sugar, etc.

* Choose whole grain products—wild or brown rice, organic brown pasta, sweet tubers or dark purple potatoes: boiled, broiled, or baked.

PROTEIN: Opt for wild if possible—seafood, fowl, deer, etc. Otherwise select pasture raised, antibiotic free poultry and eggs, grass fed beef, etc. In terms of preparation, opt for broiled, boiled, baked, roast, steamed or sashimi rather than deep-fried; also try to limit the amount to four ounces or less per day. 'Two legs or less' (poultry and seafood) are preferable to eating too much 'red' meat. Also try vegetable protein like nuts, sesame seeds, legumes, and tofu.

DAIRY: Plain Greek yogurt or sour cream for dips; samplings of cheese (preferably goat or sheep milk); an occasional scoop of ice cream (low sugar). If lactose intolerant you might prefer sugar-free almond, soya or coconut milk, etc.

SALT AND SUGAR: you can cut down on salt by using fresh or dried herbs to season. If you want to prepare sweeter meat or poultry dishes, simply add mild spices like cinnamon or try Chinese Five Spice which consists of: star anise, cassia, fennel, clove and ginger. Honey or organic stevia may also be used, but try to wean yourself of the 'sweet tooth' habit.

CONDIMENTS: Never use any type of preserved items when you can make fresh sauces or jar your own produce. Also, instead of squeeze mustard bottles which contain many ingredients, it should be made at home from only natural mustard powder and water. Instead of ketchup, use tomato paste which only has two ingredients: tomatoes and a little salt. The fewer ingredients listed on a food product the better! Refrain from using bought relishes and salad dressings—substitute with home-made savoury pickled cucumbers or a fresh lemon wedge instead.

FATS: Should come from healthful items like nuts, seeds, avocados, wild oily fish and extra virgin cold pressed olive oil. Organic coconut oil and butter can also be used, but sparingly.

LIQUID: Drink plenty of pure filtered water, sparkling mineral water or herbal teas. Limit caffeine, soda pop, and any drinks with sugar or additives—please see more under beverages below.

IMPORTANT RULES:

1. Always eat fresh, unprocessed—raw, baked, broiled, or steamed. Avoid deep-fried, and if you sauté, use a non-stick pan with very little oil.

2. Eat at home as often as possible—never eat 'fast food.' Always eat in a relaxed environment… never hectic.
3. If you like an early breakfast, choose fresh berries and fruit, rather than doughnuts or a croissant.
4. Never rush while eating a meal—masticate properly, chew a small bite of steak 10 or more times before swallowing.
5. Eat three small meals approximately four hours apart within an eight-hour window—that means fasting the other 16 hours. As an example—break the fast at 9 a.m.; luncheon at 1 p.m. and dinner at 5 o'clock.
6. Consume little or NO soft drinks, crisps, or candy. If you possess a sweet tooth, have a very small serving of sugar-free pudding, a square of very dark chocolate or a dessert of fresh fruit. For a healthful salty snack – try homemade popcorn or make a plate of sliced cucumber, tomato wedges, baby carrots and drizzle with fresh lemon—this may be topped with a little salt if desired.

Good eating and drinking habits, like most things, take some time to develop. If someone drinks two cocktails every evening, although it is unlikely that they will become an alcoholic, they might establish a habit. It is just as easy for a person to get into a healthful custom of steeping some green, camomile, or other herbal teas, and drinking one or two cups of it. Make a list of your current practises which you want to reduce or stop, and also write down new habits which you would like to form. Examples:

Reduce	Substitute
red meat	two legs or less, i.e., free range poultry/eggs, wild seafood, nuts, seeds, etc.
tinned vegetables	fresh or frozen vegetables
cakes and biscuits	berries, fruits and melons
potato crisps	homemade popcorn
coffee	herbal tea/mineral water
bottled dressing	fresh lemon, olive oil, etc.
lard	organic coconut oil or butter; extra virgin cold pressed olive oil
salt	garlic, onion, mild spices; fresh herbs like parsley, basil, coriander, chives, thyme, rosemary, tarragon, etc.

The next thing to do is discipline yourself—actually take a calendar, and monitor your progress for one month. If you gave up the items you wished to leave behind and adopted the new healthier cuisine for a whole month—congratulations! You should be well on the way to forming new and better nutritional habits.

BEVERAGES

SODA POP/ALCOHOL

If you use any soda pop, try to break the habit. It often contains sugar, caffeine, and other chemicals which the body certainly does not require. Some people do themselves a double disservice, by mixing cocktails with soft drinks.

If you consume alcohol, consider choosing the grapes: wine, champagne, sherry, port or cognac, which are never mixed; or choose a clear alcohol like vodka, which can be combined with something more nutritious like fresh orange juice, V8 or clamato.

It is a good idea for pregnant and nursing women to abstain from alcohol completely. Other women and men with a perfect bill of health (no diabetes, liver or kidney disease, immune disorders, etc.) may usually consume a couple drinks per day in safety (dry red wine is apparently the healthiest choice). However, regarding distilled spirits, wine, or other alcoholic drinks, the Healthy Heart Programme recommends not more than three units daily for women or four units daily for men and says to avoid binge drinking and have some alcohol-free days each week. We always give up alcohol completely during the 46 days of Lent until Easter—not only as an act of devotion to strengthen our character, but apparently one's liver can repair very well after 6 ½ weeks of fast and detox. Still others give up alcohol completely and become a teetotaller—which brings us to:

TEA AND COFFEE

Coffee: The caffeine it contains may cause many problems of the nervous system—heart palpitations, jitters, insomnia, and so forth. If you enjoy drinking one or two cups, avoid 'double' espresso shots and try not to drink it after 11 a.m.

Tea comes in different varieties—in order of highest caffeine to no caffeine, they are: black, oolong, green, and herbal. Herbal is sometimes preferred because it is caffeine free; however, recent studies have shown that black, oolong, and especially *green* teas, also offer a benefit. Apparently, they contain catechins (anti-cancer substances). If one is looking to choose between coffee and tea, it looks as though tea might be preferable. Never add sugar; instead, you might like herbal teas such as ginger, with a squeeze of honey or lemon; black teas can be smoothened with a little unsweetened soya milk if desired.

BOBA tea and bought ice teas: The tapioca pearls and flavoured syrups in bubble tea can be very high in starch and sugar unlike drinking plain healthful teas. Also, for iced teas try making your own—you can use a mixture of black tea and herbal flavoured teas; after steeping, let it cool, then you may add fresh squeezed lemon, some organic stevia and ice cubes. It's delicious and more nutritious!

FRUIT JUICE

Fruit juice can be a healthful drink, providing we only have it as an occasional treat and always opt for freshly made which can easily be prepared in a blender—we like to use two packages of cleaned strawberries to one package of seedless grapes. If you must buy bottled, or packaged juice, always choose

100% pure natural (not concentrate) with no added sugar or other ingredients; e.g. pure pomegranate is expensive, but one bottle contains several pomegranate fruits and can last for a few days. As an alternative, you might consider using a pure vegetable juice like V8 which is less calorific.

MILK

There is much controversy over this beverage. Some praise cow's milk as advantageous, and others conclude that it is detrimental—see "Fit for Life" by Harvey and Marilyn Diamond. I like to use small amounts of unsweetened soya, almond or coconut milk.

Finally, there is one beverage which everyone can agree upon…

WATER

Drink as much of this refreshing substance as your heart desires! You can purchase bottled mineral water (if you enjoy carbonated) or simply use *filtered* tap water from your house if you prefer 'still.'

Water should be drunk whenever we are thirsty, and throughout the day, as it transports vital nutrients in our body; aim to consume about eight glasses per day. It is also a wonderful idea to begin and end every day by consuming a glass of fresh water since water cleanses the body from the inside out.

READ THE LABELS

Whenever you go shopping for groceries or personal products, get into the habit of reading the labels. First of all, remember that on packaged products INGREDIENTS ARE LISTED IN ORDER OF AMOUNT. For example, which biscuit would be the healthier choice?

1. Ingredients: enriched flour, egg, milk, shortening, sugar.
2. Ingredients: sugar, shortening, enriched flour, milk, egg.

Number one is the healthier choice because it contains less sugar and shortening.

It is also a good idea for one to familiarise oneself with what exactly all of those long wordy ingredients really stand for. When you buy preserved foods like certain types of sausage or bacon, remember that 'sodium nitrate' is also used in **embalming fluid**. Or when you purchase that marvellous face lotion, consider that 'propylene glycol' is actually contained in **industrial anti-freeze** as well.

Pay attention, and if the product does not list the complete ingredients—**don't buy it**. Those who desire to live well, will bear in mind that inner nutrition is just as important as outer condition. You deserve to have toned muscles, healthy organs, flawless skin, and soft hair. Take good care of your body... it has to last a whole lifetime.

SOCIO-ECONOMIC CLASS AND DIET

Remember the old saying "you can never be too rich or too thin?" This is not completely true, for as we've already discussed under 'weight', we all realise that thinness caused by emotional or physical illness is certainly not desirable. Nor am I persuaded that being rich and being thin automatically go hand-in-hand, but I have noticed that those who 'live royally' tend to have less problems with obesity. Do the upper and lower classes eat differently from each other? Consider an example of one restaurant lunch with one snack at home:

Case #1

Private restaurant	Approximate calories
6 ounces tomato juice	30
4 ounces cooked cod	93
1 tablespoon fresh squeezed lemon	4
steamed asparagus (6 spears)	24
steamed okra (8 pods)	30
1 cup herbal tea	2
dessert: 1/2 cup fresh strawberries	23
with 1-ounce light cream	56
	262

Evening snack at home

a flute of chilled Perrier (mineral water)	0
2 glasses of champagne	160
a teaspoon of caviar	15
cup of raw vegetable crudité	25
6 almonds	42
1 kiwi fruit	42
	284
Total calories consumed	**546**

Case #2

Fast food franchise	**Approximate calories**
chocolate shake	380
double cheeseburger	600
4-ounce fries	320
regular sundae	310
	1610
Evening snack at home	
two bottles of beer	300
½ cup pretzels	86
100 grams of potato chips	536
	922
Total calories consumed	**2532**

Now considering that most people will have at least two meals and two snacks per day, just imagine if we doubled each total!

A moderately active person can take their present weight and times it by 15, to determine the number of calories required to maintain it. I weigh 120 pounds; therefore, I can consume 1800 calories per day without fluctuating.

If one takes regular exercise, and burns off enough of the calories which they consume, they will be unlikely to gain extra weight. If, however, one does not exercise much, they should consider eating lower calorie foods, which are generally more healthful anyway. 3500 unused calories will add approximately one pound of fat.

People who eat junk food, almost always defend their position by stating the old alibi of 'cost.' As mentioned throughout this book, money should never be a reason for deprivation. This same philosophy is true regarding the food we eat. The unaffordable excuse just doesn't measure up. One can prepare healthful meals at home for a reasonable cost.

What a contrast to the fast-food, fool-you, no service, hectic atmosphere, separate item price, bargain. Stand in line—order some greasy fries, onion rings, a hamburger, dessert and soda pop. It will be amazing if the bargain hunter pays less than $10 (not including the indigestion tablets which are later required.) If a person should try to blame poor eating habits on money, just ask them if they've been to a fast-food franchise within the past couple of months. If they answer 'no' they are probably sincere—if they say 'yes,' I wouldn't take them too seriously.

Self-Destructive Compulsions—Appendix #5

Due to weakness in human character, **almost everyone has suffered despair or oppression at some point in their life**. If one falls into despair, they must take charge of their life—regain spiritual, physical, and emotional control. **THIS CONDITION IS REVERSIBLE**. Never succumb to defeat; everyone experiences good times and bad times, especially in their younger years, before learning how to direct their destiny.

If you feel despondent from rejection or other factors, do not let self-doubt or worries drive you to take up poor habits. Try to think only of the positive, and allow any negative paradigms to become history. When I needed encouragement in my youth, I would go to the library and borrow audio cassettes like: 'Secrets of Success' by Og Mandino, 'Choose to Live and Love' by Wayne Dyer, or the book 'Think and Grow Rich' by Napoleon Hill. Not only will such forms of counselling help, but remember other important remedies for despair such as true friendships, prayer, positive thinking and actions. Get back on track, and recognise that compulsions play no part in a joyous life.

ALCOHOL —OVER-DRINKING

Why do people initially begin to drink too much? In some cases, alcohol is used as a form of painkiller to alleviate physical or emotional ailments. Rather than covering such problems with an addiction, it is far wiser to take steps to prevent the affliction from occurring. If you drink because of pain, see a doctor and discuss realistic alternatives.

Other people over-indulge because they want something which they do not have. It may be love, it may be money, or perhaps it is a combination of unfulfilled desires. If this is the situation, one must determine what their true goals are, and then create a logical outline for accomplishing them. Alcohol can offer no real support… on the contrary, in excess it only serves to weaken us.

If you do take pleasure consuming alcohol, learn to do it with moderation — 2nd Book of Machabees 15:40 "For as it is hurtful to drink always wine, or always water, but pleasant to use sometimes the one, and sometimes the other…" C-people are very traditional—the Bible mentions the drinking of wine, but clearly does not condone intemperance, and neither do they. Becoming inebriated is definitely un-C and should be avoided at all costs. Not only is intoxication damaging to your social status, but it could also be detrimental to your health. Those who imbibe large amounts of alcohol, increase their risk of accidents and might create emotional or physical disorders.

Aside from moderation, one should consider what exactly they are drinking. To avoid becoming nauseated, never imbibe both grain and grapes in the same time frame. Grains include products made with wheat, barley, rice: such as beer, brandy, vodka, whiskey, gin, sake, and so on. Grapes of course, include: wine, sherry, port, cognac, and champagne. Also, if you do drink grains, remember that mixing them with sugary beverages like eggnog or soda pop, is double injury to your diet.

For generations, people have taken an ounce of cognac for medicinal purposes, or a glass of wine as a restorative. A portion or two of wine may be beneficial, but if we were to consume a whole bottle every day, we would be inviting both illness and addiction. If one abuses their liberty to drink, they may later be forced to give it up entirely.

Garden parties, weddings, polo tournaments, and other special occasions are often celebrated with a couple glasses of champagne. At luncheon parties we may be offered champagne or sherry as an aperitif, and port as a dessert wine, not to mention a glass of red or white during the meal. Under normal conditions, we do not attend or host such engagements on a daily basis, and can refrain from continual drinking. Whenever hosting any form of entertainment, be sure to offer mineral water, tomato juice or such to those who have restricted diets or prefer to avoid inebriants.

How does our mentality affect our drinking habits? Another cause of drinking disorders originates from the familiar culprit—poverty consciousness.

Those who had little, often want too much.

Old money people tend to take alcohol, like everything else, for granted. If one has grown up in a household with a wine cellar containing a multitude of fine vintage, they are accustomed to retrieving a bottle to share with family or friends. People who have not been raised with such luxuries, often find it difficult to 'store' things. This leads to a 'consume as much as possible' attitude.

The way to remedy this syndrome is to practise the 'quality versus quantity' principle. Instead of drinking six glasses of beer or six ounces of cheap grain spirits, consume only one or two portions of a fine wine or cognac. One glass of vintage, or six measures of swill, have a similar liquor store price. Learn to substitute one splendid drink for the half dozen of poor quality—it will improve your self-image and your health. When entertaining, invite guests of tasteful discrimination. The financial cost should be equal, but the social-emotional rewards will be more gratifying.

Sometimes a person feels so happy and sociable after a couple glasses of champagne that they believe they will feel even better if they gulp down a few more glasses; alas, this is not the case. If one truly wants to be clubbable, drink slowly without getting intoxicated.

In summary, the three reasons why people drink are: pleasure, habit, or to cope. In "Brideshead Revisited" by Evelyn Waugh, it is inferred that Charles Ryder drinks for pleasure to expand in happy times, whereas, Sebastian Flyte drank to escape his miseries. Literally translated, a person may be classified as a social drinker, a problem drinker, or an alcoholic.

1. Social drinkers generally do not suffer any health consequences—in fact, recent studies have shown that people who consume one or two glasses of dry red wine per day actually live longer than those who do not drink at all.

2. A problem drinker is a person who constantly consumes in *excess* of the allowable two or three drinks per day. Habitual drinking can lead to alcohol dependency, or it can be controlled by reverting back to a social level—the choice is up to the individual. If you are problem drinker:

– Reduce your intake to two or fewer drinks per day.

– *Never* binge drink.

– For one or two days every week, abstain completely.

3. An alcoholic is a person who is beyond the problem stage, and has become fully addicted. Compulsive or continued excessive drinking should be treated professionally.

SELF-DESTRUCTIVE COMPULSIONS—SMOKING

There are three major vexations associated with the addiction of smoking. The first, and worst is related to **health**—the journal of the National Cancer Institute says *85%* of lung cancers are caused by smoking.

The second negative pertains to **money**—a 10 dollar per day habit is more than some spend on nutrition. Or consider what one could buy over the course of a year for $3,650—a reasonable annual retirementRSP, or an educational training course, or a few new wool business suits… a brighter future!

The third flaw is hazardous to our **self-image**. Studies from Health Canada show that smokers tend to have lower education, unskilled occupations and less financial savings than non-smokers. We could assume that all smokers were born into the lower socio-economic group, but this is not the case—many come from middle-class families, but regress rather than advance. Consider again the words of John Dryden "We first make our habits, and then our habits make us."

Reports indicate that most smokers begin before the age of 20 due to peer pressure, or low self-image. I used cigarettes on and off between my late teens—early twenties, and actually became fully addicted, as most smokers do. During the wild care-free days of young adulthood, our sensibility is not fully matured. One may realise that the disadvantages of this compulsion greatly outweigh the pleasures, and yet *it is necessary to select a strong reason to quit.*

Everyone is aware of why they should *not* smoke, but each person must choose a personal factor, before attempting to give it up. In my youth, one of my parents warned me of the health hazards, but I was so vitally healthy at that age… the other one mentioned the financial waste, but I knew that I had the capability of earning more money… finally it was one of my brothers who stirred my emotions. He said 'Why do you smoke? It's so out of character—you're not a low-class anxiety type. A real lady would give it up.'

Give it up… I had tried, on numerous occasions. His speech hurt my feelings, but it served a purpose, and needless to say, that time, my withdrawal became permanent. Whether one decides to quit for reasons of health, money, or status does not matter—the point is to *find a reason*.

Several decades ago, many did not fully realise how detrimental smoking was, but after years of research, we now understand that this habit is quasi-suicidal. Surely you are a person who appreciates life, otherwise you would not be reading this sort of book. If you are a non-smoker, please stay that way; if you are an ex-smoker, do accept my personal congratulations; if you are a current smoker, and you've ever, even for a moment, thought about quitting—I hope that the following information will help you to achieve that tremendous victory.

Before we proceed in working towards a solution, let's consider the severity of the problem. Most of us are aware of the health risks involved. The fact that smoking disturbs digestion, weakens our gums, creates vitamin deficiencies, induces heart disease, lung cancer and other lung related disorders, should really be reason enough for everyone to avoid this infamous killer. Why don't we even go so far as to list some of the less significant faults:

* Squinting eyes, wrinkles, ageing skin.
* Sore throats and laryngitis.
* Lingering smell, burn-holes in clothing.
* Ashtrays and filthy cigarette butts.
* Grimy windshields, walls, etc.
* Foul breath, yellow teeth, brown fingertips.
* Lower mental dexterity and possible headaches.
* Déclassé anxiety image.
* Waste of money.
* Damages the taste buds.

The list of cons is long, but what are the pros? Does one enjoy it? Perhaps, but habit and addiction can hardly be considered a pleasure.

Habit

New habits can be formed in less than a month, and old habits can be broken in the same time span. Test your personal habit time frame: at the desk where you sit and work every day, move your waste paper basket to the opposite side. i.e., if it was on the left side of your desk, move it to the right. How many days do you aimlessly throw paper on the floor? After approximately three weeks, you should be accustomed to the changeover. Habits can be formed or broken with a bit of effort.

Addiction

Addiction grows from the seed of habit, but is more serious, because not only must you break the habit and deal with physical withdrawal, you must also make the decision never to indulge again. Having a few cigarettes two years down the road can rekindle the sparks of addiction, so one must be very cautious.

So much for the problem—how to cure it? It may take several endeavours to abstain permanently, but I'm convinced that every attempt to quit is a step in the right direction—certainly better than not trying at all. When you've made the decision to give up smoking—do it… even if only for a few days. Switch to a very low tar-nicotine cigarette, prepare yourself slowly if abrupt withdrawal does not work.

When you are ready and *completely determined* to have your last cigarette, follow these important steps:

* eliminate every ashtray, tobacco product, and related accessory from your house. Do not hide them in the cupboards, but actually remove them—all ashtrays must go out with the rubbish!
* alter any other 'smoking' reminders—for example: I used to carry a silver cigarette case in my handbag. I kept it for several years later, but filled with sugar-free mints.
* write the date in your journal, circle your calendar—this becomes the first day of the rest of your life—I still remember that I quit on the late Queen's birthday!
* finally, the most important step of all—realise that *smoking is not a solitary action, but part of a complete life-style so we should avoid everything related to the compulsion.*

For example, if a person always smoked while drinking coffee or alcohol, it might be necessary to remove these beverages from their diet for a minimum of two months. Switch to fresh juices, mineral water, herbal tea—it's hard to imagine smoking a cigarette while drinking a glass of grapefruit juice. If one has a tendency to light up while watching the television, they should avoid all TV. It's interesting to note that the various destructive compulsions often co-exist.

Once you have eliminated everything which prompted the problem, additional measures should be taken to ensure permanent abandon. The next logical step is to begin doing things which 'do not' encourage smoking. **Develop a positive healthy life-style**. Since you never smoke in the swimming pool or at the opera, involve yourself more with this sort of pastime. If you notice that smokers frequent nightclubs, bars, casinos and bingo halls, try instead to associate with athletic people who enjoy tennis, riding, or some action where smoking is virtually impossible. Surround yourself with healthy people and activities—it's a complete process. You may find yourself changing some associates or much of your life-style, but the decision should prove to be one of the best you've ever made.

With regards to cigarette etiquette, there is now one recognised social code about smoking in someone's house or in public: *if you see an ashtray—you can, if you don't see an ashtray—you cannot*. It is not necessary for people to post 'no-smoking' signs, when all they have to do is remove the ashtrays. It would be baffling to hear someone ask 'do you mind if I smoke?', when it is obviously apparent that no ashtrays have been provided.

DRUGS

A lengthy composition about drugs would be redundant because much has already been discussed under smoking. Drug users generally get started for similar reasons—peer-pressure or personal dissatisfaction with life. Like smoking, the individual who succumbs to the narcotic habit, will usually become fully addicted.

Far more dangerous than cigarette smoking, drugs can also incite serious mental disorders, heart failure, and the intravenous risk—AIDS. Modern drugs like cocaine and crack are stimulants which strongly ignite the pleasure centres of the brain; unfortunately, this makes them highly addictive. Like drug dependent rats in laboratory studies, some humans become insatiable and actually 'stone' themselves to death. Preferably one should never start up, but *if one is already dependency-prone, getting treatment is a priority*.

We are all very proud of free-country libertarian attitudes, and some citizens prefer to reside in areas where marihuana has become legalised. This is one freedom which could cause serious harm. Under no circumstances will drug promotion ever create a more just and prosperous society, not to mention the additional burden on health care. Do as Nancy Reagan recommended—*JUST SAY NO!*

Index

Accents 113
Accessories 90, 100
Affirmations 27, 28, 45-48, 206
Alcohol 275, 276, 280, 282, 283
Anxiety 36, 195
Apparel .... 78, 79, 92 -98, 201
Appearance 77, 99
Associates 30, 51, 75, 122- 127
Auto-suggestion 37, 44
Avocation 150- 152, 170
  greater service = rewards 152-153

Bags 195
Balance 157-159, 196
Belts 87, 90
Billfolds 84
Brainwave states 207
Business cards 159, 160
Business wear 79, 83, 95, 100

C and un-C 67, 68
Calling cards 150, 159
Calling cards 160
Casual wear 92-94
Charisma and character 69-71
Charity 217, 229-231
Civility 66
Class . 64, 66, 67, 68, 104, 132, 143
  .... 144, 145, 146, 147, 265
Class and diet 278
Class/Civility 66
Closet 79
  de-clutter 95-97
Clothes – see apparel 78
Colours 80, 81, 86, 87, 93
Community living - condominiums
  .... 174, 175

Compulsions 208
  appendix#5 .... 280, 283, 286
Conscious and subconscious 25, 36
  .... 37, 38, 39, 40, 43, 44, 255
Consort 124, 129, 130, 131
  .... 137, 186
Contractors 163, 235
Cosmetology 103
Credit rating 224, 225
Culture 67

Diet 200, 201
  appendix#4 .... 272- 278
Dream Board 153, 244
Dreams 37-40
Drugs 33, 68, 208, 213, 286

Eager 36
Eating patterns 197-198
Education 53, 54, 55, 56, 57
  .... 110, 162, 168
  appendix#1 250-252
Emotional well-being 195, 196
Entertainment ... 139, 209, 216, 217
Enunciation 113
Enunciation
  see also Status Enuciation 256
Envy 74, 93
Exercise 202, 204, 210, 243, 279
Extremities avoidanc 71, 138

Fabrics – see material fabrics 87, 91
Fabrics see material 65
Facial care 105-107
Faith 27, 34, 40, 48, 75, 255
Fear 30, 31, 35-36, 47, 76, 255
Financial freedom 213, 216
Fireplace 43, 61, 180, 185

Flooring 178, 181
Flowers 82, 126, 141, 143
.... 181, 182, 183
Foreign speech/words 112, 113
.... 256, 271, 272
Forgiveness 68, 76
Future trend 194

Games 141, 144, 179, 208
Garden 143, 182, 199, 219
.... 220, 248
Garden Party see socialising 88
Generosity 68, 214, 231
Gift List 185, 186
Gifts 160, 231
Gloves 82, 83, 87, 90, 186
Goal setting 157, 238, 245
Gratitude 46, 48, 126, 206
.... 229, 232, 238
Greed 226, 229
Grooming .. 102, 103, 157, 180, 246

Hair 43, 65, 80, 99, 100, 101
.... 102, 103, 107
Handbags 84
Harmony 68, 138
Harmony at home 197
Hats 82, 83, 142
Health and wellbeing 194
    appendix#4 272-280
    emotional wellbeing 195, 196
    exercise 202, 204
    intimate 207
    physical diet and weight 197, 203
Hertz Vibration Scale 32
High society 73, 112, 113, 135
.... 175, 236
Hiring Help 164
Home library 57, 58
House 63, 173, 177, 180
.... 182, 216, 227, 229, 246
How does the mind work 24
How repetition affects behaviour 51

Imagery 28, 36, 43

Income tax 163, 167, 232-235
Independence 127, 219, 220, 221
Insurance 225, 227, 228
Investments 217, 220, 226, 228

Jewellery 61, 65, 88, 89, 233

Land 41, 175, 176, 182, 219, 232
Law of Attraction 29, 30, 31, 97
Lenders 161, 224
Library 54, 56, 58, 110
Location 172-176

Material fabrics 65, 82, 87, 89-91
.... 96, 97
Material Possessions 184, 188
Medical procedures 204
Mental practise/rehearsal 43
Mentors/role models 7, 53, 128, 129
Mind . 23, 24, 25, 26, 27, 28, 29, 31
.... 36, 37, 40, 44, 51, 56, 123
.appendix#2 253
appendix#2 .... 253, 255
Mind power 27
Moderation 68, 281
Money 45, 46, 47, 60, 68, 75, 90
.. 91, 94, 149, 153, 213-218, 221
.... 226, 228, 230
Morals 68, 73

Nails and manicure ... 101, 102, 109
Name 18, 19, 21, 159, 160, 272
Negativity 46, 47, 116, 125, 247

Occupation 145, 146, 147, 148
...... 150, 151, 152, 153, 154, 155
...... 158, 159, 160, 203, 215, 245
Outdoors ... 152, 174, 202, 203, 251

Partner see consort 92
Past 26, 37, 41, 42, 49, 74, 252
Patrons 161
Physical health 197
Physiology 31, 77
Positive speech 116

Posture 77, 107, 109
Poverty consciousness 38, 62, 94
    .... 149, 218, 230, 282
Power of words 37, 41, 44, 52
    .... 53, 116, 123
Prayer 48, 49, 232, 280
Pronunciation 110, 111, 112, 257
Prosperity consciousness 40, 59, 60
    .... 61, 62, 166, 174, 255

Radio 24, 25, 206, 211
    mind waves 24, 26
Reading 53, 54, 56, 58, 67, 111, 277
Reinvestment 216
Repetition 25, 26, 37, 51
Re-programming 44, 47, 211
Retirement 166, 167, 220, 221
Rewards 163, 168, 174, 229, 247
    from early investment ... 220, 226
    from greater service 153, 154
    155
RRSP 167, 220, 221, 223

Savings 167, 216, 217, 221
Scent 88, 103
Self-employed 34, 123, 126, 146
    ..... 147, 150, 155, 162, 169, 235
Service 146, 150, 155, 156
    .... 160, 163, 170
    equals greater rewards ... 153- 155
Share wealth/create a job .. 162, 163
Shoes .. 81, 82, 84-87, 90, 93, 94, 98
    .... 142, 143, 187, 228
Slang 114, 271
Sleep 205, 206
Smoking 45, 82, 208, 283- 286
Socialising 134, 136
    afternoon tea 143, 144
    entertainment 139, 140, 142
    sport and games 144, 145
    the garden party 142
Speech 18, 38, 62, 109, 110, 111- 116
    appendix#3 .... 256, 272

foreign 112, 113, 271, 272
the power of 52, 53
Speech and Class 265
Sponsors 161
Sport 57, 64, 145, 149, 151, 154
    .... 170, 202
    sports wear 81, 92, 94
Status Enunciation 113
    appendix#3 256
Sub-conscious see Conscious and
    Sub-conscious 12
Success system 216
Symphony 64, 140, 152, 159
    .... 218, 231

Tax 176, 216, 221, 231, 233
    .... 234, 252
Telephone 114, 115, 140
Television 25, 123, 146, 206
    .... 209- 211, 286
Time management 156- 159
    balance 157
    business card 159
    the agenda 156, 157

Umbrellas 88
Undergarments 87, 91, 102

Visualisation 31, 37, 43
Vitamins 203
Vocation 139, 148, 150- 155
    .... 170, 171, 247
Voice 43, 67, 110, 111
    .... 114, 116, 139

Weight 43, 200, 201, 278, 279
What is Mind 23
What you wear 78
Words 37, 41, 44, 45, 52, 53
. 55, 62, 114, 116, 123, 137, 246
Worry 31, 36, 41, 174, 218

Yard 174, 176, 182